Best of Bridge
Slow Cooker
Cookbook

200 Delicious Recipes

Robert
ROSE

Best of Bridge Slow Cooker Cookbook
Text copyright © 2012 Sally Vaughan-Johnston and The Best of Bridge Publishing Ltd.
Photographs copyright © 2012 Robert Rose Inc.
Cover and text design copyright © 2012 Robert Rose Inc.

For complete cataloguing information, see page 338.

Disclaimer

The recipes in this book have been carefully tested by our kitchen and our tasters. To the best of our knowledge, they are safe and nutritious for ordinary use and users. For those people with food or other allergies, or who have special food requirements or health issues, please read the suggested contents of each recipe carefully and determine whether or not they may create a problem for you. All recipes are used at the risk of the consumer.

We cannot be responsible for any hazards, loss or damage that may occur as a result of any recipe use.

For those with special needs, allergies, requirements or health problems, in the event of any doubt, please contact your medical adviser prior to the use of any recipe.

Design and Production: Daniella Zanchetta and Joseph Gisini/PageWave Graphics Inc.
Editor: Sue Sumeraj
Recipe editor: Jennifer MacKenzie
Proofreader: Sheila Wawanash
Indexer: Gillian Watts
Photographer: Colin Erricson
Associate Photographer: Matt Johannsson
Food Stylist: Kathryn Robertson
Prop Stylist: Charlene Erricson

Cover image: Beef Goulash (page 134)

We acknowledge the financial support of the Government of Canada through the Book Publishing Industry Development Program (BPIDP) for our publishing activities.

Published by Robert Rose Inc.
120 Eglinton Avenue East, Suite 800, Toronto, Ontario, Canada M4P 1E2
Tel: (416) 322-6552 Fax: (416) 322-6936
www.robertrose.ca

Printed and bound in Canada

2 3 4 5 6 7 8 9 FP 20 19 18 17 16 15 14 13 12

CONTENTS

INTRODUCTION

THE BEST OF BRIDGE LADIES, LIKE SO MANY OF YOU, HAVE FALLEN IN LOVE WITH OUR SLOW COOKERS ALL OVER AGAIN. THE LATEST SLOW COOKERS ARE SLEEKER, WITH A FEW MORE FEATURES THAN THOSE WE USED BACK IN THE '70S. BUT THEY ARE STILL ENDEARINGLY LOW-TECH — EVEN WE CAN FIGURE OUT HOW TO USE THEM!

WE LOVE BEING ABLE TO SWITCH ON THE SLOW COOKER IN THE MORNING, HEAD OUT THE DOOR AND COME HOME TO A HOUSE FILLED WITH THE MOUTH-WATERING AROMAS OF DINNER. SO SALLY, WHO JOINED OUR CREW THREE YEARS AGO, AGREED TO HEAD BACK INTO THE KITCHEN AND COME UP WITH MORE DELICIOUS NEW RECIPES, THIS TIME FOR THE SLOW COOKER. WE'RE DELIGHTED WITH THE RESULTS. NOT ONLY HAS SALLY CREATED SOME SENSATIONAL NEW IDEAS FOR SLOW COOKER STAPLES, SUCH AS SOUPS, POT ROASTS, CHILIS AND STEWS, BUT SHE HAS ALSO SHOWED US NEW WAYS TO USE OUR SLOW COOKERS: FOR BAKED PASTA, QUICK BREADS, PUDDINGS, FRUIT DESSERTS, SIDE DISHES AND EVEN ROASTED GARLIC! WE'RE REALLY PLEASED THAT SHE HAS ALSO ADAPTED A NUMBER OF OUR ALL-TIME FAVORITE RECIPES FOR THE SLOW COOKER — EVEN CHRISTMAS MORNING WIFE SAVER (PAGE 24)!

ENTERTAINING IS A BREEZE WHEN THE SLOW COOKER IS YOUR SOUS CHEF. BE SURE TO TRY OUR NEW GUEST-WORTHY RECIPES, SUCH AS ROCKIN' ROULADEN (PAGE 126)

OR SENSATIONAL ITALIAN POT ROAST (PAGE 112). START THEM IN THE MORNING, AND BY EVENING ALL YOU HAVE TO DO IS ADD SOME FINISHING TOUCHES, OPEN THE WINE AND ENJOY YOUR COMPANY.

WE WANT TO THANK SLOW COOKER GURU JUDITH FINLAYSON FOR HER INVALUABLE TECHNICAL ADVICE. SHE ANSWERED OUR MANY QUESTIONS WITH PATIENCE.

WHETHER YOU ARE A VETERAN SLOW COOKER COOK OR ARE JUST STARTING OUT, YOU WILL LOVE OUR NEW COLLECTION OF RECIPES AND TIPS.

SLOW COOKER 101

SLOW COOKERS ARE LIKE GOOD FRIENDS. THE BETTER YOU GET TO KNOW THEM, THE STRONGER YOUR RELATIONSHIP BECOMES.

THAT WAS OUR VERDICT AFTER SEVERAL MONTHS OF TESTING SCORES OF RECIPES FOR THIS BOOK. WE USED SLOW COOKERS RANGING IN SIZE FROM $1\frac{1}{2}$ TO 7 QUARTS. WE ALSO TESTED SEVERAL DIFFERENT BRANDS AND MODELS, RANGING FROM A TRUSTY, 30-YEAR-OLD MODEL, WITH A MANUAL DIAL AND A PLASTIC LID SO CLOUDY FROM AGE THAT WE CAN NO LONGER SEE WHAT'S INSIDE, TO THE LATEST CUISINART AND KITCHENAID MODELS. THESE HAVE REMOVABLE, EASY-TO-CLEAN INSERTS AND ELECTRONIC CONTROLS THAT AUTOMATICALLY SWITCH FROM COOKING TO KEEP WARM SETTINGS IF YOU ARE LATE GETTING HOME FOR DINNER.

WE DISCOVERED THAT, REGARDLESS OF PRICE, ALL SLOW COOKERS HAVE THEIR OWN PERSONALITIES, AND THEY DON'T ALL COOK AT THE SAME PACE. SOME MODELS COOKED SO SLOWLY ON THE LOW SETTING THAT WE THOUGHT THE NEXT ICE AGE WOULD ARRIVE BEFORE THE STEW WAS READY! IN OTHER MACHINES, THE FOOD TOOK THE SAME LENGTH OF TIME TO COOK REGARDLESS OF WHETHER WE SET IT ON LOW OR HIGH. ONE MODEL COOKED SO VIGOROUSLY ON THE HIGH SETTING THAT ITS LID RATTLED FOR SEVERAL UNNERVING HOURS AS THE SOUP COOKED. THAT'S WHY WE'VE GIVEN A RANGE OF COOKING TIMES FOR MOST OF OUR RECIPES.

THE MORE YOU USE YOUR SLOW COOKER, THE MORE FAMILIAR YOU WILL BECOME WITH ITS PERFORMANCE. UNTIL

THEN, CHECK THE FOOD FOR DONENESS AT THE SHORTER COOKING TIME INDICATED. (CONTRARY TO COMMON BELIEF, YOU CAN OVERCOOK FOOD IN THE SLOW COOKER). SOME MANUFACTURERS WARN THAT EVERY TIME YOU REMOVE THE LID TO CHECK YOUR FOOD OR STIR, YOU ADD 20 MINUTES TO THE COOKING TIME. HOWEVER, WE FOUND THAT ONE QUICK PEEK MADE NO DISCERNABLE DIFFERENCE.

BUYING A SLOW COOKER

WHEN THEY LEARNED WE WERE WRITING THIS BOOK, MANY FRIENDS AND RELATIVES ASKED OUR ADVICE ON WHICH SLOW COOKER TO PURCHASE. WE'RE NOT EXPERTS, BUT WE'RE HAPPY TO SUGGEST SOME POINTS TO CONSIDER WHEN SHOPPING FOR A SLOW COOKER.

- *SIZE:* CHOOSE A SIZE THAT'S RIGHT FOR YOUR FAMILY'S NEEDS. SMALL SLOW COOKERS (1$\frac{1}{2}$ TO 3 QUARTS) ARE PERFECT FOR HOT DIPS, SIDE DISHES AND SAUCES. A SLOW COOKER WITH A 4-QUART CAPACITY WORKS WELL FOR 4 TO 6 SERVINGS OF MOST SOUP, MAIN COURSE AND DESSERT RECIPES. A 5- TO 6-QUART SLOW COOKER COMES IN HANDY FOR ENTERTAINING AND FOR LARGER CUTS OF MEAT (POT ROASTS, BRISKETS AND RIBS). A LARGER MACHINE IS ALSO NECESSARY FOR DESSERT RECIPES, SUCH AS CUSTARDS, THAT ARE COOKED IN A WATER BATH. IF YOU DO A LOT OF SLOW COOKING, CONSIDER BUYING A MEDIUM-SIZE SLOW COOKER FOR EVERYDAY USE AND A LARGER ONE FOR ENTERTAINING.

- **CONTROLS:** WE LIKE SLOW COOKERS THAT HAVE PROGRAMMABLE AND AUTOMATIC TIMERS — THEY JUST MAKE LIFE SO MUCH EASIER. THE ONES THAT CAN AUTOMATICALLY SWITCH TO A KEEP WARM SETTING ARE ESPECIALLY HELPFUL FOR THOSE DAYS WHEN YOU GET STUCK IN TRAFFIC.

- **SHAPE:** SLOW COOKERS COME IN ROUND, OVAL AND RECTANGULAR MODELS. THE OVAL AND RECTANGULAR VERSIONS ARE THE MOST VERSATILE.

- **LIDS:** A GOOD LID SEALS IN MOISTURE, SO MAKE SURE IT FITS SNUGLY. (A LITTLE JIGGLE IS FINE.) CLEAR GLASS LIDS ALLOW YOU TO SEE WHAT'S GOING ON INSIDE AND ARE MORE DURABLE THAN PLASTIC LIDS.

- **OTHER FEATURES:** THE HANDLES ON THE SLOW COOKER INSERT HEAT UP DURING COOKING, SO THEY SHOULD BE EASY TO GRIP WITH OVEN MITTS. SOME SLOW COOKERS COME WITH A BUILT-IN TEMPERATURE PROBE, WHICH IS NICE BUT NOT NECESSARY. LIKEWISE FOR RETRACTABLE ELECTRIC CORDS THAT STORE NEATLY INSIDE THE BASE OF THE SLOW COOKER.

LOW OR HIGH?

IF YOU WANT A RECIPE TO COOK ALL DAY (FOR 7 OR 8 HOURS), USE THE LOW SETTING. IF YOU WANT IT READY FASTER, USE THE HIGH SETTING. TO GIVE A RECIPE A HEAD START, WE SOMETIMES START OUT ON HIGH FOR 1 HOUR, THEN USE LOW FOR THE REMAINDER OF THE COOKING

TIME. HOWEVER, FOR THE BEST AND MOST CONSISTENT RESULTS, WE CHOOSE THE LOW SETTING. FOR SOME QUICK BREADS AND DESSERTS, HIGH IS THE ONLY WAY TO GO.

PREPPING THE NIGHT BEFORE

IF YOU PLAN TO START YOUR SLOW COOKER BEFORE HEADING OFF TO WORK, YOU CAN PREPARE A FEW STEPS THE NIGHT BEFORE:

1. FRESH VEGETABLES CAN BE CHOPPED, PLACED IN AIRTIGHT CONTAINERS AND REFRIGERATED OVERNIGHT.

2. VEGETABLES MAY BE PARTIALLY COOKED AHEAD OF TIME. SOFTEN VEGETABLES SUCH AS ONIONS, CARROTS AND CELERY IN OIL OR BUTTER IN A SKILLET FOR A FEW MINUTES, ACCORDING TO THE RECIPE. GARLIC, TOMATO PASTE, DRIED HERBS AND SPICES MAY ALSO BE ADDED AT THIS POINT. LET COOL COMPLETELY, TRANSFER TO AN AIRTIGHT CONTAINER AND REFRIGERATE FOR UP TO 2 DAYS.

3. FROZEN VEGETABLES MAY BE THAWED OVERNIGHT IN THE REFRIGERATOR.

4. SMALL PIECES OF MEAT SUCH AS BACON, SAUSAGE OR GROUND MEAT MAY BE FULLY COOKED AHEAD. BROWN THEM IN A SKILLET UNTIL NO LONGER PINK. LET COOL, THEN REFRIGERATE IN AN AIRTIGHT CONTAINER FOR UP TO 2 DAYS.

5. OTHER TYPES OF MEAT AND POULTRY SHOULD NOT BE BROWNED THE NIGHT BEFORE, FOR FOOD SAFETY REASONS. HOWEVER, YOU CAN TRIM OFF THE FAT

AND/OR CUT THE MEAT INTO EVEN-SIZED CUBES. REFRIGERATE TRIMMED OR CUBED RAW MEAT IN AN AIRTIGHT CONTAINER, SEPARATE FROM OTHER INGREDIENTS.

6. SEASONINGS AND LIQUIDS CAN BE MEASURED OUT SO THEY'RE READY TO GO.

HOW TO BE A GOOD SLOW COOKER COOK

- USE TOUGHER CUTS OF MEAT, SUCH AS STEWING BEEF, SIMMERING STEAKS AND POT ROASTS (THESE MAY ALSO BE CALLED BONELESS BEEF CROSS RIB, BLADE OR CHUCK). PORK SHOULDER CUTS, SUCH AS ROASTS, CHOPS AND STEAKS, AND COUNTRY-STYLE RIBS WORK WELL IN THE SLOW COOKER. SO DO LAMB SHOULDER CUTS (CHOPS, STEWING CUBES AND ROASTS) AND SHANKS. SLOW COOKING BREAKS DOWN THE COLLAGEN IN THE MUSCLE'S CONNECTIVE TISSUE, LEAVING THE COOKED MEAT MOIST AND TENDER. WE'D LIKE TO SAY THAT TOUGHER CUTS OF MEAT ARE LESS EXPENSIVE, BUT THAT'S NOT NECESSARILY THE CASE. VEAL SHANKS (FOR OSSO BUCO MILANESE, PAGE 156), BEEF BRISKET AND BEEF SHORT RIBS ALL PROVED TO BE DELICIOUS BUT SURPRISINGLY COSTLY.

- CHICKEN CAN BE COOKED SUCCESSFULLY IN THE SLOW COOKER, BUT STICK TO DARK MEAT (THIGHS AND LEGS) AND, WHENEVER POSSIBLE, USE SKINLESS BONE-IN VERSIONS. FOR BEST RESULTS, COOK

CHICKEN ON LOW, AND NEVER FOR MORE THAN 6 HOURS; OTHERWISE, IT EMERGES DRY AND VERY STRINGY. YOU CAN SLOW-COOK CHICKEN ON HIGH — OUR RECIPES SUGGEST $2\frac{1}{2}$ TO 3 HOURS — BUT YOU'LL NEED TO WATCH IT CAREFULLY BECAUSE THE TEXTURE DETERIORATES PRETTY QUICKLY AFTER THAT TIME.

- DON'T EVEN THINK OF SLOW-COOKING LEAN, PREMIUM CUTS OF MEAT OR POULTRY, SUCH AS CHICKEN BREASTS, PORK CHOPS OR GRILLING STEAKS — THE RESULTS WILL BE DRY AND UNAPPEALING.

- DEFROST MEAT AND POULTRY COMPLETELY BEFORE PLACING THEM IN THE SLOW COOKER. FROZEN FRUIT AND VEGETABLES MAY BE ADDED NEAR THE END OF THE COOKING TIME AND HEATED ON HIGH UNTIL STEAMING HOT.

- IF YOU HAVE TIME, BROWN MEAT IMMEDIATELY BEFORE PLACING IT IN THE SLOW COOKER. BUT DON'T WORRY IF YOU'RE TOO BUSY. IN RECIPES THAT HAVE A LOT OF BOLD OR SPICY INGREDIENTS, SUCH AS CHILIS AND CURRIES, YOU WON'T BE ABLE TO TELL THE DIFFERENCE. IN OTHER RECIPES, BROWNING THE MEAT WILL RESULT IN A DEEPER FLAVOR THAT IS DESIRABLE BUT NOT ESSENTIAL.

- IN SOME RECIPES, WE CALL FOR TOMATO PASTE TO BE ADDED TO THE SKILLET WHEN SOFTENING VEGETABLES BEFORE ADDING THEM TO THE SLOW COOKER. WE FIND THIS SIGNIFICANTLY IMPROVES THE FLAVOR OF THE RECIPES, ESPECIALLY WHEN WE DON'T BROWN THE MEAT FIRST.

- ROOT VEGETABLES, SUCH AS POTATOES, CARROTS AND PARSNIPS, CAN TAKE LONGER TO COOK THAN MEAT PIECES OF THE SAME SIZE, SO THINLY SLICE THEM OR CUT THEM INTO CUBES NO BIGGER THAN 1 INCH (2.5 CM).

- REDUCE THE AMOUNT OF LIQUID IN YOUR STOVETOP OR OVEN RECIPES TO ADAPT THEM TO THE SLOW COOKER. UNLIKE CONVENTIONAL COOKING, THERE'S NOWHERE FOR LIQUID TO EVAPORATE IN THE SLOW COOKER. REDUCE LIQUIDS, INCLUDING BROTH, CANNED TOMATOES AND JUICE, BY ABOUT 50% FOR MOST STEWS, CHILIS AND CASSEROLES. WHEN YOU ASSEMBLE THE RECIPE IN THE SLOW COOKER, THE LIQUID MAY NOT COVER THE MEAT AND VEGETABLES. DON'T WORRY — IT WILL INCREASE AS FOODS RELEASE THEIR JUICES AND STEAM BUILDS UP.

- BE GENEROUS WITH ONIONS, CELERY, GARLIC, HERBS AND OTHER AROMATIC INGREDIENTS. LONG COOKING DULLS THEIR FLAVORS, SO YOU NEED TO COMPENSATE WITH LARGER AMOUNTS. SOME RECIPES NEED A FLAVOR PICK-ME-UP AT THE END OF THE COOKING TIME, SO WE OFTEN FINISH WITH FRESH HERBS, CITRUS JUICE AND ZEST OR EXTRA SEASONING.

- USE WHOLE RATHER THAN GROUND HERBS AND SPICES WHENEVER POSSIBLE. WHOLE SPICES (SUCH AS CINNAMON STICKS) AND WHOLE-LEAF DRIED HERBS (SUCH AS BAY LEAVES, THYME AND OREGANO) RELEASE THEIR FLAVOR SLOWLY THROUGHOUT LONG

COOKING, UNLIKE GROUND HERBS AND SPICES, WHICH TEND TO LOSE THEIR FLAVOR. SPRINKLE FRESH HERBS, SUCH AS PARSLEY, CILANTRO AND BASIL, INTO THE RECIPE JUST BEFORE SERVING.

- MILK, CREAM AND SOUR CREAM CAN ADD A RICH FINISHING TOUCH TO SOUPS AND STEWS. TO PREVENT THEM FROM SEPARATING, ALWAYS ADD THEM NEAR THE END OF THE COOKING TIME. CHEESE SHOULD BE STIRRED IN JUST BEFORE SERVING.

- BELL PEPPERS, FRESH CHILE PEPPERS AND SOME DRIED SEASONINGS, SUCH AS PAPRIKA AND CHILI POWDER, CAN TURN BITTER DURING LONG COOKING, SO ADD THEM NEAR THE END.

- SOME INGREDIENTS BECOME DISCOLORED, OVERLY SOFT AND UNAPPETIZING DURING SLOW COOKING AND SHOULD BE ADDED ONLY DURING THE LAST 30 MINUTES, AFTER THE TEMPERATURE HAS BEEN TURNED TO HIGH. THESE INCLUDE PEAS, LEAFY GREENS, ZUCCHINI AND EDAMAME.

- IN GENERAL, YOUR SLOW COOKER SHOULD BE NO LESS THAN HALF FULL AND NO MORE THAN THREE-QUARTERS FULL. LEAVE AT LEAST 2 INCHES (5 CM) BETWEEN THE TOP OF THE FOOD AND THE LID.

- A FEW OF OUR RECIPES (PUDDINGS AND CUSTARDS) NEED TO BE COOKED IN AN EXTRA DISH THAT IS PLACED IN THE SLOW COOKER AND THEN SURROUNDED BY WATER. THIS IS KNOWN AS A WATER BATH. FOR THIS PURPOSE, YOU WILL NEED A LARGE OVAL OR RECTANGULAR SLOW COOKER. WE FOUND

THAT 4-CUP (1 L) AND 6-CUP (1.5 L) OVENPROOF BAKING DISHES WORK BEST. FOR INDIVIDUAL ORANGE CRÈME CARAMEL (PAGE 326) AND CHOCOLATE POTS DE CRÈME (PAGE 324), WE WERE ABLE TO FIT FOUR 6-OZ (175 ML) RAMEKINS IN OUR MACHINE.

- IN SOME RECIPES — NOTABLY QUICK BREADS AND FRUIT CRISPS — IT'S DESIRABLE TO PROTECT THE FOOD FROM ACCUMULATED MOISTURE DRIPPING FROM THE UNDERSIDE OF THE LID. TO DO THIS, WE PLACE A CLEAN TOWEL, FOLDED IN HALF, OVER THE INSERT BEFORE REPLACING THE LID. THE TEA TOWEL ABSORBS THE EXCESS MOISTURE. WE ALSO USE THIS TECHNIQUE IN A FEW RECIPES, SUCH AS SIMPLY SUPER TOMATO SAUCE (PAGE 246), TO HELP THICKEN THE SAUCE DURING THE COOKING PROCESS. ONE TIP: MAKE SURE THE TEA TOWEL HASN'T BEEN LAUNDERED IN A HIGHLY PERFUMED DETERGENT — THE FRAGRANCE CAN TRANSFER TO THE FOOD!

- HANDLE YOUR SLOW COOKER WITH CARE: SOME CERAMIC INSERTS CHIP EASILY. ALWAYS FOLLOW THE MANUFACTURER'S INSTRUCTIONS FOR CLEANING YOUR SLOW COOKER.

- FINALLY, IF THERE IS A POWER OUTAGE AND THE FOOD IN YOUR SLOW COOKER IS ONLY PARTIALLY COOKED, DISCARD THE FOOD. IF THE FOOD IS FULLY COOKED, EAT IT WITHIN 2 HOURS.

ALL-DAY BREAKFAST

HOT CHOCOLATE MULTIGRAIN CEREAL

SET THE SLOW COOKER BEFORE BED AND WAKE UP TO A DELICIOUS HIGH-FIBER HOT BREAKFAST. IT'S ALSO WONDERFUL EATEN CHILLED AS A MID-MORNING OR LATE-NIGHT SNACK.

I CUP	MULTIGRAIN CEREAL BLEND	250 ML
4 CUPS	SWEETENED CHOCOLATE-FLAVORED ALMOND MILK (SEE TIP, PAGE 18)	I L
	SLICED BANANA	

IN A $3\frac{1}{2}$- TO 4-QUART SLOW COOKER, COMBINE CEREAL AND ALMOND MILK. COVER AND COOK ON LOW FOR ABOUT 8 HOURS, UNTIL GRAINS ARE TENDER AND LIQUID IS ABSORBED. STIR WELL AND SERVE TOPPED WITH SLICED BANANA. SERVES 4.

TIP: LOOK FOR PREPACKAGED MULTIGRAIN CEREAL BLENDS, WHICH MAY CONTAIN BARLEY, WILD OR BROWN RICE, STEEL-CUT OATS AND OTHER LONG-COOKING GRAINS.

MAKE AHEAD: LET COOL AND REFRIGERATE IN AN AIRTIGHT CONTAINER FOR UP TO 4 DAYS. REHEAT IN THE MICROWAVE OR IN A SAUCEPAN OVER LOW HEAT, STIRRING OFTEN. ADD HOT WATER TO ADJUST THE CONSISTENCY.

IRONY: THE OPPOSITE OF WRINKLY.

GOOD MORNING IRISH OATMEAL

SUPER-HEALTHY — KEEPS IN THE FRIDGE AND REHEATS BEAUTIFULLY IN THE MICROWAVE. SERVE WITH BROWN SUGAR, CREAM, MAPLE SYRUP, DRIED FRUIT OR NUTS.

2 CUPS	STEEL-CUT OATS (SEE TIP, BELOW)	500 ML
1 TSP	SALT	5 ML
8 CUPS	WATER	2 L

IN A $3\frac{1}{2}$- TO 4-QUART SLOW COOKER, COMBINE OATS, SALT AND WATER. COVER AND COOK ON LOW FOR 4 TO 6 HOURS, UNTIL OATS ARE SOFTENED AND THICKENED. SWITCH OFF SLOW COOKER AND LET STAND FOR 10 MINUTES. STIR AND SERVE. SERVES 8.

TIP: STEEL-CUT OATS, ALSO KNOWN AS IRISH OR SCOTTISH OATMEAL, ARE WHOLE OAT KERNELS THAT HAVE BEEN CUT INTO SEVERAL PIECES BUT NOT ROLLED. THEY'RE VERY NUTRITIOUS AND FLAVORFUL, AND HAVE A NICE CHEWY TEXTURE. STEEL-CUT OATS TAKE LONGER TO COOK THAN OTHER TYPES OF OATS, SO THEY'RE WELL SUITED TO THE SLOW COOKER. ALTHOUGH WE LIKED THE IDEA OF COOKING THEM OVERNIGHT AND WAKING UP TO A HOT BREAKFAST, WE FOUND THE RESULTS GLUEY AND UNAPPETIZING WHEN THE OATS COOKED FOR LONGER THAN 6 HOURS.

MAKE AHEAD: LET COOL AND REFRIGERATE IN AN AIRTIGHT CONTAINER FOR UP TO 4 DAYS. REHEAT IN THE MICROWAVE OR IN A SAUCEPAN OVER LOW HEAT, STIRRING OFTEN. ADD HOT WATER TO ADJUST THE CONSISTENCY.

CREAMY APPLE CINNAMON PORRIDGE

YOU ARE NEVER GOING BACK TO INSTANT OATMEAL AGAIN. NO MORE OF THE STIRRING AND MESS INVOLVED IN COOKING "PROPER" PORRIDGE.

$1^3/_4$ CUPS	STEEL-CUT OATS (SEE TIP, PAGE 17)	425 ML
$1/_2$ CUP	PACKED BROWN SUGAR	125 ML
$1/_2$ CUP	CHOPPED DRIED APPLES	125 ML
1 TSP	GROUND CINNAMON	5 ML
1 TSP	SALT	5 ML
4 CUPS	UNSWEETENED VANILLA-FLAVORED ALMOND MILK (SEE TIP, BELOW)	1 L
4 CUPS	WATER	1 L
$1/_2$ CUP	RAISINS	125 ML

IN A $3^1/_2$- TO 4-QUART SLOW COOKER, COMBINE OATS, BROWN SUGAR, APPLES, CINNAMON, SALT, ALMOND MILK AND WATER. COVER AND COOK ON LOW FOR 4 TO 6 HOURS, UNTIL OATS ARE SOFTENED AND THICKENED. STIR IN RAISINS. SWITCH OFF SLOW COOKER AND LET STAND FOR 10 MINUTES. STIR AND SERVE. SERVES 8.

TIP: UNLIKE REGULAR MILK, WHICH OFTEN CURDLES IN THE SLOW COOKER, ALMOND MILK STANDS UP WELL TO THE LONG COOKING TIMES. ALTHOUGH COMMONLY CALLED ALMOND MILK, IT IS GENERALLY LABELED "ALMOND NON-DAIRY BEVERAGE." IT IS AVAILABLE SWEETENED AND UNSWEETENED IN SEVERAL FLAVORS.

MAKE AHEAD: LET COOL AND REFRIGERATE IN AN AIRTIGHT CONTAINER FOR UP TO 4 DAYS. REHEAT IN THE MICROWAVE OR IN A SAUCEPAN OVER LOW HEAT, STIRRING OFTEN. ADD HOT WATER TO ADJUST THE CONSISTENCY.

OVERNIGHT RASPBERRY FRENCH TOAST

ASSEMBLE THE NIGHT BEFORE AND REFRIGERATE. SET YOUR ALARM, START THE SLOW COOKER AND HEAD BACK TO BED. HEAVENLY! SERVE WITH MAPLE SYRUP AND EXTRA FRESH BERRIES.

4 CUPS	CUBED WHITE BREAD (SEE TIP, PAGE 21)	1 L
$\frac{1}{2}$ CUP	GRANULATED SUGAR, DIVIDED	125 ML
1 TSP	GROUND CINNAMON	5 ML
1 TSP	GRATED LEMON ZEST	5 ML
6	EGGS	6
$\frac{1}{2}$ CUP	MILK	125 ML
$\frac{1}{2}$ CUP	HALF-AND-HALF (10%) CREAM	125 ML
$1\frac{1}{2}$ CUPS	FRESH OR FROZEN RASPBERRIES (NO NEED TO THAW)	375 ML

GREASE THE INSERT OF A $3\frac{1}{2}$- TO 4-QUART SLOW COOKER. PLACE BREAD IN SLOW COOKER. IN A BOWL, WHISK TOGETHER HALF THE SUGAR, CINNAMON, LEMON ZEST, EGGS, MILK AND CREAM. POUR EGG MIXTURE AND RASPBERRIES OVER BREAD AND STIR TO COMBINE, GENTLY PUSHING BREAD DOWN TO SUBMERGE. COVER AND REFRIGERATE FOR AT LEAST 4 HOURS OR OVERNIGHT. THE NEXT DAY, SPRINKLE BREAD MIXTURE WITH REMAINING SUGAR. TRANSFER INSERT TO SLOW COOKER BASE. COOK ON HIGH FOR 2 TO $2\frac{1}{2}$ HOURS, UNTIL SET AND PUFFED. SERVES 6.

VARIATION: REPLACE THE RASPBERRIES WITH BLUEBERRIES OR BLACKBERRIES, OR A COMBINATION.

SOUTHWEST BRUNCH BAKE

THIS FAVORITE BREAKFAST CASSEROLE ADAPTS EASILY TO THE SLOW COOKER.

1	CAN (14 TO 19 OZ/398 TO 540 ML) BLACK BEANS, DRAINED AND RINSED	1
1	RED BELL PEPPER, CHOPPED	1
1	ONION, FINELY CHOPPED	1
4 CUPS	FROZEN SHREDDED HASH BROWN POTATOES	1 L
1 CUP	CORN KERNELS	250 ML
2 CUPS	SHREDDED TEX-MEX CHEESE BLEND	500 ML
2 TBSP	CHOPPED FRESH CILANTRO	30 ML
8	EGGS	8
1½ CUPS	HALF-AND-HALF (10%) CREAM	375 ML
½ TSP	SALT	2 ML
¼ TSP	CAYENNE PEPPER	1 ML

GREASE THE INSERT OF A 3½- TO 4-QUART SLOW COOKER. IN SLOW COOKER, COMBINE BEANS, RED PEPPER, ONION, POTATOES AND CORN. SPRINKLE WITH CHEESE AND CILANTRO. STIR WELL. IN A BOWL, WHISK TOGETHER EGGS, CREAM, SALT AND CAYENNE. POUR EGG MIXTURE OVER BEAN MIXTURE. COVER AND REFRIGERATE FOR AT LEAST 4 HOURS OR OVERNIGHT. TRANSFER INSERT TO SLOW COOKER BASE. COOK ON LOW FOR 3 TO 4 HOURS, UNTIL EGGS ARE SET AND EDGES ARE BROWNED. LET STAND FOR 15 MINUTES BEFORE SERVING. SERVES 6 TO 8.

TIP: IF YOU PREFER TO USE COOKED DRIED BEANS INSTEAD OF CANNED, SEE BASIC BEANS (PAGE 282). YOU'LL NEED 2 CUPS (500 ML) COOKED BEANS FOR THIS RECIPE.

MEXICAN STRATA

*OLÉ! PERFECT FOR BRUNCH OR A LIGHT SUPPER.
SERVE WITH PAPAYA SALSA (PAGE 197).*

6 CUPS	CUBED WHITE BREAD (SEE TIP, BELOW)	1.5 L
2	TOMATOES, SLICED	2
4	GREEN ONIONS, CHOPPED	4
1	CAN (4$\frac{1}{2}$ OZ/127 ML) DICED MILD GREEN CHILES	1
1 CUP	SHREDDED TEX-MEX CHEESE BLEND	250 ML
4	EGGS	4
2 CUPS	HALF-AND-HALF (10%) CREAM	500 ML
1 TSP	SALT	5 ML
1 TSP	GROUND CUMIN	5 ML
$\frac{1}{4}$ TSP	CAYENNE PEPPER	1 ML

GREASE THE INSERT OF A 3$\frac{1}{2}$- TO 4-QUART SLOW COOKER.
PLACE HALF THE BREAD IN SLOW COOKER. ARRANGE
TOMATO SLICES ON TOP. SPRINKLE WITH GREEN ONIONS,
GREEN CHILES AND $\frac{3}{4}$ CUP (175 ML) OF THE CHEESE.
TOP WITH REMAINING BREAD. IN A LARGE BOWL, WHISK
TOGETHER EGGS, CREAM, SALT, CUMIN AND CAYENNE.
POUR OVER BREAD MIXTURE, GENTLY PUSHING BREAD
DOWN TO SUBMERGE. SPRINKLE WITH REMAINING CHEESE.
COVER AND REFRIGERATE FOR AT LEAST 4 HOURS OR
OVERNIGHT. TRANSFER INSERT TO SLOW COOKER BASE.
COOK ON HIGH FOR 1$\frac{1}{2}$ TO 2 HOURS, UNTIL SET AND
PUFFED. SERVES 6 TO 8.

TIP: FOR BEST RESULTS, USE STALE BREAD, AS IT BETTER
ABSORBS THE EGG MIXTURE. TO DRY THE BREAD, YOU
CAN LEAVE IT UNCOVERED AT ROOM TEMPERATURE FOR
12 HOURS OR OVERNIGHT BEFORE ASSEMBLING THE STRATA.

SUNRISE-SUNSET
APPLE BACON STRATA

THIS WORKS FOR BRUNCH OR SUPPER. SERVE
WITH MAPLE SYRUP IN THE MORNING OR
A GREEN SALAD AT NIGHT.

6	SLICES BACON, CHOPPED	6
6	EGGS	6
1 CUP	HALF-AND-HALF (10%) CREAM OR WHOLE MILK	250 ML
2 TSP	CHOPPED FRESH THYME (OR $1/4$ TSP/ 1 ML DRIED)	10 ML
1 TSP	DIJON MUSTARD	5 ML
$1/2$ TSP	SALT	2 ML
$1/8$ TSP	PEPPER	0.5 ML
4 CUPS	CUBED WHITE BREAD (SEE TIP, OPPOSITE)	1 L
4	GREEN ONIONS, CHOPPED	4
2	RED-SKINNED APPLES (UNPEELED), GRATED	2
2 CUPS	SHREDDED SMOKED GOUDA OR EXTRA-SHARP (EXTRA-OLD) CHEDDAR CHEESE, DIVIDED	500 ML

GREASE THE INSERT OF A $3^1/2$- TO 4-QUART SLOW COOKER. IN A SKILLET, BROWN BACON OVER MEDIUM-HIGH HEAT. USING A SLOTTED SPOON, TRANSFER BACON TO A PLATE LINED WITH PAPER TOWELS. IN A LARGE BOWL, WHISK TOGETHER EGGS, CREAM, THYME, MUSTARD, SALT AND PEPPER. PLACE HALF THE BREAD IN PREPARED SLOW COOKER. ARRANGE COOKED BACON, GREEN ONIONS, APPLES AND 1 CUP (250 ML) CHEESE ON TOP. POUR IN HALF THE EGG MIXTURE AND SCATTER WITH REMAINING BREAD. POUR IN REMAINING EGG MIXTURE, GENTLY PUSHING BREAD

DOWN TO SUBMERGE. COVER AND REFRIGERATE FOR AT LEAST 4 HOURS OR OVERNIGHT. TRANSFER INSERT TO SLOW COOKER BASE. COOK ON HIGH FOR 2 TO $2\frac{1}{2}$ HOURS, UNTIL SET AND PUFFED. TURN OFF SLOW COOKER. SPRINKLE REMAINING CHEESE OVER TOP; COVER AND LET STAND FOR 10 MINUTES, UNTIL CHEESE MELTS. SERVES 6.

TIP: FOR BEST RESULTS, USE STALE BREAD, AS IT BETTER ABSORBS THE EGG MIXTURE. TO DRY THE BREAD, YOU CAN LEAVE IT UNCOVERED AT ROOM TEMPERATURE FOR 12 HOURS OR OVERNIGHT BEFORE ASSEMBLING THE STRATA.

TIP: STRATAS ARE A GREAT WAY TO USE UP BREAD THAT'S A FEW DAYS OLD. STALE BREAD LENDS STRUCTURE TO THE STRATA AND PREVENTS IT FROM BECOMING TOO SOGGY.

HOW CAN YOU TELL THE MALE PANCAKES
FROM THE FEMALE PANCAKES?
THE MALE PANCAKES DON'T KNOW
WHERE TO FIND THE OTHER INGREDIENTS.
– DOUG DIRKS, RADIO SHOW HOST,
CBC RADIO, CALGARY, ALBERTA

CHRISTMAS MORNING WIFE SAVER

*WE WONDERED: COULD WE ADAPT THIS FOREVER
FAVORITE TO THE SLOW COOKER? YES, AND
IT REALLY WORKS!*

I TBSP	VEGETABLE OIL	15 ML
I	ONION, FINELY CHOPPED	I
I	RED BELL PEPPER, CHOPPED	I
12 CUPS	CUBED WHITE BREAD (SEE TIP, PAGE 21)	3 L
1 1/2 CUPS	DICED HAM	375 ML
2 1/2 CUPS	SHREDDED SHARP (OLD) CHEDDAR CHEESE, DIVIDED	625 ML
1/2 CUP	GRATED PARMESAN CHEESE	125 ML
8	EGGS	8
4 CUPS	HALF-AND-HALF (10%) CREAM	I L
2 TSP	DRY MUSTARD	10 ML
I TSP	WORCESTERSHIRE SAUCE	5 ML
1/2 TSP	SALT	2 ML
1/4 TSP	CAYENNE PEPPER	I ML
1/4 CUP	BUTTER	60 ML
I CUP	FRESH BREAD CRUMBS	250 ML

GREASE THE INSERT OF A 5- TO 6-QUART SLOW COOKER.
IN A SKILLET, HEAT OIL OVER MEDIUM HEAT. ADD ONION
AND RED PEPPER; COOK, STIRRING OCCASIONALLY, FOR
5 MINUTES. TRANSFER TO PREPARED SLOW COOKER AND
STIR IN BREAD CUBES, HAM, 2 CUPS (500 ML) CHEDDAR
AND PARMESAN. IN A LARGE BOWL, WHISK TOGETHER
EGGS, CREAM, MUSTARD, WORCESTERSHIRE SAUCE, SALT
AND CAYENNE. POUR OVER BREAD MIXTURE AND STIR TO
COMBINE, GENTLY PUSHING BREAD DOWN TO SUBMERGE.
COVER AND REFRIGERATE FOR AT LEAST 4 HOURS OR

OVERNIGHT. TRANSFER INSERT TO SLOW COOKER BASE. COOK ON HIGH FOR 2 TO $2\frac{1}{2}$ HOURS, UNTIL SET AND PUFFED. MEANWHILE, IN A SKILLET, HEAT BUTTER OVER MEDIUM HEAT. ADD BREAD CRUMBS AND COOK, STIRRING, UNTIL BROWN AND CRISPY, ABOUT 5 MINUTES. TRANSFER TO A BOWL AND LET COOL COMPLETELY; SET ASIDE. TURN OFF SLOW COOKER AND SPRINKLE REMAINING CHEDDAR OVER PUFFED STRATA. COVER AND LET STAND FOR 10 MINUTES, UNTIL CHEESE MELTS. SPRINKLE WITH RESERVED TOASTED BREAD CRUMBS AND SERVE IMMEDIATELY. SERVES 8.

TIP: THE CHRISTMAS MORNING WIFE SAVER WILL HOLD FOR UP TO 1 HOUR ON THE KEEP WARM OR BUFFET SETTING. DO NOT GARNISH WITH THE TOASTED BREAD CRUMBS UNTIL YOU ARE READY TO SERVE, OR THEY WILL LOSE THEIR CRISPINESS IN THE MOIST HEAT OF THE SLOW COOKER.

BEST-EVER BANANA BREAD

THIS IS THE WAY TO "BAKE" IN THE SUMMER WHEN IT'S TOO HOT TO SWITCH ON THE OVEN. OUR CLASSIC BANANA BREAD COOKS UNATTENDED — LEAVING YOU TIME TO CHILL. WE USUALLY SERVE THE BREAD UPSIDE DOWN, AS THE BOTTOM LOOKS NICER THAN THE TOP WHEN COOKED IN THE SLOW COOKER.

1¼ CUPS	ALL-PURPOSE FLOUR	300 ML
1 TSP	BAKING POWDER	5 ML
1 TSP	GROUND CINNAMON	5 ML
½ TSP	SALT	2 ML
1 CUP	GRANULATED SUGAR	250 ML
2	EGGS, LIGHTLY BEATEN	2
1¼ CUPS	MASHED RIPE BANANAS (ABOUT 2 LARGE)	300 ML
½ CUP	BUTTER, MELTED AND COOLED	125 ML
1 TSP	VANILLA EXTRACT	5 ML
¾ CUP	CHOPPED PECANS	175 ML

USE A 6- TO 7-QUART SLOW COOKER. GREASE AN 8- BY 4-INCH (20 BY 10 CM) GLASS LOAF DISH AND LINE THE BOTTOM WITH PARCHMENT PAPER. IN A LARGE BOWL, WHISK TOGETHER FLOUR, BAKING POWDER, CINNAMON AND SALT. IN ANOTHER BOWL, COMBINE SUGAR, EGGS, BANANAS, BUTTER AND VANILLA. POUR OVER FLOUR MIXTURE AND STIR JUST UNTIL EVENLY COMBINED. GENTLY STIR IN PECANS. SPREAD BATTER IN PREPARED LOAF DISH. COVER TIGHTLY WITH FOIL AND SECURE WITH KITCHEN STRING. PLACE IN SLOW COOKER AND POUR IN ENOUGH VERY HOT WATER TO COME HALFWAY UP THE SIDES OF THE DISH. COVER AND COOK ON HIGH FOR

2¹/₂ TO 3 HOURS, UNTIL A TESTER INSERTED IN THE CENTER COMES OUT CLEAN. TRANSFER DISH TO A WIRE RACK AND REMOVE STRING AND FOIL. LET COOL IN DISH FOR 15 MINUTES. USING A RUBBER SPATULA, LOOSEN SIDES OF LOAF. TURN OUT ONTO RACK AND REMOVE PARCHMENT. LET COOL COMPLETELY BEFORE SLICING. SERVES 12.

TIP: USE VERY RIPE BANANAS FOR THE TASTIEST RESULTS. BLACK SPOTS ON THE SKIN ARE GOOD!

TIP: OMIT THE CINNAMON FOR A BOLDER BANANA FLAVOR.

VARIATION: REPLACE THE PECANS WITH AN EQUAL AMOUNT OF RAISINS, DRIED CRANBERRIES, CHOPPED DRIED PINEAPPLE OR CHOCOLATE CHIPS. OR DRESS UP THE BREAD BY DRIZZLING MELTED CHOCOLATE OVER TOP.

CURRANT PECAN BREAD

*THE STEAM IN THE SLOW COOKER GIVES THIS BREAD
A LOVELY MOIST TEXTURE.*

1/2 CUP	ALL-PURPOSE FLOUR	125 ML
1/2 CUP	WHOLE WHEAT FLOUR	125 ML
1/2 CUP	CORNMEAL	125 ML
I TSP	GROUND CINNAMON	5 ML
1/2 TSP	BAKING SODA	2 ML
1/2 TSP	SALT	2 ML
I CUP	BUTTERMILK (SEE TIP, OPPOSITE)	250 ML
1/3 CUP	LIGHT (FANCY) MOLASSES	75 ML
	GRATED ZEST OF 1/2 LEMON	
1/2 CUP	DRIED CURRANTS OR CRANBERRIES	125 ML
1/4 CUP	CHOPPED PECANS	60 ML

USE A 6- TO 7-QUART SLOW COOKER. GREASE A 6-CUP
(1.5 L) ROUND BAKING DISH. IN A BOWL, WHISK TOGETHER
ALL-PURPOSE FLOUR, WHOLE WHEAT FLOUR, CORNMEAL,
CINNAMON, BAKING SODA AND SALT. MAKE A WELL IN
THE CENTER OF THE FLOUR MIXTURE. ADD BUTTERMILK,
MOLASSES AND LEMON ZEST TO WELL. STIR JUST
UNTIL EVENLY COMBINED. GENTLY STIR IN CURRANTS
AND PECANS. SPREAD BATTER IN PREPARED DISH. COVER
TIGHTLY WITH FOIL AND SECURE WITH KITCHEN STRING.
PLACE IN SLOW COOKER AND POUR IN ENOUGH VERY
HOT WATER TO COME HALFWAY UP THE SIDES OF THE
DISH. COVER AND COOK ON HIGH FOR 2 TO 2 1/2 HOURS,
UNTIL A TESTER INSERTED IN THE CENTER COMES OUT
CLEAN. TRANSFER DISH TO A WIRE RACK AND LET COOL,
COVERED, FOR 5 MINUTES. REMOVE STRING AND FOIL.

USING A RUBBER SPATULA, LOOSEN SIDES OF LOAF. TURN OUT ONTO RACK AND LET COOL COMPLETELY. CUT INTO WEDGES. SERVES 8.

TIP: IF YOU DON'T HAVE BUTTERMILK, COMBINE 1½ TSP (7 ML) VINEGAR WITH ENOUGH MILK TO MAKE ½ CUP (125 ML). LET STAND FOR 5 MINUTES BEFORE ADDING TO THE RECIPE.

TIP: A FEW RECIPES IN THIS BOOK NEED TO BE COOKED IN AN EXTRA DISH PLACED IN THE SLOW COOKER. YOU'LL NEED A LARGE (6- TO 7-QUART) SLOW COOKER TO ACCOMMODATE THE DISH. WE FOUND THAT 6- TO 8-OZ (175 TO 250 ML) RAMEKINS, 4-CUP (1 L) AND 6-CUP (1.5 L) ROUND BAKING DISHES AND 8- BY 4-INCH (20 BY 10 CM) LOAF PANS ALL FIT IN OUR 6-QUART OVAL OR RECTANGULAR SLOW COOKER.

IF YOU'RE NOT LIVING ON THE EDGE,
YOU'RE TAKING UP TOO MUCH ROOM.
– FLO KENNEDY

BANANA DATE BREAD

A WHOLESOME SNACK FOR YOUR CREW.

1 CUP	WHOLE WHEAT FLOUR	250 ML
1/2 CUP	WHEAT GERM	125 ML
1/2 CUP	WHEAT OR OAT BRAN	125 ML
1 TSP	BAKING POWDER	5 ML
1 TSP	BAKING SODA	5 ML
1 TSP	GROUND CINNAMON	5 ML
1/2 TSP	SALT	2 ML
1/2 CUP	PACKED BROWN SUGAR	125 ML
1	EGG, LIGHTLY BEATEN	1
1 1/4 CUPS	MASHED RIPE BANANAS (ABOUT 2 LARGE)	300 ML
1/2 CUP	BUTTERMILK (SEE TIP, PAGE 29)	125 ML
1/4 CUP	VEGETABLE OIL	60 ML
3/4 CUP	CHOPPED DATES	175 ML

GREASE THE INSERT OF A 3 1/2- TO 4-QUART SLOW COOKER. IN A LARGE BOWL, WHISK TOGETHER FLOUR, WHEAT GERM, BRAN, BAKING POWDER, BAKING SODA, CINNAMON AND SALT. IN ANOTHER BOWL, COMBINE BROWN SUGAR, EGG, BANANAS, BUTTERMILK AND OIL. POUR OVER FLOUR MIXTURE AND STIR JUST UNTIL EVENLY COMBINED. GENTLY STIR IN DATES. SPREAD BATTER IN PREPARED SLOW COOKER. PLACE A CLEAN TEA TOWEL, FOLDED IN HALF (SO YOU HAVE TWO LAYERS), OVER TOP OF INSERT. COVER AND COOK ON HIGH FOR 1 1/2 TO 2 HOURS, UNTIL A TESTER INSERTED IN THE CENTER COMES OUT CLEAN. TRANSFER INSERT TO A CUTTING BOARD AND LET COOL FOR 10 MINUTES. USING A RUBBER SPATULA, LOOSEN SIDES OF LOAF. TURN OUT ONTO RACK TO COOL COMPLETELY. CUT INTO WEDGES. SERVES 8.

SWEET POTATO RAISIN BREAD

HEARTY AND NUTRITIOUS. TRY IT — YOU'LL LIKE IT!

3/4 CUP	ALL-PURPOSE FLOUR	175 ML
1/2 CUP	WHOLE WHEAT FLOUR	125 ML
1/2 CUP	GROUND FLAX SEEDS (FLAXSEED MEAL)	125 ML
1 TSP	GROUND CINNAMON	5 ML
1 TSP	BAKING POWDER	5 ML
1/4 TSP	BAKING SODA	1 ML
1 1/2 CUPS	GRATED PEELED SWEET POTATO	375 ML
3/4 CUP	RAISINS	175 ML
3/4 CUP	GRANULATED SUGAR	175 ML
2	EGGS, LIGHTLY BEATEN	2
1/3 CUP	VEGETABLE OIL	75 ML
2 TBSP	GRATED ORANGE ZEST	30 ML
2 TBSP	FRESHLY SQUEEZED ORANGE JUICE	30 ML

GREASE THE INSERT OF A 3 1/2 - TO 4-QUART SLOW COOKER.
IN A LARGE BOWL, WHISK TOGETHER ALL-PURPOSE FLOUR,
WHOLE WHEAT FLOUR, FLAX SEEDS, CINNAMON, BAKING
POWDER AND BAKING SODA. IN ANOTHER BOWL, COMBINE
SWEET POTATO, RAISINS, SUGAR, EGGS, OIL, ORANGE
ZEST AND ORANGE JUICE. POUR OVER FLOUR MIXTURE
AND STIR JUST UNTIL EVENLY COMBINED. SPREAD BATTER
IN PREPARED SLOW COOKER. PLACE A CLEAN TEA TOWEL,
FOLDED IN HALF (SO YOU HAVE TWO LAYERS), OVER TOP OF
INSERT. COVER AND COOK ON HIGH FOR 1 1/2 TO 2 HOURS,
UNTIL A TESTER INSERTED IN THE CENTER COMES OUT
CLEAN. TRANSFER INSERT TO A CUTTING BOARD AND LET
COOL FOR 10 MINUTES. USING A RUBBER SPATULA, LOOSEN
SIDES OF LOAF. TURN OUT ONTO A WIRE RACK TO COOL
COMPLETELY. CUT INTO WEDGES. SERVES 8.

LEMONY ZUCCHINI FLAXSEED LOAF

GOODY! OUR FAVORITE MUFFIN RECIPE, ADAPTED TO THE SLOW COOKER. THE BREAD DOESN'T GET AS BROWN AS WHEN COOKED IN THE OVEN, BUT IT TASTES JUST AS GOOD.

1 1/4 CUPS	ALL-PURPOSE FLOUR	300 ML
1/2 CUP	GROUND FLAX SEEDS (FLAXSEED MEAL)	125 ML
1 TSP	BAKING POWDER	5 ML
1/2 TSP	GROUND CINNAMON	2 ML
1/4 TSP	BAKING SODA	1 ML
1 1/2 CUPS	GRATED ZUCCHINI	375 ML
3/4 CUP	DRIED CRANBERRIES	175 ML
3/4 CUP	GRANULATED SUGAR	175 ML
2	EGGS, LIGHTLY BEATEN	2
1/3 CUP	VEGETABLE OIL	75 ML
2 TBSP	GRATED LEMON ZEST	30 ML
2 TBSP	FRESHLY SQUEEZED LEMON JUICE	30 ML

GREASE THE INSERT OF A 3 1/2- TO 4-QUART SLOW COOKER. IN A LARGE BOWL, WHISK TOGETHER FLOUR, FLAX SEEDS, BAKING POWDER, CINNAMON AND BAKING SODA. IN ANOTHER BOWL, COMBINE ZUCCHINI, CRANBERRIES, SUGAR, EGGS, OIL, LEMON ZEST AND LEMON JUICE. POUR OVER FLOUR MIXTURE AND STIR JUST UNTIL EVENLY COMBINED. SPREAD BATTER IN PREPARED SLOW COOKER. PLACE A CLEAN TEA TOWEL, FOLDED IN HALF (SO YOU HAVE TWO LAYERS), OVER TOP OF INSERT. COVER AND COOK ON HIGH FOR 1 1/2 TO 2 HOURS, UNTIL A TESTER INSERTED IN THE CENTER COMES OUT CLEAN. TRANSFER INSERT TO A CUTTING BOARD AND LET COOL FOR 10 MINUTES. USING A RUBBER SPATULA, LOOSEN SIDES OF LOAF. TURN OUT ONTO A WIRE RACK TO COOL COMPLETELY. CUT INTO WEDGES. SERVES 8.

Good Morning Irish Oatmeal (page 17)

Sunrise-Sunset Apple Bacon Strata (page 22)

Cranberry Party Meatballs (page 38)

Honey Nuts (page 42) and
Chipotle Cashews (page 43)

EASY CORNBREAD

EVEN BETTER THAN CORNBREAD BAKED IN THE OVEN. SERVE WARM WITH SOUPS AND CHILIS, OR SPREAD WITH BUTTER AND JAM FOR BREAKFAST.

4 TBSP	MELTED BUTTER, DIVIDED	60 ML
1 CUP	ALL-PURPOSE FLOUR	250 ML
1 CUP	CORNMEAL	250 ML
1 1/2 TSP	BAKING POWDER	7 ML
1/2 TSP	BAKING SODA	2 ML
1/2 TSP	SALT	2 ML
3 TBSP	PACKED BROWN SUGAR	45 ML
2	EGGS, LIGHTLY BEATEN	2
1 1/3 CUPS	BUTTERMILK (SEE TIP, PAGE 29)	325 ML

BRUSH 1 TBSP (15 ML) BUTTER OVER THE BOTTOM AND SIDES OF THE INSERT OF A 3 1/2- TO 4-QUART SLOW COOKER (SEE TIP, PAGE 35). IN A BOWL, WHISK TOGETHER FLOUR, CORNMEAL, BAKING POWDER, BAKING SODA AND SALT. MAKE A WELL IN THE CENTER OF THE FLOUR MIXTURE. ADD BROWN SUGAR, EGGS, BUTTERMILK AND REMAINING BUTTER TO WELL. STIR JUST UNTIL EVENLY COMBINED. SPREAD BATTER IN PREPARED SLOW COOKER. PLACE A CLEAN TEA TOWEL, FOLDED IN HALF (SO YOU HAVE TWO LAYERS), OVER TOP OF INSERT. COVER AND COOK ON HIGH FOR 1 1/2 TO 2 HOURS, UNTIL A TESTER INSERTED IN THE CENTER COMES OUT CLEAN. TRANSFER INSERT TO A CUTTING BOARD AND LET COOL FOR 10 MINUTES. USING A RUBBER SPATULA, LOOSEN SIDES OF LOAF. TURN OUT ONTO CUTTING BOARD. CUT INTO WEDGES AND SERVE WARM. SERVES 6.

TEX-MEX CORNBREAD

*MOIST AND CRUMBLY, WITH A CRUNCHY EXTERIOR —
THIS MILDLY SPICED CORNBREAD IS IRRESISTIBLE EATEN
WARM WITH BUTTER.*

4 TBSP	MELTED BUTTER, DIVIDED	60 ML
I CUP	ALL-PURPOSE FLOUR	250 ML
I CUP	CORNMEAL	250 ML
1½ TSP	BAKING POWDER	7 ML
½ TSP	BAKING SODA	2 ML
½ TSP	SALT	2 ML
½ TSP	GROUND CUMIN	2 ML
¼ TSP	CAYENNE PEPPER	I ML
I CUP	SHREDDED TEX-MEX CHEESE BLEND OR JALAPEÑO JACK CHEESE	250 ML
3 TBSP	PACKED BROWN SUGAR	45 ML
2	EGGS, LIGHTLY BEATEN	2
I CUP	BUTTERMILK (SEE TIP, PAGE 29)	250 ML
¾ CUP	CHOPPED DRAINED ROASTED RED BELL PEPPERS	175 ML

BRUSH I TBSP (15 ML) BUTTER OVER THE BOTTOM AND
SIDES OF THE INSERT OF A 3½- TO 4-QUART SLOW
COOKER. IN A BOWL, WHISK TOGETHER FLOUR, CORNMEAL,
BAKING POWDER, BAKING SODA, SALT, CUMIN AND
CAYENNE. MAKE A WELL IN THE CENTRE OF THE FLOUR
MIXTURE. ADD CHEESE, BROWN SUGAR, EGGS, BUTTERMILK,
ROASTED PEPPERS AND REMAINING BUTTER TO WELL.
STIR JUST UNTIL EVENLY COMBINED. SPREAD BATTER
IN PREPARED SLOW COOKER. PLACE A CLEAN TEA TOWEL,
FOLDED IN HALF (SO YOU HAVE TWO LAYERS), OVER
TOP OF INSERT. COVER AND COOK ON HIGH FOR 1½ TO

2 HOURS, UNTIL A TESTER INSERTED IN THE CENTER COMES OUT CLEAN. TRANSFER INSERT TO A CUTTING BOARD AND LET COOL FOR 10 MINUTES. USING A RUBBER SPATULA, LOOSEN SIDES OF LOAF. TURN OUT ONTO CUTTING BOARD. CUT INTO WEDGES AND SERVE WARM. SERVES 6.

TIP: CONVENIENT BAGS OF SHREDDED TEX-MEX CHEESE BLEND CAN BE FOUND IN THE REFRIGERATED SECTION OF THE SUPERMARKET. THE BLEND USUALLY INCLUDES CHEDDAR, MOZZARELLA AND JALAPENO-FLAVORED MONTEREY-JACK CHEESE. IF YOU PREFER, SHRED YOUR OWN CHEESE USING ONE OR A COMBINATION OF THE TYPES SUGGESTED.

TIP: DON'T FORGET TO BRUSH THE SLOW COOKER INSERT WITH MELTED BUTTER BEFORE ADDING THE BATTER, AND DON'T SUBSTITUTE OIL OR BAKING SPRAY. THE BUTTER HELPS GIVE THE CORNBREAD ITS CHARACTERISTIC GOLDEN CRUST.

MY TRAIN OF THOUGHT HAS LEFT THE STATION.

UNATTENDED APPLESAUCE

AREN'T YOU A SMART MOM!

3 LBS	APPLES, PEELED AND CUT INTO 1½-INCH (4 CM) CHUNKS	1.5 KG
2 TBSP	GRANULATED SUGAR, OR TO TASTE	30 ML
1 CUP	UNSWEETENED APPLE JUICE (APPROX.)	250 ML

IN A MINIMUM 3½- TO 4-QUART SLOW COOKER, COMBINE APPLES, SUGAR AND JUICE. COVER AND COOK ON LOW FOR ABOUT 4 HOURS, UNTIL APPLES ARE VERY SOFT AND FALLING APART. USING A POTATO MASHER, MASH APPLES. STIR IN EXTRA SUGAR, IF DESIRED. ADJUST CONSISTENCY WITH ADDITIONAL JUICE, IF DESIRED. SERVE WARM, AT ROOM TEMPERATURE OR CHILLED. MAKES ABOUT 4 CUPS (1 L).

TIP: THE BEST APPLES FOR THIS RECIPE ARE GOLDEN DELICIOUS, MCINTOSH OR JONAGOLD.

MAKE AHEAD: LET COOL AND REFRIGERATE IN AN AIRTIGHT CONTAINER FOR UP TO 1 WEEK.

VARIATION

CRANBERRY APPLESAUCE: ADD 1 CUP (250 ML) FRESH OR FROZEN CRANBERRIES AND AN ADDITIONAL 2 TBSP (30 ML) GRANULATED SUGAR TO SLOW COOKER WITH APPLES.

NIBBLES, DIPS AND DRINKS

CRANBERRY PARTY MEATBALLS

THEY'LL ASK FOR THIS AGAIN!

2	CLOVES GARLIC, MINCED	2
1/4 CUP	FRESH BREAD CRUMBS	60 ML
2 TBSP	DRIED CRANBERRIES, FINELY CHOPPED	30 ML
1 TSP	CRUMBLED DRIED SAGE	5 ML
1 TSP	SALT	5 ML
1/4 TSP	PEPPER	1 ML
1	EGG, LIGHTLY BEATEN	1
1 LB	LEAN GROUND TURKEY	500 G
1/2 CUP	FINELY CHOPPED TOASTED PECANS	125 ML
1 TBSP	VEGETABLE OIL	15 ML
1/4 CUP	GRATED ONION	60 ML
1 CUP	JELLIED CRANBERRY SAUCE	250 ML
1/4 CUP	CHICKEN BROTH	60 ML
2 TBSP	TOMATO PASTE	30 ML
1 TBSP	DIJON MUSTARD	15 ML
1 TBSP	CIDER VINEGAR	15 ML

USE A 3 1/2 TO 4-QUART SLOW COOKER. IN A LARGE BOWL, COMBINE GARLIC, BREAD CRUMBS, CRANBERRIES, SAGE, SALT, PEPPER AND EGG. LET STAND FOR 5 MINUTES. ADD TURKEY AND PECANS. MIX WELL. USING ABOUT 2 TSP (10 ML) FOR EACH, SHAPE INTO MEATBALLS. IN A SKILLET, HEAT OIL OVER MEDIUM-HIGH HEAT. BROWN MEATBALLS IN TWO BATCHES. (THE MEATBALLS MIGHT STILL BE PINK INSIDE. DON'T WORRY; THEY WILL FINISH COOKING IN THE SAUCE). TRANSFER TO SLOW COOKER. IN A SAUCEPAN, COMBINE ONION, CRANBERRY SAUCE, BROTH, TOMATO PASTE, MUSTARD AND VINEGAR; BRING TO A

BOIL. REDUCE HEAT AND SIMMER, STIRRING OCCASIONALLY, FOR 5 MINUTES. POUR OVER MEATBALLS. COVER AND COOK ON LOW FOR 5 TO 6 HOURS OR ON HIGH FOR $2\frac{1}{2}$ TO 3 HOURS, UNTIL MEATBALLS ARE NO LONGER PINK INSIDE AND SAUCE IS THICKENED. SET THE SLOW COOKER TO KEEP WARM AND LET GUESTS HELP THEMSELVES. MAKES ABOUT 30 MEATBALLS.

TIP: BE SURE TO USE CRUMBLED DRIED SAGE AND NOT GROUND DRIED SAGE, WHICH HAS AN INTENSE AND OVERPOWERING FLAVOR.

TIP: WE USE TOMATO PASTE IN MANY OF OUR SLOW COOKER RECIPES BECAUSE IT GREATLY BOOSTS FLAVOR AND RICHNESS. THE LONG, MOIST COOKING DULLS OTHER AROMATIC INGREDIENTS, SUCH AS ONIONS, GARLIC AND HERBS. MICROWAVING OR BROWNING A DOLLOP OR TWO OF TOMATO PASTE WITH THESE INGREDIENTS MAKES ALL THE DIFFERENCE.

MANY PEOPLE HAVE EATEN MY COOKING
AND GONE ON TO LEAD NORMAL LIVES.

JELLY BALLS

EVERYONE LOVES THIS CLASSIC. THE SLOW COOKER CAN GO STRAIGHT TO THE BUFFET TABLE WITH COCKTAIL STICKS AND PLENTY OF NAPKINS.

1/4 CUP	FRESH BREAD CRUMBS	60 ML
1	EGG, LIGHTLY BEATEN	1
1 LB	LEAN GROUND BEEF	500 G
1/2 CUP	GRATED ONION	125 ML
1/2 TSP	SALT	2 ML
1/4 TSP	PEPPER	1 ML
1 TBSP	WORCESTERSHIRE SAUCE	15 ML
1 TBSP	VEGETABLE OIL	15 ML
2 TBSP	PACKED BROWN SUGAR	30 ML
1 CUP	TOMATO-BASED CHILI SAUCE	250 ML
3/4 CUP	GRAPE JELLY	175 ML
1 TBSP	FRESHLY SQUEEZED LEMON JUICE	15 ML
1 TBSP	SOY SAUCE	15 ML

USE A 3 1/2- TO 4-QUART SLOW COOKER. IN A LARGE BOWL, COMBINE BREAD CRUMBS AND EGG; LET SOAK FOR 5 MINUTES. ADD BEEF, ONION, SALT, PEPPER AND WORCESTERSHIRE SAUCE. MIX WELL. USING ABOUT 2 TSP (10 ML) FOR EACH, SHAPE INTO MEATBALLS. IN A SKILLET, HEAT OIL OVER MEDIUM-HIGH HEAT. BROWN MEATBALLS, IN TWO BATCHES. (THE MEATBALLS MIGHT STILL BE PINK INSIDE. DON'T WORRY; THEY WILL FINISH COOKING IN THE SAUCE). TRANSFER TO SLOW COOKER. IN A SMALL BOWL, WHISK TOGETHER BROWN SUGAR, CHILI SAUCE, GRAPE JELLY, LEMON JUICE AND SOY SAUCE. POUR OVER MEATBALLS. COVER AND COOK ON LOW FOR 5 TO 6 HOURS

OR ON HIGH FOR 2½ TO 3 HOURS, UNTIL MEATBALLS ARE NO LONGER PINK INSIDE AND SAUCE IS THICKENED. SET THE SLOW COOKER TO KEEP WARM AND LET GUESTS HELP THEMSELVES. MAKES ABOUT 30 MEATBALLS.

TIP: FRESH BREAD CRUMBS CAN BE MADE EASILY IN A FOOD PROCESSOR WITH WHATEVER SLIGHTLY STALE BREAD YOU HAVE LYING AROUND, SUCH AS SANDWICH LOAF, ENGLISH MUFFINS, DINNER ROLLS OR PITA BREAD. NO MACHINE? SIMPLY RUB THE BREAD ON A BOX GRATER. FROZEN BREAD IS EASIER TO GRATE THAN ROOM TEMPERATURE BREAD. FREEZE EXTRA BREAD CRUMBS IN SEALABLE PLASTIC BAGS.

TIP: WHEN SQUEEZING JUICE FROM A LEMON, LIME OR ORANGE, AIM TO HAVE THE FRUIT AT ROOM TEMPERATURE — IT WILL GIVE UP JUICE MORE EASILY THAN IF SQUEEZED STRAIGHT FROM THE REFRIGERATOR. IF YOU FORGET TO REMOVE IT FROM THE FRIDGE AHEAD OF TIME, PRICK THE FRUIT WITH A FORK AND MICROWAVE IT ON HIGH FOR ABOUT 20 SECONDS TO WARM IT SLIGHTLY.

SOME MISTAKES ARE TOO MUCH FUN
TO MAKE ONLY ONCE.

HONEY NUTS

WARMLY SPICED NUTS — AND YOU MADE THEM YOURSELF!

1 TSP	CHINESE FIVE-SPICE POWDER	5 ML
1/2 TSP	COARSE SEA SALT OR KOSHER SALT	2 ML
1/4 TSP	CAYENNE PEPPER	1 ML
1/2 CUP	LIQUID HONEY	125 ML
4 CUPS	UNSALTED RAW NUTS (SEE TIP, BELOW)	1 L

USE A 2- TO 3½-QUART SLOW COOKER. GREASE A LARGE RIMMED BAKING SHEET. IN A LARGE MICROWAVE-SAFE BOWL, COMBINE FIVE-SPICE POWDER, SALT, CAYENNE AND HONEY. MICROWAVE ON HIGH UNTIL BUBBLY, ABOUT 45 SECONDS. PLACE NUTS IN SLOW COOKER. POUR HONEY MIXTURE OVER NUTS AND STIR WELL. COVER AND COOK ON HIGH FOR 2 HOURS, STIRRING EVERY 30 MINUTES, UNTIL NUTS ARE HOT AND GLAZED. SPREAD ON PREPARED BAKING SHEET AND LET COOL COMPLETELY. BREAK INTO BITE-SIZED CLUSTERS. MAKES ABOUT 4 CUPS (1 L).

TIP: WE LOVE TO MAKE THIS WITH HAZELNUTS, BUT CASHEWS, PECANS, WHOLE ALMONDS AND PEANUTS WORK EQUALLY WELL.

MAKE AHEAD: STORE LAYERED BETWEEN WAXED PAPER IN AIRTIGHT CONTAINER FOR UP TO 2 DAYS.

CHIPOTLE CASHEWS

HOT ROASTED NUTS — GREAT WITH BEER.

2 CUPS	RAW CASHEWS	500 ML
1 TSP	CHIPOTLE CHILE POWDER	5 ML
1/4 TSP	CAYENNE PEPPER	1 ML
1 TBSP	OLIVE OIL	15 ML
2 TSP	FINE SEA SALT	10 ML

IN A 2- TO 3 1/2-QUART SLOW COOKER, COMBINE CASHEWS, CHIPOTLE CHILE POWDER AND CAYENNE. COVER AND COOK ON HIGH FOR 1 1/2 HOURS, STIRRING EVERY 30 MINUTES, UNTIL NUTS ARE TOASTED. STIR IN OIL AND SPRINKLE WITH SALT. MAKES 2 CUPS (500 ML).

TIP: JARS OF CHIPOTLE CHILE POWDER ARE AVAILABLE IN MOST SUPERMARKETS. THE REDDISH-BROWN POWDER IS MADE FROM DRIED SMOKED JALAPEÑO PEPPERS. IT LENDS AN AUTHENTIC MEXICAN TOUCH TO SOUPS, STEWS AND CHILIS. REGULAR CHILI POWDER CAN BE SUBSTITUTED IF YOU PREFER TO NOT HAVE A SMOKY FLAVOR.

SHE WHO WAITS FOR HER KNIGHT MUST REMEMBER:
SHE WILL HAVE TO CLEAN UP AFTER HIS HORSE.

POLENTA CROSTINI, THREE WAYS

SOMETHING NEW. BITE-SIZED PIECES OF CRISPY ITALIAN CORNMEAL CROSTINI, SERVED WITH THREE DIFFERENT TOPPINGS.

1 CUP	CORNMEAL	250 ML
1/2 TSP	SALT	2 ML
1/8 TSP	PEPPER	0.5 ML
3 1/2 CUPS	BOILING WATER	875 ML
1/3 CUP	GRATED PARMESAN CHEESE	75 ML
2 TBSP	MELTED BUTTER	30 ML
	OLIVE OIL	

GREASE THE INSERT OF A 3 1/2- TO 4-QUART SLOW COOKER. GREASE A LARGE RIMMED BAKING SHEET. PLACE CORNMEAL, SALT AND PEPPER IN PREPARED SLOW COOKER. GRADUALLY ADD BOILING WATER, WHISKING CONSTANTLY UNTIL BLENDED. COVER AND COOK ON LOW FOR ABOUT 1 1/2 HOURS, UNTIL LIQUID IS ABSORBED AND CORNMEAL IS TENDER. STIR IN CHEESE AND BUTTER. IMMEDIATELY POUR COOKED POLENTA ONTO PREPARED BAKING SHEET AND SPREAD EVENLY TO 1/4-INCH (0.5 CM) THICKNESS. LET COOL, COVER AND REFRIGERATE FOR AT LEAST 1 HOUR, UNTIL FIRM. MEANWHILE, PREHEAT OVEN TO 400°F (200°C). GREASE 2 LARGE BAKING SHEETS. CUT CHILLED POLENTA INTO 2- BY 1 1/2-INCH (5 BY 3 CM) PIECES OR USE A SMALL COOKIE CUTTER TO CUT ROUNDS, DISCARDING TRIMMINGS. TRANSFER POLENTA PIECES TO PREPARED BAKING SHEET, SPACING THEM ABOUT 1/2 INCH (1 CM) APART. BRUSH TOPS WITH OIL. BAKE FOR ABOUT 30 MINUTES, UNTIL GOLDEN BROWN AND CRISP. LET COOL FOR 5 MINUTES. ADD TOPPING AND SERVE IMMEDIATELY. *MAKES 50 PIECES.*

MAKE AHEAD: SPREAD COOKED POLENTA ON PREPARED BAKING SHEET. LET COOL, COVER AND REFRIGERATE FOR UP TO 3 DAYS. PROCEED WITH BAKING INSTRUCTIONS.

SUNNY TOMATO CROSTINI TOPPING

THIS MAKES ENOUGH TO TOP ABOUT HALF A BATCH — OR 25 PIECES — OF POLENTA CROSTINI (SEE RECIPE, PAGE 44).

1/4 CUP	CHOPPED FRESH BASIL	60 ML
3 TBSP	CRUMBLED GOAT CHEESE	45 ML
6 TBSP	CHOPPED DRAINED OIL-PACKED SUN-DRIED TOMATOES	90 ML
1 TBSP	OIL FROM SUN-DRIED TOMATOES	15 ML
	SALT AND PEPPER	

IN A SMALL BOWL, COMBINE BASIL, GOAT CHEESE, TOMATOES AND OIL. SEASON TO TASTE WITH SALT AND PEPPER. STIR WELL. DOLLOP A TEASPOON (5 ML) OF TOPPING ONTO EACH PIECE OF WARM CROSTINI. SERVE IMMEDIATELY. MAKES ABOUT 1 CUP (250 ML), ENOUGH FOR ABOUT 25 CROSTINI.

CONTINUED ON NEXT PAGE...

FIG AND PECAN CROSTINI TOPPING

A SENSATIONAL SWEET AND SAVORY APPETIZER.

2	CLOVES GARLIC, MINCED	2
$3/4$ CUP	FINELY CHOPPED STEMMED DRIED FIGS	175 ML
$1/4$ CUP	FINELY CHOPPED TOASTED PECANS	60 ML
PINCH	CAYENNE PEPPER	PINCH
	SALT	
1 TBSP	PURE MAPLE SYRUP	15 ML
1 TBSP	BALSAMIC VINEGAR	15 ML
	SHAVED PARMESAN CHEESE (SEE TIP, BELOW)	

IN A SMALL BOWL, COMBINE GARLIC, FIGS, PECANS, CAYENNE, SALT TO TASTE, MAPLE SYRUP AND VINEGAR. COVER AND REFRIGERATE FOR UP TO 1 HOUR TO BLEND THE FLAVORS. DOLLOP 2 TSP (10 ML) TOPPING ONTO EACH PIECE OF WARM CROSTINI (SEE RECIPE, PAGE 44). GARNISH WITH 1 OR 2 PARMESAN SHAVINGS. SERVE IMMEDIATELY. MAKES ABOUT 1 CUP (250 ML), ENOUGH FOR ABOUT 25 CROSTINI.

TIP: TO MAKE ATTRACTIVE PARMESAN SHAVINGS, USE A VEGETABLE PEELER TO SHAVE SMALL, THIN SLICES OFF A WEDGE OF FRESH PARMESAN CHEESE.

OLIVE CROSTINI TOPPING

OLIVE FANS, REJOICE!

1	TOMATO, SEEDED AND FINELY CHOPPED	1
1	CLOVE GARLIC, MINCED	1
1	ANCHOVY FILLET, FINELY CHOPPED	1
1/4 CUP	FINELY CHOPPED PITTED GREEN OLIVES	60 ML
1/4 CUP	FINELY CHOPPED PITTED KALAMATA OLIVES (SEE TIP, PAGE 49)	60 ML
1 TBSP	OLIVE OIL	15 ML
1/4 TSP	DRIED OREGANO	1 ML
	SALT AND PEPPER	
	GRATED PARMESAN CHEESE	

IN A SMALL BOWL, COMBINE TOMATO, GARLIC, ANCHOVY, GREEN OLIVES, KALAMATA OLIVES, OIL AND OREGANO. SEASON TO TASTE WITH SALT AND PEPPER. COVER AND LET STAND FOR 1 HOUR TO BLEND THE FLAVORS. DOLLOP 2 TSP (10 ML) OLIVE TOPPING ONTO EACH PIECE OF WARM CROSTINI (SEE RECIPE, PAGE 44). GARNISH WITH PARMESAN. SERVE IMMEDIATELY. MAKES ABOUT 1 CUP (250 ML), ENOUGH FOR ABOUT 25 CROSTINI.

TIP: WHEN A RECIPE CALLS FOR JUST 1 OR 2 ANCHOVIES, YOU CAN SUBSTITUTE 1/4 TSP (1 ML) ANCHOVY PASTE FOR EACH FILLET. IF THE RECIPE REQUIRES MORE, IT IS BEST TO STICK WITH JARRED OR CANNED ANCHOVIES, AS THE PASTE CAN BE A BIT OVERWHELMING IN LARGER AMOUNTS.

CARAMELIZED ONION AND OLIVE FLATBREAD

PREPARE THE CARAMELIZED ONIONS IN THE SLOW COOKER AND ASSEMBLE THESE MUNCHIES JUST BEFORE YOUR GUESTS ARRIVE.

2	LARGE ONIONS, THINLY SLICED	2
2 TBSP	BUTTER, MELTED	30 ML
I TSP	SALT	5 ML
1/2 TSP	PEPPER	2 ML
1/4 TSP	CAYENNE PEPPER (OR TO TASTE)	I ML
4	7-INCH (18 CM) GREEK-STYLE PITAS (NO POCKET) OR MINI PIZZA SHELLS	4
2 TBSP	OLIVE OIL	30 ML
1/2 CUP	GRATED PARMESAN CHEESE	125 ML
2 CUPS	SHREDDED SWISS CHEESE	500 ML
1/2 CUP	KALAMATA OLIVES, HALVED AND PITTED	125 ML
I TSP	DRIED OREGANO	5 ML

IN A 2- TO 4-QUART SLOW COOKER, COMBINE ONIONS AND BUTTER, STIRRING WELL. COVER AND COOK ON HIGH FOR 45 TO 90 MINUTES, STIRRING TWICE, UNTIL ONIONS ARE SOFTENED. ADD SALT, PEPPER AND CAYENNE. PLACE TWO CLEAN TEA TOWELS, EACH FOLDED IN HALF (SO YOU HAVE FOUR LAYERS), OVER TOP OF INSERT. COVER AND COOK ON HIGH FOR 3 TO 4 HOURS, STIRRING TWICE, UNTIL ONIONS ARE GOLDEN BROWN. TRANSFER ONIONS TO A BOWL AND LET COOL TO ROOM TEMPERATURE. MEANWHILE, PREHEAT OVEN TO 375°F (190°C). PLACE PITAS ON 2 LARGE BAKING SHEETS. BRUSH WITH OIL AND SPRINKLE WITH PARMESAN. SPREAD COOLED ONION MIXTURE OVER PITAS. SPRINKLE WITH SWISS CHEESE,

OLIVES AND OREGANO. BAKE FOR ABOUT 15 MINUTES OR UNTIL CHEESE IS BUBBLY AND PITAS ARE BROWNED AND CRISP ON THE BOTTOM. CUT EACH PITA INTO 8 THIN WEDGES. MAKES 32 PIECES.

TIP: BUY OLIVES FROM THE REFRIGERATED OR DELI SECTION OF THE SUPERMARKET, RATHER THAN BUYING CANNED. THE CANNED ONES HAVE AN UNDESIRABLE TEXTURE AND LITTLE FLAVOR.

MAKE AHEAD: TRANSFER COOLED ONIONS TO AN AIRTIGHT CONTAINER AND REFRIGERATE FOR UP TO 5 DAYS OR FREEZE FOR UP TO 1 MONTH.

ZIPPY CHICKPEA SPREAD

DEFINITELY DELICIOUS — AND IT'S GOOD FOR YOU!

I	CAN (14 TO 19 OZ/398 TO 540 ML) CHICKPEAS, DRAINED AND RINSED	I
4	GREEN ONIONS, CHOPPED, DIVIDED	4
4 OZ	CREAM CHEESE, CUBED AND SOFTENED	125 G
1 1/2 CUPS	SHREDDED TEX-MEX CHEESE BLEND, DIVIDED	375 ML
1/2 CUP	SOUR CREAM	125 ML
1/4 TSP	CAYENNE PEPPER	I ML
I	TOMATO, CHOPPED	I

USE A 3 1/2- TO 4-QUART SLOW COOKER. IN A FOOD PROCESSOR, PURÉE CHICKPEAS UNTIL SMOOTH. SCRAPE INTO SLOW COOKER. ADD HALF THE GREEN ONIONS, CREAM CHEESE, I CUP (250 ML) TEX-MEX CHEESE, SOUR CREAM AND CAYENNE. COVER AND COOK ON HIGH FOR I HOUR. STIR WELL. COVER AND COOK ON HIGH FOR 30 TO 60 MINUTES, UNTIL HOT AND BUBBLY. STIR. SPRINKLE WITH REMAINING GREEN ONIONS, REMAINING TEX-MEX CHEESE AND TOMATO. SERVE IMMEDIATELY. SERVES 6 TO 8 AN APPETIZER.

TIP: IF YOU PREFER TO USE COOKED DRIED CHICKPEAS INSTEAD OF CANNED, SEE BASIC BEANS (PAGE 282). YOU'LL NEED 2 CUPS (500 ML) COOKED CHICKPEAS FOR THIS RECIPE.

CREAMY BLACK BEAN DIP

EVERYONE WILL BE FIGHTING FOR THE LAST SCOOP.
SERVE WITH TORTILLA CHIPS.

I TBSP	VEGETABLE OIL	15 ML
I CUP	FINELY CHOPPED ONION	250 ML
2	CLOVES GARLIC, MINCED	2
$\frac{1}{2}$ TSP	GROUND CUMIN	2 ML
$\frac{1}{4}$ TSP	CAYENNE PEPPER	I ML
I	CAN (14 TO 19 OZ/398 TO 540 ML) BLACK BEANS, DRAINED AND RINSED (SEE TIP, PAGE 20)	I
8 OZ	BLOCK PROCESSED CHEESE (SUCH AS VELVEETA), CUBED	250 G
I CUP	SALSA	250 ML
2 TBSP	CHOPPED FRESH CILANTRO (OPTIONAL)	30 ML

USE A 2- TO $3\frac{1}{2}$-QUART SLOW COOKER. IN A SKILLET, HEAT OIL OVER MEDIUM HEAT. ADD ONION, GARLIC, CUMIN AND CAYENNE; COOK, STIRRING OCCASIONALLY, FOR 3 MINUTES. SCRAPE INTO SLOW COOKER. STIR IN BEANS, CHEESE AND SALSA. COVER AND COOK ON HIGH FOR I HOUR. STIR WELL. COVER AND COOK FOR 30 TO 60 MINUTES, UNTIL CHEESE IS MELTED AND MIXTURE IS HOT AND BUBBLY. STIR IN CILANTRO, IF USING. SERVE WARM. MAKES ABOUT 3 CUPS (750 ML).

TIP: BLOCK PROCESSED CHEESE, SUCH AS VELVEETA, IS A BLAST FROM THE PAST, BUT IT'S GOT WHAT IT TAKES WHEN IT COMES TO MELTING QUALITIES. IT'S PERFECT IN RECIPES WHERE YOU WANT A REALLY SMOOTH AND CREAMY TEXTURE. YOU CAN SUBSTITUTE I CUP (250 ML) SHREDDED EXTRA-SHARP (EXTRA-OLD) CHEDDAR CHEESE IN THIS RECIPE, IF YOU PREFER.

CARAMELIZED ONION DIP

ONIONS THAT GENTLY CARAMELIZE IN THE
SLOW COOKER. AND IT ONLY TOOK US 30 YEARS
TO FIGURE THIS OUT!

I	LARGE ONION, THINLY SLICED	I
2 TBSP	BUTTER, MELTED	30 ML
I TSP	SALT	5 ML
1/2 TSP	PEPPER	2 ML
1/4 TSP	CAYENNE PEPPER (APPROX.)	I ML
4 OZ	CREAM CHEESE, CUBED AND SOFTENED	125 G
1/2 CUP	SOUR CREAM	125 ML
1/2 CUP	MAYONNAISE	125 ML

IN A 2- TO 4-QUART SLOW COOKER, COMBINE ONIONS AND
BUTTER, STIRRING WELL. COVER AND COOK ON HIGH FOR
45 TO 90 MINUTES, STIRRING TWICE, UNTIL ONIONS ARE
SOFTENED. ADD SALT, PEPPER AND CAYENNE. PLACE TWO
CLEAN TEA TOWELS, EACH FOLDED IN HALF (SO YOU HAVE
FOUR LAYERS), OVER TOP OF INSERT. COVER AND COOK ON
HIGH FOR 3 TO 4 HOURS, STIRRING TWICE, UNTIL ONIONS
ARE GOLDEN BROWN. TRANSFER ONIONS TO A BOWL AND
LET COOL TO ROOM TEMPERATURE. IN ANOTHER BOWL,
BEAT CREAM CHEESE, SOUR CREAM AND MAYONNAISE UNTIL
SMOOTH. SCRAPE ONIONS AND ACCUMULATED JUICES INTO
CHEESE MIXTURE; STIR WELL. ADJUST SEASONING WITH
ADDITIONAL CAYENNE, IF DESIRED. TRANSFER TO A SERVING
BOWL. MAKES ABOUT 2 CUPS (500 ML).

MAKE AHEAD: TRANSFER COOLED ONIONS TO AN AIRTIGHT
CONTAINER AND REFRIGERATE FOR UP TO 5 DAYS OR
FREEZE FOR UP TO 1 MONTH.

CRAB AND ARTICHOKE DIP

A PERENNIAL CROWD-PLEASER. SERVE WITH YOUR FAVORITE CHIPS, CRACKERS OR VEGETABLES.

1	JAR (12 OZ/340 ML) MARINATED ARTICHOKE HEARTS, DRAINED AND CHOPPED	1
1	CLOVE GARLIC, MINCED	1
8 OZ	CREAM CHEESE, CUBED AND SOFTENED	250 G
1/2 CUP	MAYONNAISE	125 ML
1/2 CUP	SOUR CREAM	125 ML
1/4 CUP	GRATED PARMESAN CHEESE	60 ML
1/4 TSP	CAYENNE PEPPER	1 ML
8 OZ	COOKED CRABMEAT (SEE TIP, BELOW), CHOPPED	250 G
	SALT (OPTIONAL)	
	CHOPPED GREEN ONIONS	

IN A 2- TO 4-QUART SLOW COOKER, COMBINE ARTICHOKES, GARLIC, CREAM CHEESE, MAYONNAISE, SOUR CREAM, PARMESAN AND CAYENNE. COVER AND COOK ON HIGH FOR 1 1/2 TO 2 HOURS, STIRRING TWICE, UNTIL HOT AND BUBBLY. STIR IN CRABMEAT. COVER AND COOK ON HIGH FOR 30 MINUTES, UNTIL HEATED THROUGH. STIR WELL. IF DESIRED, SEASON WITH SALT TO TASTE. GARNISH WITH GREEN ONIONS. MAKES ABOUT 3 CUPS (750 ML).

TIP: EITHER CANNED OR THAWED DRAINED FROZEN CRABMEAT WILL WORK IN THIS RECIPE.

BACON, ARTICHOKE AND SPINACH DIP

ALWAYS A HIT.

9	SLICES BACON, CHOPPED	9
1 TBSP	VEGETABLE OIL	15 ML
1/2 CUP	FINELY CHOPPED ONION	125 ML
3	CLOVES GARLIC, MINCED	3
1/2 TSP	SWEET SMOKED PAPRIKA	2 ML
1	CAN (14 OZ/398 ML) ARTICHOKES, DRAINED AND FINELY CHOPPED	1
2 CUPS	PACKED BABY SPINACH, CHOPPED	500 ML
3/4 CUP	GRATED PARMESAN CHEESE	175 ML
1/2 CUP	SOUR CREAM	125 ML
1/2 CUP	MAYONNAISE	125 ML
1 TBSP	FRESHLY SQUEEZED LEMON JUICE	15 ML

USE A 2- TO 4-QUART SLOW COOKER. IN A SKILLET, COOK BACON OVER MEDIUM-HIGH HEAT UNTIL CRISPY. USING A SLOTTED SPOON, TRANSFER BACON TO A BOWL. COVER AND REFRIGERATE. DRAIN FAT FROM SKILLET AND WIPE CLEAN WITH A PAPER TOWEL. ADD OIL TO SKILLET AND HEAT OVER MEDIUM HEAT. ADD ONION, GARLIC AND PAPRIKA; COOK, STIRRING, FOR 3 MINUTES. SCRAPE INTO SLOW COOKER. ADD ARTICHOKES, SPINACH, PARMESAN, SOUR CREAM, MAYONNAISE AND LEMON JUICE; STIR WELL. COVER AND COOK ON HIGH FOR 1 1/2 TO 2 HOURS, UNTIL HOT AND BUBBLY. STIR WELL. ADD RESERVED BACON AND STIR UNTIL BACON IS HEATED THROUGH. MAKES ABOUT 3 CUPS (750 ML).

TIP: SPANISH SMOKED PAPRIKA LENDS A WARM, SMOKY FLAVOR TO FOOD. IT COMES IN THREE LEVELS OF INTENSITY: SWEET, BITTERSWEET AND HOT. IT IS AVAILABLE ON THE SPICE SHELF AT MOST SUPERMARKETS. YOU CAN SUBSTITUTE REGULAR SWEET PAPRIKA IN THIS RECIPE, BUT THE RESULT WILL BE MILDER.

TIP: YOU CAN BUY GRATED PARMESAN CHEESE AT THE SUPERMARKET, BUT WE RECOMMEND GRATING YOUR OWN. WEDGES OF FRESH PARMESAN MAY SEEM EXPENSIVE, BUT THEY TASTE SO MUCH BETTER THAN THE PACKAGED STUFF. TO GRATE, USE A RASP-STYLE GRATER, SUCH AS A MICROPLANE, OR THE SMALLEST HOLES OF A BOX GRATER. WRAPPED IN PLASTIC WRAP, FRESH PARMESAN WILL KEEP FOR WEEKS IN THE REFRIGERATOR. BEST OF ALL, THE "HEEL," OR RIND, AT THE END OF THE WEDGE CAN BE THROWN INTO A SOUP OR STEW FOR ADDED FLAVORING.

ALWAYS BEING PERFECT
IS AN AWESOME RESPONSIBILITY.

CHEESE AND BEER FONDUE

YOUR SLOW COOKER WORKS AS A FONDUE POT.
NO FLAMMABLE FUEL, PERFECT FOR KIDS.

1	CLOVE GARLIC, HALVED	1
4 CUPS	SHREDDED EXTRA-SHARP (EXTRA-OLD) OR SHARP (OLD) CHEDDAR CHEESE	1 L
2 TBSP	ALL-PURPOSE FLOUR	30 ML
1 TSP	DRY MUSTARD	5 ML
1 1/4 CUPS	LIGHT OR MEDIUM BEER	300 ML
	PEPPER	

RUB THE INSIDE OF THE INSERT OF A 3 1/2- TO 4-QUART SLOW COOKER WITH CUT SIDES OF GARLIC; DISCARD GARLIC. COVER SLOW COOKER AND SET TO HIGH. IN A BOWL, TOSS TOGETHER CHEESE, FLOUR AND MUSTARD. SET ASIDE. IN A SAUCEPAN, BRING BEER TO A BOIL. POUR INTO SLOW COOKER. ADD CHEESE MIXTURE IN HANDFULS, STIRRING THOROUGHLY AFTER EACH ADDITION. COVER AND COOK ON HIGH FOR ABOUT 30 MINUTES, UNTIL CHEESE IS MELTED. SEASON TO TASTE WITH PEPPER. SERVES 6 AS AN APPETIZER.

TIP: USE A LIGHT TO MEDIUM BEER RATHER THAN A DARK OR BITTER BEER, WHICH MIGHT OVERWHELM THE FONDUE FLAVORS. BE SURE TO BRING THE BEER TO A BOIL BEFORE ADDING THE CHEESE — IT'S THE KEY TO A SUCCESSFUL CHEESE FONDUE IN THE SLOW COOKER.

HOT CRANBERRY SIPPER

A WARM WELCOME AFTER SKATING, SKIING, SKATEBOARDING OR SHOVELING THE SIDEWALK!

6	WHOLE CLOVES	6
2	3-INCH (7.5 CM) CINNAMON STICKS	2
1/2 CUP	PACKED BROWN SUGAR	125 ML
6 CUPS	RED CRANBERRY COCKTAIL	1.5 L
3 CUPS	ORANGE JUICE	750 ML
1 CUP	DARK RUM (OPTIONAL)	250 ML
1/4 CUP	ORANGE LIQUEUR (OPTIONAL)	60 ML

IN A 3 1/2- TO 4-QUART SLOW COOKER, COMBINE CLOVES, CINNAMON STICKS, BROWN SUGAR, CRANBERRY COCKTAIL AND ORANGE JUICE. COVER AND COOK ON LOW FOR ABOUT 4 HOURS, UNTIL STEAMING HOT. USING A SLOTTED SPOON, SCOOP OUT AND DISCARD CLOVES AND CINNAMON. IF DESIRED, STIR IN RUM AND ORANGE LIQUEUR. SET THE SLOW COOKER TO KEEP WARM. SERVES 8.

MULLED WINE

FILL YOUR HOUSE WITH WONDERFUL AROMAS. THIS RECIPE CAN BE EASILY DOUBLED.

6	WHOLE CLOVES	6
1	3-INCH (7.5 CM) CINNAMON STICK	1
	ZEST OF 1 ORANGE, CUT INTO 1/4-INCH (0.5 CM) WIDE STRIPS	
1 CUP	PACKED BROWN SUGAR	250 ML
2 1/2 CUPS	ORANGE JUICE	625 ML
1 CUP	WATER	250 ML
1	BOTTLE (750 ML) DRY RED WINE	1
	ORANGE SLICES	

IN A 4- TO 6-QUART SLOW COOKER, COMBINE CLOVES, CINNAMON STICK, ORANGE ZEST, BROWN SUGAR, ORANGE JUICE AND WATER. COVER AND COOK ON LOW FOR ABOUT 4 HOURS, UNTIL STEAMING HOT. USING A SLOTTED SPOON, SCOOP OUT AND DISCARD CLOVES, CINNAMON STICK AND ORANGE ZEST. STIR IN WINE. COVER AND COOK ON LOW FOR ABOUT 1 HOUR, UNTIL STEAMING HOT. LADLE INTO MUGS OR HEATPROOF GLASSES AND GARNISH WITH ORANGE SLICES. SERVES 8 TO 10.

SOUPS

BEET AND APPLE SOUP

JEWEL-COLORED AND WITH A HINT OF FRUITINESS, THIS SMOOTH VERSION OF BORSCHT IS DELICIOUS HOT OR CHILLED.

1 1/2 LBS	BEETS, PEELED AND CUT INTO 1/2-INCH (1 CM) CUBES	750 G
2	APPLES, PEELED AND CHOPPED	2
2	BAY LEAVES	2
1 TBSP	VEGETABLE OIL	15 ML
2	ONIONS, CHOPPED	2
4	CLOVES GARLIC, MINCED	4
4 CUPS	BEEF OR VEGETABLE BROTH	1 L
	SALT AND PEPPER	
2 TBSP	PACKED BROWN SUGAR	30 ML
1/3 CUP	ORANGE JUICE	75 ML
	SOUR CREAM	
	CHOPPED FRESH DILL (OPTIONAL)	

IN A 4- TO 6-QUART SLOW COOKER, COMBINE BEETS, APPLES AND BAY LEAVES. IN A SKILLET, HEAT OIL OVER MEDIUM HEAT. ADD ONIONS AND GARLIC; COOK, STIRRING OCCASIONALLY, FOR 5 MINUTES. ADD BROTH, 1/2 TSP (2 ML) SALT AND PEPPER TO TASTE; BRING TO A BOIL. POUR INTO SLOW COOKER. COVER AND COOK ON LOW FOR 6 TO 8 HOURS OR ON HIGH FOR 3 TO 4 HOURS, UNTIL BEETS ARE TENDER. WORKING IN BATCHES, TRANSFER SOUP TO A BLENDER OR FOOD PROCESSOR (OR USE AN IMMERSION BLENDER IN THE SLOW COOKER) AND PURÉE UNTIL SMOOTH. RETURN SOUP TO SLOW COOKER, IF NECESSARY, AND STIR IN BROWN SUGAR AND ORANGE JUICE. ADJUST SEASONING WITH SALT AND PEPPER, IF DESIRED. (IF

SERVING COLD, TRANSFER TO A LARGE BOWL, COVER AND CHILL THOROUGHLY, PREFERABLY OVERNIGHT). COVER AND COOK ON HIGH FOR 15 MINUTES, UNTIL STEAMING. LADLE INTO BOWLS AND TOP WITH A DOLLOP OF SOUR CREAM. SPRINKLE WITH DILL (IF USING). SERVES 6 TO 8.

TIP: WHEN SQUEEZING JUICE FROM A LEMON, LIME OR ORANGE, AIM TO HAVE THE FRUIT AT ROOM TEMPERATURE — IT WILL GIVE UP JUICE MORE EASILY THAN IF SQUEEZED STRAIGHT FROM THE REFRIGERATOR. IF YOU FORGET TO REMOVE IT FROM THE FRIDGE AHEAD OF TIME, PRICK THE FRUIT WITH A FORK AND MICROWAVE IT ON HIGH FOR ABOUT 20 SECONDS TO WARM IT SLIGHTLY.

APPARENTLY, IF YOU PLAY A BLUES SONG BACKWARDS,
YOUR LOVER RETURNS, YOUR DOG COMES BACK,
AND YOU CEASE TO BE AN ALCOHOLIC.

CARROT AND FENNEL SOUP WITH MAPLE SOUR CREAM

A LIGHT AND ELEGANT SOUP FOR A DINNER PARTY.

2 TBSP	VEGETABLE OIL, DIVIDED	30 ML
2	LARGE ONIONS, CHOPPED	2
2	FENNEL BULBS, TRIMMED AND THINLY SLICED	2
4	CLOVES GARLIC, MINCED	4
	SALT AND PEPPER	
4	LARGE CARROTS, THINLY SLICED	4
I TBSP	PACKED BROWN SUGAR	15 ML
6 CUPS	CHICKEN OR VEGETABLE BROTH, DIVIDED	1.5 L
2 TSP	DRIED DILLWEED	10 ML
1/3 CUP	SOUR CREAM	75 ML
I TBSP	PURE MAPLE SYRUP	15 ML
	CHOPPED FENNEL FRONDS (OPTIONAL)	

USE A 4- TO 6-QUART SLOW COOKER. IN A SKILLET, HEAT HALF THE OIL OVER MEDIUM HEAT. ADD ONIONS, FENNEL, GARLIC, I TSP (5 ML) SALT AND 1/4 TSP (I ML) PEPPER; COOK, STIRRING OCCASIONALLY, FOR 5 MINUTES. TRANSFER TO SLOW COOKER. ADD REMAINING OIL TO SKILLET. ADD CARROTS AND BROWN SUGAR; COOK, STIRRING OCCASIONALLY, FOR 5 MINUTES. ADD I CUP (250 ML) BROTH AND BRING TO A BOIL. TRANSFER TO SLOW COOKER. STIR IN REMAINING BROTH AND DILL. COVER AND COOK ON LOW FOR 6 TO 8 HOURS OR ON HIGH FOR 3 TO 4 HOURS, UNTIL VEGETABLES ARE TENDER. WORKING IN BATCHES, TRANSFER SOUP TO A BLENDER OR FOOD PROCESSOR (OR USE AN IMMERSION BLENDER IN THE SLOW COOKER)

AND PURÉE UNTIL SMOOTH. RETURN TO SLOW COOKER, IF NECESSARY. COVER AND COOK ON HIGH FOR 15 MINUTES, UNTIL STEAMING. ADJUST SEASONING WITH SALT AND PEPPER, IF DESIRED. IN A BOWL, COMBINE SOUR CREAM AND MAPLE SYRUP. LADLE SOUP INTO BOWLS AND TOP WITH A DOLLOP OF SOUR CREAM MIXTURE. SPRINKLE WITH FENNEL FRONDS (IF USING). SERVES 6 TO 8.

TIP: IF THE FENNEL BULB HAS STALKS ATTACHED, TRIM THEM OFF ABOUT 1 INCH (2.5 CM) ABOVE THE BULB. RESERVE SOME OF THE FEATHERY FRONDS FOR GARNISH — THEY TASTE LIKE DILL. CUT THE BULB IN HALF VERTICALLY AND REMOVE THE WOODY CORE FROM EACH HALF. CUT EACH HALF CROSSWISE INTO VERY THIN STRIPS.

CLASSIC FRENCH ONION SOUP

AH, BLISS! THE SLOW COOKER TAKES THE EFFORT OUT OF CARAMELIZING THE ONIONS. THE SOY SAUCE IS UNUSUAL, BUT IT BEEFS UP THE FLAVOR.

6	LARGE ONIONS, THINLY SLICED	6
1/4 CUP	MELTED BUTTER	60 ML
1 TBSP	PACKED BROWN SUGAR	15 ML
1 TSP	SALT	5 ML
1/2 TSP	PEPPER	2 ML
1/4 CUP	SOY SAUCE	60 ML
4 CUPS	BEEF BROTH	1 L
4 CUPS	CHICKEN BROTH	1 L
2 TBSP	DRY SHERRY OR BRANDY (OPTIONAL)	30 ML
12	SLICES BAGUETTE, ABOUT 1/2-INCH (1 CM) THICK	12
2 CUPS	SHREDDED SWISS OR CHEDDAR CHEESE (APPROX.)	500 ML

IN A 5- TO 6-QUART SLOW COOKER, COMBINE ONIONS AND BUTTER, STIRRING WELL. COVER AND COOK ON HIGH FOR 45 TO 90 MINUTES, STIRRING TWICE, UNTIL ONIONS ARE SOFTENED. ADD BROWN SUGAR, SALT, PEPPER AND SOY SAUCE. PLACE TWO CLEAN TEA TOWELS, EACH FOLDED IN HALF (SO YOU HAVE FOUR LAYERS), OVER TOP OF INSERT. COVER AND COOK ON HIGH FOR 3 TO 4 HOURS, STIRRING THREE OR FOUR TIMES TO PREVENT ONIONS FROM STICKING AND BURNING ON EDGES OF INSERT, UNTIL ONIONS ARE VERY SOFT AND DEEP BROWN. STIR IN BEEF BROTH, CHICKEN BROTH AND SHERRY (IF USING). LEAVE TEA TOWELS OFF. COVER AND COOK ON HIGH FOR 1 1/2 TO 2 HOURS, UNTIL VERY

HOT. PREHEAT BROILER. PLACE BAGUETTE SLICES ON A BAKING SHEET AND TOAST ON BOTH SIDES. SPRINKLE CHEESE ON ONE SIDE OF EACH SLICE AND BROIL FOR 2 TO 3 MINUTES, UNTIL CHEESE IS MELTED AND BUBBLY. LADLE SOUP INTO SERVING BOWLS AND TOP WITH CHEESY BREAD. SERVES 6.

THEY SAY IT'S BETTER TO BE POOR AND HAPPY THAN RICH AND MISERABLE. BUT COULDN'T SOME COMPROMISE BE WORKED OUT, LIKE BEING MODERATELY WEALTHY AND A LITTLE MOODY?

FOREST MUSHROOM CHOWDER

UNASHAMEDLY RICH! SERVE AS A STARTER,
WITH A SIMPLE GRILLED STEAK AND SALAD
TO FOLLOW.

1 TBSP	VEGETABLE OIL	15 ML
2	ONIONS, FINELY CHOPPED	2
2	CARROTS, THINLY SLICED	2
4 CUPS	SLICED EXOTIC MUSHROOMS	1 L
4	CLOVES GARLIC, MINCED	4
	SALT AND PEPPER	
2	BAY LEAVES	2
1	SMALL POTATO, PEELED AND CHOPPED	1
1	APPLE, PEELED AND CHOPPED	1
3 CUPS	CHICKEN OR VEGETABLE BROTH	750 ML
1 TBSP	SOY SAUCE	15 ML
$\frac{1}{2}$ CUP	CORN KERNELS, THAWED IF FROZEN	125 ML
2 TBSP	CHOPPED FRESH PARSLEY	30 ML
1 CUP	HEAVY OR WHIPPING (35%) CREAM, WARMED	250 ML
2 TBSP	DRY SHERRY	30 ML

USE A 4- TO 6-QUART SLOW COOKER. IN A SKILLET,
HEAT OIL OVER MEDIUM HEAT. ADD ONIONS, CARROTS,
MUSHROOMS, GARLIC, 1 TSP (5 ML) SALT AND $\frac{1}{4}$ TSP (1 ML)
PEPPER; COOK, STIRRING OCCASIONALLY, FOR 5 MINUTES.
TRANSFER TO SLOW COOKER. STIR IN BAY LEAVES,
POTATO, APPLE, BROTH AND SOY SAUCE. COVER AND COOK
ON LOW FOR ABOUT 6 HOURS OR ON HIGH FOR ABOUT
3 HOURS, UNTIL VEGETABLES ARE TENDER. STIR IN CORN,
PARSLEY, CREAM AND SHERRY. COVER AND COOK ON HIGH

FOR 15 MINUTES, UNTIL STEAMING. ADJUST SEASONING WITH SALT AND PEPPER, IF DESIRED. SERVES 6.

TIP: EXOTIC MUSHROOMS, SUCH AS CREMINI, PORTOBELLO, OYSTER AND SHIITAKE, ARE MORE FLAVORFUL THAN REGULAR WHITE (BUTTON) MUSHROOMS AND ARE AVAILABLE IN MOST SUPERMARKETS. THEY CAN BE USED INTERCHANGEABLY IN THIS AND MANY OTHER RECIPES. ALTHOUGH SOMETIMES CALLED "WILD" MUSHROOMS, THE EXOTIC MUSHROOMS YOU FIND IN THE PRODUCE AISLE ARE GENERALLY CULTIVATED. SPECIALTY FOOD STORES AND FARMERS' MARKETS ARE GOOD SOURCES OF TRUE WILD MUSHROOMS THAT HAVE BEEN PLUCKED FROM FIELD AND FOREST.

I DON'T SUFFER FROM INSANITY —
I ENJOY EVERY MINUTE OF IT!

MUSHROOM BARLEY SOUP

MUSHROOMS MAKE MAGIC IN THIS EARTHY SOUP.
VEGETARIANS WILL BE GLAD TO KNOW THAT IT'S
EQUALLY DELICIOUS MADE WITH VEGETABLE BROTH.

2 TBSP	VEGETABLE OIL, DIVIDED	30 ML
2	LARGE ONIONS, FINELY CHOPPED	2
2	STALKS CELERY, THINLY SLICED	2
1	LARGE CARROT, HALVED LENGTHWISE AND THINLY SLICED	1
6 CUPS	SLICED CREMINI MUSHROOMS	1.5 L
4	CLOVES GARLIC, MINCED	4
1 TSP	DRIED OREGANO	5 ML
	SALT AND PEPPER	
2 TBSP	TOMATO PASTE	30 ML
4 CUPS	BEEF OR VEGETABLE BROTH, DIVIDED	1 L
1/4 CUP	BARLEY, RINSED	60 ML
2 TBSP	SOY SAUCE	30 ML
1/4 CUP	CHOPPED FRESH PARSLEY	60 ML
1 TBSP	DRY SHERRY (OPTIONAL)	15 ML

USE A 4- TO 6-QUART SLOW COOKER. IN A SKILLET,
HEAT HALF THE OIL OVER MEDIUM HEAT. ADD ONIONS,
CELERY AND CARROT; COOK, STIRRING OCCASIONALLY,
FOR 5 MINUTES. TRANSFER TO SLOW COOKER. ADD
REMAINING OIL TO SKILLET. ADD MUSHROOMS AND COOK,
STIRRING OCCASIONALLY, FOR 5 MINUTES, UNTIL ANY
LIQUID HAS EVAPORATED. ADD GARLIC, OREGANO, 1 TSP
(5 ML) SALT, 1/4 TSP (1 ML) PEPPER AND TOMATO PASTE;
COOK, STIRRING, FOR 1 MINUTE. STIR IN 1 CUP (250 ML)
BROTH, SCRAPING UP ANY BROWN BITS FROM BOTTOM
OF PAN; BRING TO A BOIL. TRANSFER TO SLOW COOKER.

STIR IN BARLEY, REMAINING BROTH AND SOY SAUCE. COVER AND COOK ON LOW FOR ABOUT 8 HOURS OR ON HIGH FOR ABOUT 4 HOURS, UNTIL BARLEY IS TENDER. STIR IN PARSLEY AND SHERRY, IF USING. ADJUST SEASONING WITH SALT AND PEPPER, IF DESIRED. SERVES 6.

TIP: CREMINI MUSHROOMS (SOMETIMES LABELED "BROWN MUSHROOMS") ARE ACTUALLY MINI PORTOBELLO MUSHROOMS, BUT ARE LESS EXPENSIVE. CREMINI MUSHROOMS HAVE MORE FLAVOR THAN REGULAR WHITE (BUTTON) MUSHROOMS, BUT USE WHITE MUSHROOMS IF YOU PREFER.

CURRIED SWEET POTATO SOUP

A CREAMY, SPICY SOUP TO WARM A WINTER'S DAY.

1 TBSP	VEGETABLE OIL	15 ML
2	ONIONS, CHOPPED	2
4	CLOVES GARLIC, MINCED	4
1 TBSP	FINELY CHOPPED GINGERROOT	15 ML
2 TBSP	MILD OR MEDIUM INDIAN CURRY PASTE (SEE TIP, PAGE 235)	30 ML
1	POTATO, PEELED AND CHOPPED	1
3 CUPS	CHOPPED PEELED SWEET POTATOES	750 ML
1 CUP	CHOPPED PARSNIPS	250 ML
4 CUPS	CHICKEN OR VEGETABLE BROTH	1 L
1/2 CUP	LIGHT COCONUT MILK	125 ML
1 TBSP	FRESHLY SQUEEZED LIME JUICE	15 ML
	SALT (OPTIONAL)	
	TOASTED SLIVERED ALMONDS (OPTIONAL)	

USE A 5- TO 6-QUART SLOW COOKER. IN A SKILLET, HEAT OIL OVER MEDIUM HEAT. ADD ONIONS, GARLIC, GINGER AND CURRY PASTE; COOK, STIRRING OCCASIONALLY, FOR 5 MINUTES. SCRAPE INTO SLOW COOKER. ADD POTATO, SWEET POTATOES, PARSNIPS AND BROTH. COVER AND COOK ON LOW FOR 6 TO 8 HOURS OR ON HIGH FOR 3 TO 4 HOURS, UNTIL VEGETABLES ARE TENDER. WORKING IN BATCHES, TRANSFER SOUP TO A BLENDER OR FOOD PROCESSOR (OR USE AN IMMERSION BLENDER IN THE SLOW COOKER) AND PURÉE UNTIL SMOOTH. RETURN SOUP TO SLOW COOKER, IF NECESSARY, AND STIR IN COCONUT MILK AND LIME JUICE. SEASON TO TASTE WITH SALT, IF DESIRED. COVER AND COOK ON HIGH FOR 15 MINUTES,

UNTIL STEAMING. SERVE GARNISHED WITH ALMONDS (IF USING). SERVES 6.

TIP: COCONUT MILK IS NOT THE LIQUID FOUND INSIDE A COCONUT (THAT'S CALLED COCONUT WATER). RATHER, IT'S A PRODUCT MADE BY SIMMERING AND THEN STRAINING COCONUT MEAT AND WATER. ALTHOUGH DELICIOUS, FULL-FAT COCONUT MILK HAS A VERY HIGH FAT CONTENT, SO WE GENERALLY OPT FOR A LIGHT (FAT-REDUCED) VERSION. EITHER WORKS IN THIS RECIPE.

VARIATION: USE AN EQUAL AMOUNT OF CHOPPED CARROTS, BUTTERNUT SQUASH OR ADDITIONAL SWEET POTATO IN PLACE OF THE PARSNIPS, IF YOU PREFER.

BEST-EVER CREAM OF TOMATO SOUP

YOUR FAVORITE CHILDHOOD SOUP, ALL GROWN UP. CHECK OUT THE VARIATIONS OPPOSITE.

1 TBSP	OLIVE OIL	15 ML
2	ONIONS, CHOPPED	2
2	CARROTS, CHOPPED	2
4	CLOVES GARLIC, MINCED	4
1 TBSP	GRANULATED SUGAR	15 ML
1 TSP	DRIED BASIL	5 ML
	SALT AND PEPPER	
1/4 CUP	TOMATO PASTE	60 ML
1	CAN (28 OZ/796 ML) CRUSHED TOMATOES	1
3 CUPS	CHICKEN OR VEGETABLE BROTH	750 ML
1/2 CUP	CHOPPED DRAINED OIL-PACKED SUN-DRIED TOMATOES	125 ML
3/4 CUP	HEAVY OR WHIPPING (35%) CREAM, WARMED, DIVIDED	175 ML

USE A 4- TO 6-QUART SLOW COOKER. IN A SKILLET, HEAT OIL OVER MEDIUM HEAT. ADD ONIONS, CARROTS, GARLIC, SUGAR, BASIL, 1 TSP (5 ML) SALT, 1/4 TSP (1 ML) PEPPER AND TOMATO PASTE; COOK, STIRRING OCCASIONALLY, FOR 7 MINUTES. TRANSFER TO SLOW COOKER. STIR IN CANNED TOMATOES, BROTH AND SUN-DRIED TOMATOES. COVER AND COOK ON LOW FOR ABOUT 8 HOURS OR ON HIGH FOR ABOUT 4 HOURS, UNTIL VEGETABLES ARE TENDER. WORKING IN BATCHES, TRANSFER SOUP TO A BLENDER OR FOOD PROCESSOR (OR USE AN IMMERSION BLENDER IN THE SLOW COOKER) AND PURÉE UNTIL SMOOTH.

RETURN TO SLOW COOKER, IF NECESSARY, AND STIR IN 1/2 CUP (125 ML) CREAM. ADJUST SEASONING WITH SALT AND PEPPER, IF DESIRED. COVER AND COOK ON HIGH FOR 15 MINUTES, UNTIL STEAMING. LADLE INTO BOWLS AND SWIRL A LITTLE OF THE REMAINING CREAM OVER TOP OF EACH BOWL. SERVES 6.

VARIATIONS

SPICY CREAM OF TOMATO SOUP: REDUCE CHICKEN BROTH TO 2 1/2 CUPS (625 ML). ADD 1/2 CUP (125 ML) SPICY TOMATO CLAM JUICE WITH THE BROTH. GARNISH WITH SHREDDED CHEDDAR CHEESE AND YOUR FAVORITE GARLIC CROUTONS.

TOMATO AND ROASTED RED PEPPER SOUP: OMIT THE SUN-DRIED TOMATOES. JUST BEFORE PURÉEING THE SOUP, STIR IN 1 CUP (250 ML) CHOPPED DRAINED ROASTED RED BELL PEPPERS (THE ONES IN A JAR ARE PERFECT FOR THIS SOUP). PROCEED WITH THE RECIPE.

TOMATO SOUP WITH SMOKED PAPRIKA

SPANISH SMOKED PAPRIKA AND BACON PUT A MELLOW, SMOKY SPIN ON THIS FAMILIAR SOUP.

4	SLICES BACON, CHOPPED	4
2	ONIONS, CHOPPED	2
1	LARGE CARROT, CHOPPED	1
4	CLOVES GARLIC, MINCED	4
1 TBSP	GRANULATED SUGAR	15 ML
1 TSP	DRIED OREGANO	5 ML
	SALT AND PEPPER	
1/4 CUP	TOMATO PASTE	60 ML
1	CAN (28 OZ/796 ML) CRUSHED TOMATOES	1
3 CUPS	CHICKEN BROTH	750 ML
1 TSP	SWEET OR HOT SMOKED PAPRIKA (SEE TIP, OPPOSITE)	5 ML
1 TBSP	FRESHLY SQUEEZED LIME JUICE	15 ML
	SOUR CREAM AND CRUSHED CORN TORTILLA CHIPS	

USE A 4- TO 6-QUART SLOW COOKER. IN A SKILLET, FRY BACON OVER MEDIUM-HIGH HEAT UNTIL CRISPY. USING A SLOTTED SPOON, TRANSFER BACON TO A PLATE LINED WITH PAPER TOWELS. COVER AND REFRIGERATE. REDUCE HEAT TO MEDIUM. ADD ONIONS, CARROT, GARLIC, SUGAR, OREGANO, 1/2 TSP (2 ML) SALT, 1/4 TSP (1 ML) PEPPER AND TOMATO PASTE TO SKILLET AND COOK, STIRRING OCCASIONALLY, FOR 5 MINUTES. TRANSFER TO SLOW COOKER. STIR IN TOMATOES AND BROTH. COVER AND COOK ON LOW FOR ABOUT 8 HOURS OR ON HIGH FOR

ABOUT 4 HOURS, UNTIL VEGETABLES ARE TENDER. WORKING IN BATCHES, TRANSFER SOUP TO A BLENDER OR FOOD PROCESSOR (OR USE AN IMMERSION BLENDER IN THE SLOW COOKER) AND PURÉE UNTIL SMOOTH. RETURN TO SLOW COOKER, IF NECESSARY. IN A BOWL, COMBINE PAPRIKA AND LIME JUICE. STIR PAPRIKA MIXTURE AND RESERVED BACON INTO SOUP. COVER AND COOK ON HIGH FOR 15 MINUTES, TO BLEND THE FLAVORS. ADJUST SEASONING WITH SALT AND PEPPER, IF DESIRED. LADLE INTO BOWLS AND GARNISH WITH A DOLLOP OF SOUR CREAM AND A SPRINKLE OF TORTILLA CHIPS. SERVES 6.

TIP: SPANISH SMOKED PAPRIKA LENDS A WARM, SMOKY FLAVOR TO FOOD. IT COMES IN THREE LEVELS OF INTENSITY: SWEET, BITTERSWEET AND HOT. IT IS AVAILABLE ON THE SPICE SHELF AT MOST SUPERMARKETS. YOU CAN SUBSTITUTE REGULAR SWEET PAPRIKA IN THIS RECIPE, BUT THE RESULT WILL BE MILDER.

I DON'T HAVE AGE SPOTS,
I HAVE MATURE FRECKLES.

ROASTED RED PEPPER AND BEAN SOUP

SERVE WITH A GRILLED CHEESE SANDWICH, AND YOU HAVE A SIMPLE, NOURISHING SUPPER.

1 TBSP	VEGETABLE OIL	15 ML
2	ONIONS, CHOPPED	2
2	CARROTS, CHOPPED	2
2	CLOVES GARLIC, MINCED	2
1 TSP	DRIED ITALIAN SEASONING	5 ML
	SALT AND PEPPER	
1	CAN (28 OZ/796 ML) CRUSHED TOMATOES	1
1	CAN (14 TO 19 OZ/398 TO 540 ML) SMALL WHITE BEANS, DRAINED AND RINSED (SEE TIP, PAGE 79)	1
4 CUPS	CHICKEN OR VEGETABLE BROTH	1 L
1 TSP	GRANULATED SUGAR	5 ML
1 CUP	CHOPPED DRAINED ROASTED RED BELL PEPPERS (SEE TIP, OPPOSITE)	250 ML
2 TBSP	CHOPPED FRESH BASIL (OPTIONAL)	30 ML

USE A 4- TO 6-QUART SLOW COOKER. IN A SKILLET, HEAT OIL OVER MEDIUM HEAT. ADD ONIONS, CARROTS, GARLIC, ITALIAN SEASONING, 1 TSP (5 ML) SALT AND $1/4$ TSP (1 ML) PEPPER; COOK, STIRRING OCCASIONALLY, FOR 5 MINUTES. STIR IN TOMATOES. TRANSFER TO SLOW COOKER. STIR IN BEANS, BROTH AND SUGAR. COVER AND COOK ON LOW FOR ABOUT 6 HOURS OR ON HIGH FOR ABOUT 3 HOURS, UNTIL VEGETABLES ARE TENDER. STIR IN ROASTED PEPPERS. WORKING IN BATCHES, TRANSFER SOUP TO A BLENDER OR FOOD PROCESSOR (OR USE AN IMMERSION BLENDER IN THE SLOW COOKER) AND PURÉE UNTIL SMOOTH. RETURN

TO SLOW COOKER, IF NECESSARY. COVER AND COOK ON HIGH FOR 20 MINUTES, UNTIL HOT. ADJUST SEASONING WITH SALT AND PEPPER, IF DESIRED. LADLE INTO BOWLS AND GARNISH WITH BASIL (IF USING). SERVES 6 TO 8.

TIP: ROASTED RED BELL PEPPERS ARE SOLD IN JARS OR IN THE DELI SECTION OF THE SUPERMARKET. BUT IT IS EASY TO ROAST YOUR OWN. PREHEAT OVEN TO 425°F (220°C). BRUSH WHOLE PEPPERS GENEROUSLY WITH OLIVE OIL. PLACE ON A BAKING SHEET LINED WITH GREASED FOIL. ROAST FOR ABOUT 30 MINUTES, TURNING OCCASIONALLY, UNTIL SKINS ARE BLACKENED AND PUFFED. TRANSFER PEPPERS TO A BOWL, COVER AND LET STAND FOR 15 MINUTES. PEEL OFF SKINS AND REMOVE CORES, RIBS AND SEEDS. STORE IN AN AIRTIGHT CONTAINER IN THE REFRIGERATOR FOR UP TO 5 DAYS. OR CUT INTO STRIPS, SPREAD IN A SINGLE LAYER ON A BAKING SHEET AND FREEZE. PACK FROZEN PEPPER PIECES INTO FREEZER BAGS AND STORE FOR UP TO 3 MONTHS.

MINESTRONE

THE CLASSIC ITALIAN SOUP, COOKED LENTAMENTE.
(THAT'S SLOWLY, TO YOU!)

I TBSP	VEGETABLE OIL	15 ML
2	ONIONS, FINELY CHOPPED	2
2	CARROTS, HALVED LENGTHWISE AND CHOPPED	2
2	STALKS CELERY, THINLY SLICED	2
4	CLOVES GARLIC, MINCED	4
I TSP	DRIED ITALIAN SEASONING	5 ML
	SALT AND PEPPER	
2 TBSP	TOMATO PASTE	30 ML
I	CAN (14 OZ/398 ML) TOMATO SAUCE	I
2	BAY LEAVES	2
I	CAN (14 TO 19 OZ/398 TO 540 ML) CANNELLINI (WHITE KIDNEY) OR SMALL WHITE BEANS, DRAINED AND RINSED (SEE TIP, OPPOSITE)	I
4 CUPS	CHICKEN OR VEGETABLE BROTH	I L
I	ZUCCHINI, DICED	I
2 CUPS	SHREDDED GREEN CABBAGE	500 ML
	GRATED PARMESAN CHEESE	

USE A 4- TO 6-QUART SLOW COOKER. IN A SKILLET, HEAT OIL OVER MEDIUM HEAT. ADD ONIONS, CARROTS, CELERY, GARLIC, ITALIAN SEASONING, $\frac{1}{2}$ TSP (2 ML) SALT, $\frac{1}{4}$ TSP (I ML) PEPPER AND TOMATO PASTE; COOK, STIRRING OCCASIONALLY, FOR 5 MINUTES. STIR IN TOMATO SAUCE. TRANSFER TO SLOW COOKER. STIR IN BAY LEAVES, BEANS AND BROTH. COVER AND COOK ON LOW FOR 5 TO 6 HOURS OR ON HIGH FOR $2\frac{1}{2}$ TO 3 HOURS, UNTIL VEGETABLES ARE TENDER. STIR IN ZUCCHINI AND CABBAGE. COVER AND

COOK ON HIGH FOR 20 TO 30 MINUTES, UNTIL ZUCCHINI AND CABBAGE ARE TENDER. DISCARD BAY LEAVES. ADJUST SEASONING WITH SALT AND PEPPER, IF DESIRED. LADLE INTO BOWLS AND SPRINKLE WITH PARMESAN. SERVES 6 TO 8.

TIP: IF YOU PREFER TO USE COOKED DRIED BEANS INSTEAD OF CANNED, SEE BASIC BEANS (PAGE 282). YOU'LL NEED 2 CUPS (500 ML) COOKED BEANS FOR THIS RECIPE.

VARIATIONS: REPLACE THE CABBAGE WITH CHOPPED SWISS CHARD OR KALE (STEMS REMOVED). REPLACE THE ZUCCHINI WITH 1 CUP (250 ML) CHOPPED GREEN BEANS. OR ADD 2 CUPS (500 ML) COOKED SMALL PASTA SHAPES (SUCH AS MACARONI), A FEW MINUTES BEFORE SERVING.

WINE IMPROVES WITH AGE. THE OLDER I GET,
THE MORE I LIKE IT.

LEMONY LENTIL SOUP

A FRESH-TASTING SOUP FOR LENTIL LOVERS.

I TBSP	VEGETABLE OIL	15 ML
2	STALKS CELERY, THINLY SLICED	2
2	CARROTS, THINLY SLICED	2
I	LARGE ONION, FINELY CHOPPED	I
I TBSP	GROUND CORIANDER	15 ML
1½ TSP	DRIED MARJORAM OR ITALIAN SEASONING	7 ML
	SALT AND PEPPER	
I CUP	DRIED BROWN OR GREEN LENTILS, RINSED	250 ML
I TSP	GRATED LEMON ZEST	5 ML
6 CUPS	CHICKEN OR VEGETABLE BROTH, DIVIDED	1.5 L
I	BAY LEAF	I

USE A 4- TO 6-QUART SLOW COOKER. IN A SKILLET, HEAT OIL OVER MEDIUM HEAT. ADD CELERY, CARROTS AND ONION; COOK, STIRRING OCCASIONALLY, FOR 5 MINUTES. ADD CORIANDER, MARJORAM, I TSP (5 ML) SALT AND ¼ TSP (1 ML) PEPPER; COOK, STIRRING, FOR 15 SECONDS. STIR IN LENTILS, LEMON ZEST AND I CUP (250 ML) BROTH; BRING TO A BOIL. TRANSFER TO SLOW COOKER. STIR IN REMAINING BROTH AND BAY LEAF. COVER AND COOK ON LOW FOR 6 TO 8 HOURS OR ON HIGH FOR 3 TO 4 HOURS, UNTIL VEGETABLES AND LENTILS ARE TENDER. DISCARD BAY LEAF. ADJUST SEASONING WITH SALT AND PEPPER, IF DESIRED.

SERVES 4 TO 6.

SPICED LENTIL VEGETABLE SOUP

SO GOOD! GUARANTEED TO WIN SOME LENTIL CONVERTS.

1 TBSP	VEGETABLE OIL	15 ML
2	LARGE ONIONS, FINELY CHOPPED	2
2	STALKS CELERY, THINLY SLICED	2
2	CARROTS, QUARTERED LENGTHWISE AND CHOPPED	2
4	CLOVES GARLIC, MINCED	4
2 TBSP	MILD OR MEDIUM INDIAN CURRY PASTE (SEE TIP, PAGE 235)	30 ML
2 TBSP	TOMATO PASTE	30 ML
1 1/2 CUPS	DRIED RED LENTILS, RINSED	375 ML
4 CUPS	CHICKEN OR VEGETABLE BROTH, DIVIDED	1 L
2	BAY LEAVES	2
	SALT AND PEPPER	

USE A 4- TO 6-QUART SLOW COOKER. IN A SKILLET, HEAT OIL OVER MEDIUM HEAT. ADD ONIONS, CELERY, CARROTS, GARLIC, CURRY PASTE AND TOMATO PASTE; COOK, STIRRING OCCASIONALLY, FOR 5 MINUTES. ADD LENTILS AND STIR TO COAT. STIR IN 1 CUP (250 ML) BROTH; BRING TO A BOIL. TRANSFER TO SLOW COOKER. STIR IN REMAINING BROTH AND BAY LEAVES. COVER AND COOK ON LOW FOR 6 TO 8 HOURS OR ON HIGH FOR 3 TO 4 HOURS, UNTIL VEGETABLES AND LENTILS ARE TENDER. DISCARD BAY LEAVES. ADJUST SEASONING WITH SALT AND PEPPER, IF DESIRED (BUT BE WARY — SOME CURRY PASTES ADD A FAIR BIT OF SALT). SERVES 6.

SEAFOOD AND TOMATO CHOWDER

TOMATO-BASED SEAFOOD CHOWDERS ARE LIGHTER THAN THEIR CREAMY COUSINS, BUT EVERY BIT AS TASTY.

1 TBSP	VEGETABLE OIL	15 ML
2	ONIONS, FINELY CHOPPED	2
2	CARROTS, FINELY CHOPPED	2
2	STALKS CELERY, FINELY CHOPPED	2
4	CLOVES GARLIC, MINCED	4
1 TSP	DRIED OREGANO	5 ML
	SALT AND PEPPER	
1	CAN (28 OZ/796 ML) DICED TOMATOES, WITH JUICE	1
2	BAY LEAVES	2
1	LARGE POTATO, PEELED AND DICED	1
3 CUPS	CHICKEN OR VEGETABLE BROTH	750 ML
1 TSP	WORCESTERSHIRE SAUCE	5 ML
1 1/2 LBS	SKINLESS FIRM WHITE FISH FILLETS (SUCH AS COD, SNAPPER, TILAPIA OR HALIBUT, OR A COMBINATION), CUT INTO BITE-SIZE PIECES	750 G
8 OZ	RAW MEDIUM SHRIMP, PEELED AND DEVEINED	250 G
1/4 CUP	CHOPPED FRESH PARSLEY	60 ML
2 TBSP	DRY SHERRY (OPTIONAL)	30 ML

USE A 5- TO 6-QUART SLOW COOKER. IN A LARGE SKILLET, HEAT OIL OVER MEDIUM HEAT. ADD, ONIONS, CARROTS, CELERY, GARLIC, OREGANO, 1/2 TSP (2 ML) SALT AND 1/4 TSP (1 ML) PEPPER; COOK, STIRRING OCCASIONALLY, FOR 5 MINUTES. ADD TOMATOES AND BRING TO A BOIL. POUR INTO SLOW COOKER. ADD BAY LEAVES, POTATO,

BROTH AND WORCESTERSHIRE SAUCE. COVER AND COOK ON LOW FOR ABOUT 6 HOURS OR ON HIGH FOR ABOUT 3 HOURS, UNTIL VEGETABLES ARE TENDER. STIR IN FISH AND SHRIMP. COVER AND COOK ON HIGH FOR ABOUT 30 MINUTES, UNTIL FISH IS OPAQUE AND IS JUST STARTING TO FLAKE WHEN TESTED WITH A FORK, AND SHRIMP ARE PINK AND OPAQUE. DISCARD BAY LEAVES. STIR IN PARSLEY AND SHERRY (IF USING). ADJUST SEASONING WITH SALT AND PEPPER, IF DESIRED. SERVE IMMEDIATELY. SERVES 6 TO 8.

TIP: WORCESTERSHIRE SAUCE (PRONOUNCED *WOOS-TUHR-SHEER*) IS A DARK BROWN SAUCE WITH A PIQUANT, SPICY FLAVOR THAT WAS DEVELOPED FOR BRITISH COLONIALS IN INDIA. IT TAKES ITS NAME FROM WORCESTER, ENGLAND, WHERE IT WAS FIRST BOTTLED. THE SAUCE IS USED TO SEASON MEATS, SAUCES AND SOUPS, AND IS AN ESSENTIAL INGREDIENT IN A BLOODY MARY COCKTAIL. ONCE OPENED, IT KEEPS FOR SEVERAL MONTHS IN THE REFRIGERATOR.

TURKEY AND WILD RICE SOUP

A FRESH TURKEY THIGH MAKES GREAT SOUP!
SERVE WITH WARM EASY CORNBREAD (PAGE 33).

1	SKINLESS BONE-IN TURKEY THIGH OR DRUMSTICK	1
1 TBSP	VEGETABLE OIL	15 ML
2	ONIONS, CHOPPED	2
2	CARROTS, CHOPPED	2
2	STALKS CELERY, THINLY SLICED	2
4	CLOVES GARLIC, MINCED	4
1/2 TSP	DRIED THYME	2 ML
	SALT AND PEPPER	
1 TBSP	TOMATO PASTE	15 ML
4 CUPS	CHICKEN BROTH, DIVIDED	1 L
2	BAY LEAVES	2
1 CUP	COOKED WILD RICE	250 ML
1/2 CUP	FROZEN PEAS (NO NEED TO THAW)	125 ML
2 TBSP	CHOPPED FRESH PARSLEY	30 ML

PLACE TURKEY IN A 4- TO 6-QUART SLOW COOKER. IN A SKILLET, HEAT OIL OVER MEDIUM HEAT. ADD ONIONS, CARROTS, CELERY, GARLIC, THYME, 1/2 TSP (2 ML) SALT, 1/4 TSP (1 ML) PEPPER AND TOMATO PASTE; COOK, STIRRING OCCASIONALLY, FOR 5 MINUTES. STIR IN 1 CUP (250 ML) BROTH; BRING TO A BOIL. POUR OVER TURKEY. ADD BAY LEAVES AND REMAINING BROTH. COVER AND COOK ON LOW FOR 5 TO 6 HOURS OR ON HIGH FOR 2 1/2 TO 3 HOURS, UNTIL JUICES RUN CLEAR WHEN TURKEY IS PIERCED. DISCARD BAY LEAVES. TRANSFER TURKEY TO A CUTTING BOARD AND USE TWO FORKS TO SHRED MEAT, DISCARDING BONES. RETURN SHREDDED TURKEY TO SLOW

COOKER AND STIR IN RICE AND PEAS. COVER AND COOK ON HIGH FOR 15 MINUTES, UNTIL STEAMING. LADLE INTO BOWLS AND SPRINKLE WITH PARSLEY. SERVES 4.

TIP: WE USE TOMATO PASTE IN MANY OF OUR SLOW COOKER RECIPES BECAUSE IT GREATLY BOOSTS FLAVOR AND RICHNESS. THE LONG, MOIST COOKING DULLS OTHER AROMATIC INGREDIENTS, SUCH AS ONIONS, GARLIC AND HERBS. MICROWAVING OR BROWNING A DOLLOP OR TWO OF TOMATO PASTE WITH THESE INGREDIENTS MAKES ALL THE DIFFERENCE.

TIP: WE LIKE TO USE COOKED WILD RICE IN THIS RECIPE, BUT COOKED WHITE OR BROWN RICE WORK WELL TOO. NEXT TIME YOU HAVE RICE FOR SUPPER, COOK EXTRA. FREEZE LEFTOVERS IN 1-CUP (250 ML) PORTIONS IN SMALL SEALABLE BAGS. FROZEN RICE CAN BE ADDED DIRECTLY TO SOUPS, STIR-FRIES AND CASSEROLES.

SUPER SUPPER SOUP

TURKEY MEATBALLS, PASTA AND A GENEROUS HELPING OF VEGETABLES. WHAT'S NOT TO LIKE?

1/4 CUP	DRY BREAD CRUMBS	60 ML
1	EGG, LIGHTLY BEATEN	1
2	CLOVES GARLIC, MINCED	2
1 LB	LEAN GROUND TURKEY	500 G
1/2 CUP	GRATED PARMESAN CHEESE	125 ML
2 TBSP	CHOPPED FRESH PARSLEY	30 ML
1/2 TSP	CRUMBLED DRIED SAGE	2 ML
	SALT AND PEPPER	
1 TBSP	VEGETABLE OIL	15 ML
2	STALKS CELERY, THINLY SLICED	2
1	LARGE ONION, CHOPPED	1
1	LARGE CARROT, CHOPPED	1
1 TBSP	TOMATO PASTE	15 ML
6 CUPS	CHICKEN BROTH, DIVIDED	1.5 L
1 CUP	BROKEN SPAGHETTINI PASTA OR OTHER THIN NOODLES	250 ML
1/2 CUP	FROZEN PEAS, THAWED	125 ML

USE A 4- TO 6-QUART SLOW COOKER. IN A BOWL, COMBINE BREAD CRUMBS AND EGG. LET SOAK FOR 5 MINUTES. ADD GARLIC, TURKEY, CHEESE, PARSLEY, SAGE, 1/2 TSP (2 ML) SALT AND 1/4 TSP (1 ML) PEPPER; MIX WELL. SCOOP UP TABLESPOONFULS (15 ML) OF TURKEY MIXTURE AND ROLL INTO MEATBALLS. IN A LARGE SKILLET, HEAT OIL OVER MEDIUM-HIGH HEAT. BROWN MEATBALLS, IN BATCHES IF NECESSARY. (THE MEATBALLS WILL STILL BE PINK INSIDE. DON'T WORRY; THEY WILL FINISH COOKING IN THE SOUP). TRANSFER TO SLOW COOKER. ADD CELERY, ONION, CARROT

AND TOMATO PASTE TO SKILLET AND COOK, STIRRING OCCASIONALLY, FOR 5 MINUTES. STIR IN I CUP (250 ML) BROTH, SCRAPING UP BROWN BITS FROM BOTTOM OF PAN; BRING TO A BOIL. POUR OVER MEATBALLS. STIR IN REMAINING BROTH. COVER AND COOK ON LOW FOR 5 TO 6 HOURS OR ON HIGH FOR $2\frac{1}{2}$ TO 3 HOURS, UNTIL VEGETABLES ARE TENDER AND MEATBALLS ARE NO LONGER PINK INSIDE. MEANWHILE, IN A LARGE POT OF BOILING WATER, COOK PASTA ACCORDING TO PACKAGE INSTRUCTIONS UNTIL AL DENTE. DRAIN AND STIR INTO SOUP, ALONG WITH PEAS. COVER AND COOK ON HIGH FOR 5 MINUTES, UNTIL PEAS ARE HOT. SERVES 4 TO 6.

VARIATION: IF YOUR GANG ENJOYS LEAFY GREENS, REPLACE THE PEAS WITH A COUPLE OF GENEROUS HANDFULS OF CHOPPED KALE OR SWISS CHARD LEAVES (STEMS REMOVED). ADD THE GREENS AT THE END OF THE COOKING TIME, BEFORE ADDING THE COOKED PASTA. COVER AND COOK ON HIGH FOR 10 MINUTES, UNTIL GREENS ARE TENDER. STIR IN COOKED SPAGHETTINI AND SERVE IMMEDIATELY.

A REALLY GOOD CHICKEN NOODLE SOUP

. . . FOR YOUR SOUL!

6	SKINLESS BONE-IN CHICKEN THIGHS OR DRUMSTICKS	6
2	BAY LEAVES	2
I TBSP	VEGETABLE OIL	15 ML
2	CARROTS, THINLY SLICED	2
2	STALKS CELERY, THINLY SLICED	2
I	LARGE ONION, FINELY CHOPPED	I
I CUP	SLICED MUSHROOMS	250 ML
4	CLOVES GARLIC, MINCED	4
	SALT AND PEPPER	
$1/4$ TSP	DRIED THYME	I ML
I TBSP	TOMATO PASTE	15 ML
6 CUPS	CHICKEN BROTH, DIVIDED	1.5 L
$1^1/2$ CUPS	BROAD EGG NOODLES	375 ML
$1/2$ CUP	FROZEN PEAS (NO NEED TO THAW)	125 ML
2 TBSP	CHOPPED FRESH PARSLEY (OPTIONAL)	30 ML

PLACE CHICKEN AND BAY LEAVES IN A 5- TO 6-QUART SLOW COOKER. IN A SKILLET, HEAT OIL OVER MEDIUM HEAT. ADD CARROTS, CELERY, ONION, MUSHROOMS, GARLIC, I TSP (5 ML) SALT, $1/4$ TSP (I ML) PEPPER, THYME AND TOMATO PASTE; COOK, STIRRING OCCASIONALLY, FOR ABOUT 5 MINUTES, UNTIL ANY LIQUID HAS EVAPORATED. STIR IN I CUP (250 ML) BROTH AND BRING TO A BOIL. POUR OVER CHICKEN. ADD REMAINING BROTH. COVER AND COOK ON LOW FOR ABOUT 6 HOURS OR ON HIGH FOR ABOUT 3 HOURS, UNTIL JUICES RUN CLEAR WHEN CHICKEN IS PIERCED. DISCARD BAY LEAVES. TRANSFER CHICKEN TO

A CUTTING BOARD AND USE TWO FORKS TO SHRED MEAT, DISCARDING BONES. MEANWHILE, COOK NOODLES ACCORDING TO PACKAGE INSTRUCTIONS UNTIL AL DENTE. DRAIN AND STIR INTO SOUP, ALONG WITH SHREDDED CHICKEN, PEAS AND PARSLEY (IF USING). COVER AND COOK ON HIGH FOR 15 MINUTES, UNTIL HOT. ADJUST SEASONING WITH SALT AND PEPPER, IF DESIRED. SERVES 6.

TIP: YOU'LL PROBABLY HAVE TO BUY THE BONE-IN CHICKEN THIGHS WITH THE SKIN ON. TO REMOVE THE SKIN, USE A PIECE OF PAPER TOWEL TO GRAB THE SKIN AT ONE END. PULL FIRMLY. THE SKIN SHOULD PEEL RIGHT OFF.

DON'T BELIEVE EVERYTHING YOU THINK.

CASABLANCA CHICKEN SOUP

*FRAGRANT AND NOURISHING. A SALAD TO START,
A BOWL OF SOUP AND FRESH CRUSTY BREAD.
DINNER IS SERVED!*

2	BONE-IN CHICKEN LEGS, SKIN REMOVED	2
1	CAN (14 TO 19 OZ/398 TO 540 ML) CHICKPEAS, DRAINED AND RINSED (SEE TIP, PAGE 50)	1
1 TBSP	VEGETABLE OIL	15 ML
2	ONIONS, FINELY CHOPPED	2
4	CLOVES GARLIC, MINCED	4
2 TSP	GROUND CUMIN	10 ML
	SALT AND PEPPER	
1	CAN (28 OZ/796 ML) WHOLE TOMATOES, WITH JUICE	1
1	2-INCH (5 CM) CINNAMON STICK	1
1 TBSP	GRANULATED SUGAR	15 ML
2 CUPS	CHICKEN BROTH	500 ML
1 CUP	CHOPPED DRAINED ROASTED RED BELL PEPPERS (SEE TIP, PAGE 77)	250 ML
1/4 TSP	CAYENNE PEPPER	1 ML
1 TBSP	FRESHLY SQUEEZED LEMON JUICE	15 ML
2 CUPS	PACKED BABY SPINACH	500 ML

PLACE CHICKEN AND CHICKPEAS IN A 4- TO 6-QUART SLOW COOKER. IN A LARGE SAUCEPAN, HEAT OIL OVER MEDIUM HEAT. ADD ONIONS, GARLIC, CUMIN, 1 TSP (5 ML) SALT AND 1/4 TSP (1 ML) PEPPER; COOK, STIRRING, FOR 3 MINUTES. STIR IN TOMATOES, CINNAMON STICK, SUGAR AND BROTH, BREAKING TOMATOES UP WITH A SPOON. POUR OVER CHICKEN MIXTURE. COVER AND COOK ON LOW FOR 5 TO

6 HOURS OR ON HIGH FOR ABOUT $2\frac{1}{2}$ TO 3 HOURS, UNTIL JUICES RUN CLEAR WHEN CHICKEN IS PIERCED. TRANSFER CHICKEN TO A CUTTING BOARD AND USE TWO FORKS TO SHRED MEAT, DISCARDING BONES. RETURN SHREDDED CHICKEN TO SLOW COOKER AND STIR IN ROASTED PEPPERS, CAYENNE AND LEMON JUICE. COVER AND COOK ON HIGH FOR 20 MINUTES, UNTIL STEAMING. ADD SPINACH AND STIR UNTIL WILTED. ADJUST SEASONING WITH SALT AND PEPPER, IF DESIRED. SERVES 6.

TIP: CHICKEN LEGS ARE A THRIFTY AND TASTY CHOICE FOR THE SLOW COOKER. IT'S WORTH BUYING THEM WHEN THEY'RE ON SALE AND POPPING THEM IN THE FREEZER. SINCE LEGS DON'T LOOK PARTICULARLY APPEALING ON A PLATE, WE MOSTLY USE THEM IN SOUPS AND SHRED THE COOKED CHICKEN OFF THE BONE BEFORE SERVING.

TUESDAY TORTILLA SOUP

QUICK TO ASSEMBLE — IDEAL FOR MAD MIDWEEK MORNINGS. IT COOKS ALL DAY; JUST ADD THE FINISHING TOUCHES WHEN YOU GET HOME.

3	CLOVES GARLIC, MINCED	3
1	LARGE ONION, FINELY CHOPPED	1
1	CAN (28 OZ/796 ML) DICED TOMATOES, WITH JUICE	1
2 CUPS	CHOPPED COOKED CHICKEN	500 ML
1 CUP	CORN KERNELS (NO NEED TO THAW IF FROZEN)	250 ML
1 TBSP	GROUND CUMIN	15 ML
1 TBSP	DRIED OREGANO	15 ML
	SALT AND PEPPER	
4 CUPS	CHICKEN BROTH	1 L
2 CUPS	CRUSHED CORN TORTILLA CHIPS, DIVIDED	500 ML
1 TBSP	CHOPPED FRESH CILANTRO	15 ML
1 TSP	CHIPOTLE CHILE POWDER (SEE TIP, OPPOSITE)	5 ML
2 TBSP	FRESHLY SQUEEZED LIME JUICE	30 ML
	SHREDDED TEX-MEX CHEESE BLEND OR CHEDDAR CHEESE	
	SOUR CREAM	

IN A 4- TO 6-QUART SLOW COOKER, COMBINE GARLIC, ONION, TOMATOES, CHICKEN, CORN, CUMIN, OREGANO, $1/2$ TSP (2 ML) SALT, $1/4$ TSP (1 ML) PEPPER AND BROTH. COVER AND COOK ON LOW FOR ABOUT 8 HOURS OR ON HIGH FOR ABOUT 4 HOURS, UNTIL ONIONS ARE TENDER AND SOUP IS BUBBLING. STIR IN HALF THE TORTILLA CHIPS AND THE CILANTRO. IN A SMALL BOWL, COMBINE CHIPOTLE

CHILE POWDER AND LIME JUICE UNTIL SMOOTH. STIR INTO SOUP. COOK ON HIGH FOR 20 MINUTES, UNTIL TORTILLA CHIPS ARE SOFTENED AND SOUP IS THICKENED. ADJUST SEASONING WITH SALT AND PEPPER, IF DESIRED. LADLE INTO BOWLS AND GARNISH WITH REMAINING TORTILLA CHIPS, CHEESE AND SOUR CREAM. SERVES 4.

TIP: JARS OF CHIPOTLE CHILE POWDER ARE AVAILABLE IN MOST SUPERMARKETS. THE REDDISH-BROWN POWDER IS MADE FROM DRIED SMOKED JALAPEÑO PEPPERS. IT LENDS AN AUTHENTIC MEXICAN TOUCH TO SOUPS, STEWS AND CHILIS. REGULAR CHILI POWDER CAN BE SUBSTITUTED IF YOU PREFER TO NOT HAVE A SMOKY FLAVOR.

CHILD LOGIC: DALMATIANS RIDE WITH THE FIREMEN
SO THEY CAN FIND THE FIRE HYDRANTS.

CHICKEN AND CORN CHOWDER

A SOUP THAT THINKS IT'S A MAIN COURSE!
SERVE WITH FRESH CRUSTY BREAD.

4	SLICES BACON, CHOPPED	4
2	ONIONS, FINELY CHOPPED	2
4	CLOVES GARLIC, MINCED	4
1 TBSP	TOMATO PASTE	15 ML
3 TBSP	ALL-PURPOSE FLOUR	45 ML
3 CUPS	CHICKEN BROTH	750 ML
	SALT AND PEPPER	
1	LARGE CARROT, QUARTERED LENGTHWISE AND CHOPPED	1
1	LARGE POTATO, PEELED AND CUT INTO $1/2$-INCH (1 CM) CUBES	1
2	BAY LEAVES	2
4	SKINLESS BONE-IN CHICKEN THIGHS	4
1	RED BELL PEPPER, CHOPPED	1
2 CUPS	CORN KERNELS, THAWED IF FROZEN	500 ML
2 TBSP	CHOPPED FRESH PARSLEY	30 ML
1	CAN (12 OZ OR 370 ML) EVAPORATED MILK, WARMED	1

USE A 4- TO 6-QUART SLOW COOKER. IN A SKILLET, FRY BACON OVER MEDIUM-HIGH HEAT UNTIL CRISPY. USING A SLOTTED SPOON, TRANSFER BACON TO A PLATE LINED WITH PAPER TOWELS. COVER AND REFRIGERATE. DRAIN ALL BUT 1 TBSP (15 ML) FAT FROM SKILLET. REDUCE HEAT TO MEDIUM. ADD ONIONS, GARLIC AND TOMATO PASTE TO SKILLET AND COOK, STIRRING, FOR 3 MINUTES. STIR IN FLOUR. GRADUALLY WHISK IN BROTH, 1 TSP (5 ML) SALT AND $1/4$ TSP (1 ML) PEPPER. PLACE CARROTS, POTATOES

AND BAY LEAVES IN SLOW COOKER. PLACE CHICKEN ON TOP OF VEGETABLES. POUR ONION MIXTURE OVER CHICKEN. COVER AND COOK ON LOW FOR 5 TO 6 HOURS OR ON HIGH FOR $2^{1}/_{2}$ TO 3 HOURS, UNTIL JUICES RUN CLEAR WHEN CHICKEN IS PIERCED. TRANSFER CHICKEN TO A CUTTING BOARD AND USE TWO FORKS TO SHRED MEAT, DISCARDING BONES. RETURN SHREDDED CHICKEN TO SLOW COOKER AND STIR IN RESERVED BACON, RED PEPPER, CORN, PARSLEY AND EVAPORATED MILK. COVER AND COOK ON HIGH FOR 20 MINUTES, UNTIL RED PEPPER IS TENDER AND SOUP IS HOT. DISCARD BAY LEAVES. ADJUST SEASONING WITH SALT AND PEPPER, IF DESIRED. SERVES 6 TO 8.

VARIATION

CHICKEN, CORN AND BEAN CHOWDER: ADD I CAN (14 TO 19 OZ/398 TO 540 ML) SMALL WHITE BEANS, DRAINED AND RINSED (SEE TIP, PAGE IOI), WHEN ADDING THE ONION MIXTURE TO THE SLOW COOKER.

ZUPPA DU JOUR

A BEST OF BRIDGE CLASSIC.

6	SLICES BACON, CHOPPED	6
3	STALKS CELERY, THINLY SLICED	3
2	ONIONS, FINELY CHOPPED	2
3	CLOVES GARLIC, MINCED	3
I TSP	DRIED ITALIAN SEASONING	5 ML
	SALT AND PEPPER	
I	CAN (28 OZ/796 ML) DICED TOMATOES, WITH JUICE	I
4 CUPS	CHICKEN OR VEGETABLE BROTH	I L
I	CAN (14 OZ/398 ML) ARTICHOKES, DRAINED AND QUARTERED	I
1/3 CUP	SMALL PASTA SHAPES (SEE TIP, OPPOSITE)	75 ML
1/4 TSP	HOT PEPPER FLAKES (OR TO TASTE)	I ML
2 TSP	BALSAMIC VINEGAR	10 ML
	GRATED PARMESAN CHEESE	

USE A 5- TO 6-QUART SLOW COOKER. IN A SKILLET, FRY BACON OVER MEDIUM-HIGH HEAT UNTIL CRISPY. USING A SLOTTED SPOON, TRANSFER BACON TO A PLATE LINED WITH PAPER TOWELS. COVER AND REFRIGERATE. DRAIN OFF ALL BUT I TBSP (15 ML) FAT FROM SKILLET. REDUCE HEAT TO MEDIUM. ADD CELERY, ONIONS, GARLIC, ITALIAN SEASONING, 1/2 TSP (2 ML) SALT AND 1/4 TSP (I ML) PEPPER TO SKILLET AND COOK, STIRRING OCCASIONALLY, FOR 5 MINUTES. STIR IN TOMATOES AND BRING TO A BOIL. TRANSFER TO SLOW COOKER. STIR IN BROTH. COVER AND COOK ON LOW FOR ABOUT 6 HOURS OR ON HIGH FOR ABOUT 3 HOURS, UNTIL VEGETABLES ARE TENDER. STIR IN

CONTINUED ON PAGE 97...

Hot Cranberry Sipper
(page 57)

Casablanca Chicken Soup (page 90)

Tuesday Tortilla Soup (page 92)

Cowboy Pot Roast with Sweet Potatoes (page 110)

ARTICHOKES, PASTA, HOT PEPPER FLAKES AND VINEGAR. COVER AND COOK ON HIGH FOR ABOUT 15 MINUTES, UNTIL PASTA IS TENDER AND ARTICHOKES ARE HOT. ADJUST SEASONING WITH SALT AND PEPPER, IF DESIRED. LADLE INTO BOWLS AND SPRINKLE WITH PARMESAN AND RESERVED BACON. SERVES 4 TO 6.

TIP: FOR THIS SOUP, WE LIKE TO USE SMALL PASTA SHAPES LABELED "SOUP NOODLES." THEY COME IN FUN SHAPES THAT APPEAL TO KIDS, SUCH AS MINI BOWS, SHELLS, WHEELS AND ALPHABET LETTERS. THEY CAN BE COOKED DIRECTLY IN THE SOUP. BROKEN SPAGHETTINI PIECES ALSO WORK WELL.

CLASSIC PEA SOUP WITH SAUSAGE AND BACON

A CONTEMPORARY VERSION OF TRADITIONAL SPLIT PEA SOUP. LOOK, MA — NO HAM BONE!

1 TBSP	VEGETABLE OIL	15 ML
1	HOT ITALIAN SAUSAGE, CASING REMOVED, CRUMBLED	1
4	SLICES BACON, CHOPPED	4
2	ONIONS, CHOPPED	2
2	STALKS CELERY, THINLY SLICED	2
1	LARGE CARROT, CHOPPED	1
1	BAY LEAF	1
1 CUP	DRIED GREEN SPLIT PEAS, RINSED	250 ML
	PEPPER	
5 CUPS	CHICKEN BROTH OR WATER	1.25 L
1 TBSP	FRESHLY SQUEEZED LEMON JUICE	15 ML
	SALT (OPTIONAL)	
	HOT PEPPER SAUCE (OPTIONAL)	

USE A 4- TO 6-QUART SLOW COOKER. IN A SKILLET, HEAT OIL OVER MEDIUM-HIGH HEAT. BROWN SAUSAGE. USING A SLOTTED SPOON, TRANSFER SAUSAGE TO A PLATE LINED WITH PAPER TOWELS. COVER AND REFRIGERATE. ADD BACON TO SKILLET AND FRY UNTIL CRISPY. USING A SLOTTED SPOON, SCOOP UP BACON AND PRESS AGAINST SIDE OF PAN TO EXTRACT EXCESS FAT; TRANSFER TO SLOW COOKER. POUR OFF ALL BUT 1 TBSP (15 ML) FAT FROM SKILLET. REDUCE HEAT TO MEDIUM. ADD ONIONS, CELERY AND CARROT; COOK, STIRRING OCCASIONALLY, FOR 5 MINUTES. STIR IN BAY LEAF, PEAS, 1/4 TSP (1 ML) PEPPER AND BROTH; BRING TO A BOIL. TRANSFER TO

SLOW COOKER. COVER AND COOK ON LOW FOR 10 TO 12
HOURS OR ON HIGH FOR 5 TO 6 HOURS, UNTIL PEAS ARE
VERY SOFT. DISCARD BAY LEAF. WORKING IN BATCHES,
TRANSFER SOUP TO A BLENDER OR FOOD PROCESSOR (OR
USE AN IMMERSION BLENDER IN THE SLOW COOKER) AND
PURÉE UNTIL SMOOTH. STIR IN RESERVED SAUSAGE AND
LEMON JUICE. COVER AND COOK ON HIGH FOR 15 MINUTES,
UNTIL SAUSAGE IS HOT. ADJUST SEASONING WITH SALT,
PEPPER AND HOT PEPPER SAUCE, IF DESIRED. SERVES 4.

WHEN DID MY BROAD MIND
AND MY NARROW WAIST CHANGE PLACES?

BAJA SAUSAGE AND BEAN SOUP

ANOTHER DINNER-IN-A-BOWL! OLÉ!

I TBSP	VEGETABLE OIL	15 ML
4	FRESH CHORIZO OR HOT ITALIAN SAUSAGES, CASINGS REMOVED, CRUMBLED	4
2	ONIONS, FINELY CHOPPED	2
2	CARROTS, HALVED LENGTHWISE AND THINLY SLICED	2
2	STALKS CELERY, THINLY SLICED	2
4	CLOVES GARLIC, MINCED	4
2 TSP	GROUND CUMIN	10 ML
I TSP	DRIED OREGANO	5 ML
I	CAN (28 OZ/796 ML) DICED TOMATOES, WITH JUICE	I
2	CANS (EACH 14 TO 19 OZ/398 TO 540 ML) BLACK BEANS, DRAINED AND RINSED (SEE TIP, OPPOSITE)	2
2 CUPS	CHICKEN BROTH	500 ML
I CUP	CORN KERNELS (NO NEED TO THAW IF FROZEN)	250 ML
2 TBSP	CHOPPED FRESH CILANTRO	30 ML
	SOUR CREAM AND DICED AVOCADO	

USE A 5- TO 6-QUART SLOW COOKER. IN A SKILLET, HEAT OIL OVER MEDIUM HEAT. BROWN SAUSAGE. USING A SLOTTED SPOON, TRANSFER SAUSAGE TO SLOW COOKER. ADD ONIONS, CARROTS, CELERY, GARLIC, CUMIN AND OREGANO; COOK, STIRRING OCCASIONALLY, FOR 5 MINUTES. STIR IN TOMATOES AND BRING TO A BOIL. TRANSFER TO SLOW COOKER. STIR IN BEANS AND BROTH. COVER AND COOK ON LOW FOR ABOUT 6 HOURS OR ON HIGH

FOR ABOUT 3 HOURS, UNTIL VEGETABLES ARE TENDER. STIR IN CORN AND CILANTRO. COVER AND COOK ON HIGH FOR ABOUT 20 MINUTES, UNTIL CORN IS HOT. LADLE INTO BOWLS AND TOP WITH A DOLLOP OF SOUR CREAM. SPRINKLE WITH AVOCADO. SERVES 6.

TIP: CHORIZO IS A SPICY, FLAVORFUL SAUSAGE THAT IS WIDELY AVAILABLE IN SUPERMARKETS, EITHER FRESH OR CURED LIKE SALAMI. FOR THIS RECIPE, YOU NEED FRESH. A GOOD SUBSTITUTE IS HOT ITALIAN SAUSAGE. BOTH CHORIZO AND ITALIAN SAUSAGE ARE HIGHLY SEASONED, SO WE DON'T RECOMMEND ADDING EXTRA SALT OR PEPPER TO THE SOUP. FOR MORE HEAT, PASS HOT PEPPER SAUCE AT THE TABLE.

TIP: IF YOU PREFER TO USE COOKED DRIED BEANS INSTEAD OF CANNED, SEE BASIC BEANS (PAGE 282). YOU'LL NEED 2 CUPS (500 ML) COOKED BEANS FOR THIS RECIPE.

BUSY DAY BEEF AND BARLEY SOUP

SO SIMPLE TO START IN THE MORNING, AND SO GOOD TO COME HOME TO AT NIGHT.

3	CLOVES GARLIC, MINCED	3
2	ONIONS, FINELY CHOPPED	2
1 TSP	DRIED OREGANO	5 ML
	SALT AND PEPPER	
2 TBSP	TOMATO PASTE	30 ML
1 TBSP	VEGETABLE OIL	15 ML
2	CARROTS, FINELY CHOPPED	2
2	BAY LEAVES	2
1 1/2 LBS	STEWING BEEF, CUT INTO 1/2-INCH (1 CM) CUBES	750 G
1/4 CUP	BARLEY, RINSED	60 ML
4 to 5 CUPS	BEEF BROTH	1 to 1.25 L
1 CUP	FROZEN PEAS (NO NEED TO THAW)	250 ML
2 TBSP	CHOPPED FRESH PARSLEY	30 ML
1 TBSP	BALSAMIC VINEGAR	15 ML

USE A 4- TO 6-QUART SLOW COOKER. IN A MICROWAVE-SAFE BOWL, COMBINE GARLIC, ONIONS, OREGANO, 1 TSP (5 ML) SALT, 1/4 TSP (1 ML) PEPPER, TOMATO PASTE AND OIL. MICROWAVE ON HIGH FOR ABOUT 7 MINUTES, STOPPING THREE TIMES TO STIR, UNTIL ONIONS ARE SOFTENED. TRANSFER TO SLOW COOKER. STIR IN CARROTS, BAY LEAVES, BEEF, BARLEY AND 4 CUPS (1 L) BROTH. COVER AND COOK ON LOW FOR ABOUT 8 HOURS OR ON HIGH FOR ABOUT 4 HOURS, UNTIL BEEF AND BARLEY ARE TENDER. STIR IN REMAINING BROTH IF SOUP IS THICKER THAN DESIRED. STIR IN PEAS, PARSLEY AND VINEGAR. COVER AND

COOK ON HIGH FOR 20 MINUTES, UNTIL PEAS ARE HOT. DISCARD BAY LEAVES. ADJUST SEASONING WITH SALT AND PEPPER, IF DESIRED. SERVES 6.

TIP: WE USE TOMATO PASTE IN MANY OF OUR SLOW COOKER RECIPES BECAUSE IT GREATLY BOOSTS FLAVOR AND RICHNESS. THE LONG, MOIST COOKING DULLS OTHER AROMATIC INGREDIENTS, SUCH AS ONIONS, GARLIC AND HERBS. MICROWAVING OR BROWNING A DOLLOP OR TWO OF TOMATO PASTE WITH THESE INGREDIENTS MAKES ALL THE DIFFERENCE.

TIP: MOST SUPERMARKETS SELL PACKAGES OF CUBED BEEF LABELED AS "STEWING BEEF." ALTERNATIVELY, LOOK FOR OTHER BRAISING BEEF CUTS SUCH AS BONELESS CROSS-RIB, BLADE OR CHUCK IN THE FORM OF STEAKS OR POT ROASTS. TRIM OFF EXCESS FAT AND CUT INTO DESIRED-SIZED PIECES.

BEEF NOODLE SOUP

A SATISFYING WINTER SOUP!

I TBSP	VEGETABLE OIL	15 ML
2	ONIONS, FINELY CHOPPED	2
2	CARROTS, HALVED LENGTHWISE AND THINLY SLICED	2
2	STALKS CELERY, THINLY SLICED	2
4	CLOVES GARLIC, MINCED	4
	SALT AND PEPPER	
2 TBSP	TOMATO PASTE	30 ML
I	BAY LEAF	I
I LB	STEWING BEEF, CUT INTO $1/2$-INCH (I CM) CUBES	500 G
3 CUPS	SLICED MUSHROOMS	750 ML
4 CUPS	BEEF BROTH	I L
I TBSP	WORCESTERSHIRE SAUCE	15 ML
3 CUPS	MEDIUM EGG NOODLES	750 ML

USE A 4- TO 6-QUART SLOW COOKER. IN A SKILLET, HEAT OIL OVER MEDIUM HEAT. ADD ONIONS, CARROTS, CELERY, GARLIC, I TSP (5 ML) SALT, $1/4$ TSP (I ML) PEPPER AND TOMATO PASTE; COOK, STIRRING OCCASIONALLY, FOR 5 MINUTES. TRANSFER TO SLOW COOKER. STIR IN BAY LEAF, BEEF, MUSHROOMS, BROTH AND WORCESTERSHIRE SAUCE. COVER AND COOK ON LOW FOR ABOUT 8 HOURS OR ON HIGH FOR ABOUT 4 HOURS, UNTIL BEEF AND VEGETABLES ARE TENDER. MEANWHILE, IN A POT OF BOILING SALTED WATER, COOK NOODLES ACCORDING TO PACKAGE INSTRUCTIONS UNTIL AL DENTE. DRAIN AND STIR INTO SOUP. DISCARD BAY LEAF. ADJUST SEASONING WITH SALT AND PEPPER, IF DESIRED. SERVES 4 TO 6.

BEEF, VEAL AND LAMB

CONTINUED ON NEXT PAGE...

MMM-MUSHROOM POT ROAST

USING CANNED CREAM OF MUSHROOM SOUP IN A CASSEROLE SURE IS OLD SCHOOL. BUT IT WORKS! SERVE WITH BUTTERED NOODLES AND STEAMED BROCCOLI.

1	BONELESS BEEF CHUCK, BLADE OR CROSS RIB ROAST (3 TO 4 LBS/1.5 TO 2 KG)	1
	SALT AND PEPPER	
2 TBSP	VEGETABLE OIL, DIVIDED	30 ML
2	ONIONS, THINLY SLICED	2
2 CUPS	QUARTERED CREMINI MUSHROOMS	500 ML
4	CLOVES GARLIC, MINCED	4
1 TSP	DRIED OREGANO	5 ML
1	CAN (10 OZ/284 ML) CONDENSED CREAM OF MUSHROOM SOUP	1
1/2 CUP	BEEF BROTH	125 ML
2 TBSP	SOY SAUCE	30 ML

USE A 5- TO 6-QUART SLOW COOKER. SEASON BEEF WELL WITH SALT AND PEPPER. IN A LARGE SKILLET, HEAT HALF THE OIL OVER MEDIUM-HIGH HEAT. ADD BEEF AND BROWN ON ALL SIDES. TRANSFER TO SLOW COOKER. REDUCE HEAT TO MEDIUM AND ADD REMAINING OIL TO SKILLET. ADD ONIONS, MUSHROOMS, GARLIC, OREGANO AND 1/4 TSP (1 ML) PEPPER; COOK, STIRRING OCCASIONALLY, FOR 5 MINUTES. WHISK IN SOUP, BROTH AND SOY SAUCE; BRING TO A BOIL. POUR OVER BEEF. COVER AND COOK ON LOW FOR ABOUT 8 HOURS OR ON HIGH FOR ABOUT 4 HOURS, UNTIL BEEF IS TENDER. TRANSFER BEEF TO A CUTTING BOARD, COVER LOOSELY WITH FOIL AND LET REST FOR 10 MINUTES. ADJUST GRAVY SEASONING WITH SALT AND PEPPER, IF DESIRED. SLICE BEEF ACROSS THE GRAIN OR PULL APART INTO CHUNKS. SERVE TOPPED WITH GRAVY. SERVES 6 TO 8.

POT ROAST WITH CREAMY MUSTARD GRAVY

IDEAL FOR EASY ENTERTAINING.

I	BONELESS BEEF CHUCK, BLADE OR CROSS RIB ROAST (3 TO 4 LBS/1.5 TO 2 KG)	I
	SALT AND PEPPER	
2 TBSP	VEGETABLE OIL, DIVIDED	30 ML
2	CARROTS, CHOPPED	2
2	STALKS CELERY, CHOPPED	2
2	LARGE ONIONS, THINLY SLICED	2
4	CLOVES GARLIC, MINCED	4
2 TBSP	TOMATO PASTE	30 ML
2 TBSP	ALL-PURPOSE FLOUR	30 ML
I CUP	DRY WHITE WINE	250 ML
$\frac{1}{2}$ CUP	BEEF BROTH	125 ML
2 TBSP	SOUR CREAM	30 ML
I TBSP	DIJON MUSTARD	15 ML
2 TSP	PREPARED HORSERADISH	10 ML

USE A 5- TO 6-QUART SLOW COOKER. SEASON BEEF WELL WITH SALT AND PEPPER. IN A LARGE SKILLET, HEAT HALF THE OIL OVER MEDIUM-HIGH HEAT. ADD BEEF AND BROWN ON ALL SIDES. TRANSFER TO SLOW COOKER. REDUCE HEAT TO MEDIUM AND ADD REMAINING OIL TO SKILLET. ADD CARROTS, CELERY, ONIONS, GARLIC, I TSP (5 ML) SALT, $\frac{1}{4}$ TSP (I ML) PEPPER AND TOMATO PASTE; COOK, STIRRING OCCASIONALLY, FOR 7 MINUTES. STIR IN FLOUR. WHISK IN WINE AND BROTH, SCRAPING UP BROWN BITS FROM BOTTOM OF PAN. POUR OVER BEEF. COVER AND COOK ON LOW FOR ABOUT 8 HOURS OR ON HIGH FOR

ABOUT 4 HOURS, UNTIL BEEF IS TENDER. TRANSFER BEEF TO A CUTTING BOARD, COVER LOOSELY WITH FOIL AND LET REST FOR 10 MINUTES. MEANWHILE, IN A BOWL, COMBINE SOUR CREAM, MUSTARD, HORSERADISH AND ABOUT $\frac{1}{2}$ CUP (125 ML) OF THE COOKING LIQUID. WHISK INTO SLOW COOKER. ADJUST SEASONING WITH SALT AND PEPPER, IF DESIRED. COVER AND COOK ON HIGH FOR 10 MINUTES, UNTIL STEAMING. SLICE BEEF ACROSS THE GRAIN OR PULL APART INTO CHUNKS. SERVE TOPPED WITH VEGETABLES AND GRAVY. SERVES 6 TO 8.

TIP: WE USE TOMATO PASTE IN MANY OF OUR SLOW COOKER RECIPES BECAUSE IT GREATLY BOOSTS FLAVOR AND RICHNESS. THE LONG, MOIST COOKING DULLS OTHER AROMATIC INGREDIENTS, SUCH AS ONIONS, GARLIC AND HERBS. MICROWAVING OR BROWNING A DOLLOP OR TWO OF TOMATO PASTE WITH THESE INGREDIENTS MAKES ALL THE DIFFERENCE.

I'M MUCH TOO YOUNG TO BE THIS OLD.

COWBOY POT ROAST WITH SWEET POTATOES

YAHOO! A POT ROAST WITH SASS. THIS IS AN ADAPTATION OF ONE OF OUR LONG-TIME FAVORITES! SERVE WITH LAZY DAYS BUTTERMILK BISCUITS (PAGE 224).

1	BONELESS BEEF CHUCK, BLADE OR CROSS RIB ROAST (3 TO 4 LBS/1.5 TO 2 KG)	1
	SALT AND PEPPER	
2 TBSP	VEGETABLE OIL, DIVIDED	30 ML
1	LARGE SWEET POTATO, CUT INTO 2-INCH (5 CM) CUBES	1
3	STALKS CELERY, CHOPPED	3
3	CARROTS, CUT INTO 2-INCH (5 CM) CHUNKS	3
2	ONIONS, THINLY SLICED	2
4	CLOVES GARLIC, MINCED	4
2 TSP	GROUND CUMIN	10 ML
1 TSP	DRIED OREGANO	5 ML
2 TBSP	ALL-PURPOSE FLOUR	30 ML
1 CUP	TOMATO-BASED CHILI SAUCE	250 ML
1 CUP	BEEF BROTH	250 ML
2 TSP	CHILI POWDER	10 ML
2 TSP	RED WINE VINEGAR	10 ML
2	JALAPEÑO PEPPERS, SEEDED AND FINELY CHOPPED	2

USE A 5- TO 6-QUART SLOW COOKER. SEASON BEEF WELL WITH SALT AND PEPPER. IN A LARGE SKILLET, HEAT HALF THE OIL OVER MEDIUM-HIGH HEAT. ADD BEEF AND BROWN ON ALL SIDES. TRANSFER TO SLOW COOKER.

ARRANGE SWEET POTATO AROUND BEEF. REDUCE HEAT TO MEDIUM AND ADD REMAINING OIL TO SKILLET. ADD CELERY, CARROTS, ONIONS, GARLIC, CUMIN, OREGANO AND 1 TSP (5 ML) SALT; COOK, STIRRING OCCASIONALLY, FOR 7 MINUTES. STIR IN FLOUR. WHISK IN CHILI SAUCE AND BROTH; BRING TO A BOIL, SCRAPING UP BROWN BITS FROM BOTTOM OF PAN. POUR OVER BEEF. COVER AND COOK ON LOW FOR ABOUT 8 HOURS OR ON HIGH FOR ABOUT 4 HOURS, UNTIL BEEF IS TENDER. TRANSFER BEEF TO A CUTTING BOARD, COVER LOOSELY WITH FOIL AND LET REST FOR 10 MINUTES. MEANWHILE, IN A SMALL BOWL, COMBINE CHILI POWDER AND VINEGAR UNTIL SMOOTH. STIR INTO SLOW COOKER, ALONG WITH JALAPEÑOS. COVER AND COOK ON HIGH FOR 10 MINUTES TO BLEND THE FLAVORS. ADJUST SEASONING WITH SALT, IF DESIRED. SLICE BEEF ACROSS THE GRAIN OR PULL APART INTO CHUNKS. SERVE TOPPED WITH VEGETABLES AND GRAVY. SERVES 6 TO 8.

SENSATIONAL ITALIAN POT ROAST

WOW! THE BEEF IS SO TENDER IT FALLS APART, AND THE GRAVY IS DIVINE. SERVE WITH MUSHROOM PARMESAN POLENTA (PAGE 298) AND A STEAMED GREEN VEGETABLE.

1	BONELESS BEEF CHUCK, BLADE OR CROSS RIB ROAST (3 TO 4 LBS/1.5 TO 2 KG)	1
	SALT AND PEPPER	
2 TBSP	VEGETABLE OIL, DIVIDED	30 ML
2	ONIONS, THINLY SLICED	2
3 CUPS	SLICED MUSHROOMS	750 ML
4	CLOVES GARLIC, MINCED	4
1½ TSP	DRIED ITALIAN SEASONING OR BASIL	7 ML
2 TBSP	TOMATO PASTE	30 ML
2 TBSP	ALL-PURPOSE FLOUR	30 ML
½ CUP	DRY RED WINE	125 ML
1 CUP	BEEF BROTH	250 ML
½ CUP	TOMATO SAUCE	125 ML
½ CUP	OIL-PACKED SUN-DRIED TOMATOES, DRAINED AND CHOPPED	125 ML
3 TBSP	CHOPPED FRESH PARSLEY	45 ML
	GRATED ZEST OF ½ LEMON	

USE A 5- TO 6-QUART SLOW COOKER. SEASON BEEF WELL WITH SALT AND PEPPER. IN A LARGE SKILLET, HEAT HALF THE OIL OVER MEDIUM-HIGH HEAT. ADD BEEF AND BROWN ON ALL SIDES. TRANSFER TO SLOW COOKER. REDUCE HEAT TO MEDIUM AND ADD REMAINING OIL TO SKILLET. ADD ONIONS, MUSHROOMS, GARLIC, ITALIAN SEASONING, ½ TSP (2 ML) SALT, ¼ TSP (1 ML) PEPPER AND TOMATO PASTE; COOK, STIRRING OCCASIONALLY, FOR 5 MINUTES.

STIR IN FLOUR. WHISK IN WINE, SCRAPING UP BROWN BITS FROM BOTTOM OF PAN. WHISK IN BROTH, TOMATO SAUCE AND SUN-DRIED TOMATOES. POUR OVER BEEF. COVER AND COOK ON LOW FOR ABOUT 8 HOURS OR ON HIGH FOR ABOUT 4 HOURS, UNTIL BEEF IS TENDER. TRANSFER BEEF TO A CUTTING BOARD, COVER LOOSELY WITH FOIL AND LET REST FOR 10 MINUTES. ADJUST GRAVY SEASONING WITH SALT AND PEPPER, IF DESIRED. IN A SMALL BOWL, COMBINE PARSLEY AND LEMON ZEST. SLICE BEEF ACROSS THE GRAIN OR PULL APART INTO CHUNKS. SERVE BEEF TOPPED WITH GRAVY. GARNISH WITH PARSLEY MIXTURE. SERVES 6 TO 8.

BEEF IN BEER POT ROAST

EVERYTHING TASTES BETTER WITH BEER.
THE RICH GRAVY IS SO GOOD WITH CRUSTY BREAD.

3	CARROTS, CHOPPED	3
1	LARGE SWEET POTATO, PEELED AND CUT INTO 2-INCH (5 CM) CUBES	1
1 LB	POTATOES, PEELED AND CUT INTO 1/2-INCH (1 CM) CUBES	500 G
1	BONELESS BEEF CHUCK, BLADE OR CROSS RIB ROAST (3 TO 4 LBS/1.5 TO 2 KG)	1
	SALT AND PEPPER	
2 TBSP	VEGETABLE OIL, DIVIDED	30 ML
2	LARGE ONIONS, CHOPPED	2
4	CLOVES GARLIC, MINCED	4
1 TSP	DRIED THYME	5 ML
2 TBSP	TOMATO PASTE	30 ML
2 TBSP	ALL-PURPOSE FLOUR	30 ML
1	BOTTLE (12 OZ/341 ML) LIGHT-COLORED BEER	1
1 CUP	BEEF BROTH	250 ML
1 TBSP	WORCESTERSHIRE SAUCE	15 ML
1 CUP	FROZEN PEAS (NO NEED TO THAW)	250 ML
1 TBSP	PACKED BROWN SUGAR	15 ML
1 TBSP	BALSAMIC VINEGAR	15 ML
	CHOPPED FRESH PARSLEY	

IN A 5- TO 6-QUART SLOW COOKER, COMBINE CARROTS, SWEET POTATO AND POTATOES. SEASON BEEF WELL WITH SALT AND PEPPER. IN A LARGE SKILLET, HEAT HALF THE OIL OVER MEDIUM-HIGH HEAT. ADD BEEF AND BROWN ON ALL SIDES. TRANSFER TO SLOW COOKER. REDUCE HEAT

TO MEDIUM AND ADD REMAINING OIL TO SKILLET. ADD ONIONS, GARLIC, THYME, $\frac{1}{2}$ TSP (2 ML) SALT, $\frac{1}{4}$ TSP (I ML) PEPPER AND TOMATO PASTE; COOK, STIRRING OCCASIONALLY, FOR 5 MINUTES. STIR IN FLOUR. WHISK IN BEER, BROTH AND WORCESTERSHIRE SAUCE, STIRRING TO SCRAPE UP BROWN BITS FROM BOTTOM OF PAN; BRING TO A BOIL. POUR OVER BEEF. COVER AND COOK ON LOW FOR ABOUT 8 HOURS OR ON HIGH FOR ABOUT 4 HOURS, UNTIL BEEF IS TENDER. TRANSFER BEEF TO A CUTTING BOARD, COVER LOOSELY WITH FOIL AND LET REST FOR IO MINUTES. MEANWHILE, STIR PEAS, BROWN SUGAR AND VINEGAR INTO SLOW COOKER. ADJUST SEASONING WITH SALT AND PEPPER, IF DESIRED. COVER AND COOK ON HIGH FOR I5 MINUTES, UNTIL PEAS ARE HOT. SLICE BEEF ACROSS THE GRAIN OR PULL APART INTO CHUNKS. SERVE TOPPED WITH VEGETABLES AND GRAVY. GARNISH WITH PARSLEY. SERVES 6 TO 8.

JAVA JIVE POT ROAST

COFFEE IS THE SUBTLE SECRET TO THIS GREAT-TASTING DISH. SERVE WITH MASHED SWEET POTATO.

8	GARLIC CLOVES, LIGHTLY CRUSHED	8
3	CARROTS, CHOPPED	3
2	STALKS CELERY, CHOPPED	2
1	LARGE ONION, THINLY SLICED	1
1	BONELESS BEEF CHUCK, BLADE OR CROSS RIB ROAST (3 TO 4 LBS/1.5 TO 2 KG)	1
	SALT AND PEPPER	
1 TBSP	VEGETABLE OIL	15 ML
1/4 CUP	ALL-PURPOSE FLOUR	60 ML
1/4 CUP	PACKED BROWN SUGAR	60 ML
1 TSP	DRIED THYME	5 ML
1 CUP	STRONG BREWED COFFEE	250 ML
1/2 CUP	BEEF BROTH	125 ML
1/4 CUP	TOMATO PASTE	60 ML
3 TBSP	WORCESTERSHIRE SAUCE	45 ML
1 TBSP	RED WINE VINEGAR	15 ML

IN A 5- TO 6-QUART SLOW COOKER, COMBINE GARLIC, CARROTS, CELERY AND ONION. SEASON BEEF WELL WITH SALT AND PEPPER. IN A LARGE SKILLET, HEAT OIL OVER MEDIUM-HIGH HEAT. ADD BEEF AND BROWN ON ALL SIDES. TRANSFER TO SLOW COOKER. IN A BOWL, WHISK TOGETHER FLOUR, BROWN SUGAR, THYME, 1 TSP (5 ML) SALT, 1/4 TSP (1 ML) PEPPER, COFFEE, BROTH, TOMATO PASTE AND WORCESTERSHIRE SAUCE. POUR OVER BEEF. COVER AND COOK ON LOW FOR ABOUT 8 HOURS OR ON HIGH FOR ABOUT 4 HOURS, UNTIL BEEF IS TENDER.

TRANSFER BEEF TO A CUTTING BOARD, COVER LOOSELY WITH FOIL AND LET REST FOR 10 MINUTES. STIR VINEGAR INTO SAUCE. ADJUST SEASONING WITH SALT AND PEPPER, IF DESIRED. SLICE BEEF ACROSS THE GRAIN OR PULL APART INTO CHUNKS. SERVE TOPPED WITH VEGETABLES AND SAUCE. SERVES 6 TO 8.

TIP: WORCESTERSHIRE SAUCE (PRONOUNCED *WOOS-TUHR-SHEER*) IS A DARK BROWN SAUCE WITH A PIQUANT, SPICY FLAVOR THAT WAS DEVELOPED FOR BRITISH COLONIALS IN INDIA. IT TAKES ITS NAME FROM WORCESTER, ENGLAND, WHERE IT WAS FIRST BOTTLED. THE SAUCE IS USED TO SEASON MEATS, SAUCES AND SOUPS, AND IS AN ESSENTIAL INGREDIENT IN A BLOODY MARY COCKTAIL. ONCE OPENED, IT KEEPS FOR SEVERAL MONTHS IN THE REFRIGERATOR.

IF THE DAY I CAME OUT OF YOUR TUMMY
IS CALLED MY BIRTHDAY, WHAT IS
THE DAY I WENT IN CALLED?

GLAZED BRAISED ONION BRISKET

THE SWEET AND TANGY SAUCE BEGS TO BE SERVED
WITH STEAMED RICE AND A SLIGHTLY BITTER GREEN
VEGETABLE, SUCH AS STEAMED RAPINI OR BROCCOLINI.

4 to 5 LB	DOUBLE BEEF BRISKET (SEE TIP, PAGE 121)	2 to 2.5 KG
4	CLOVES GARLIC, MINCED	4
1½	ENVELOPES (EACH 1.4 OZ/38.5 G) ONION SOUP MIX	1½
1½ CUPS	RED PEPPER JELLY	375 ML
½ CUP	BALSAMIC VINEGAR	125 ML
2 TBSP	CORNSTARCH	30 ML
3 TBSP	COLD WATER	45 ML

USE A 5- TO 6-QUART SLOW COOKER. PLACE BRISKET
IN A LARGE BOWL OR BAKING DISH. IN ANOTHER BOWL,
COMBINE GARLIC, SOUP MIX, RED PEPPER JELLY AND
VINEGAR. POUR OVER BEEF AND, USING A SPATULA,
SPREAD EVENLY OVER ALL SIDES OF BEEF. COVER AND
REFRIGERATE FOR AT LEAST 12 HOURS OR UP TO 24
HOURS. TRANSFER BEEF TO SLOW COOKER, SCRAPING IN
ALL JELLY MIXTURE FROM BOTTOM OF BOWL. COVER AND
COOK ON LOW FOR 8 TO 10 HOURS OR ON HIGH FOR 4
TO 5 HOURS, UNTIL BRISKET IS VERY TENDER. TRANSFER
BRISKET TO A CUTTING BOARD, COVER LOOSELY WITH FOIL
AND LET REST FOR 10 MINUTES. USING A SPOON, REMOVE
EXCESS FAT FROM SURFACE OF COOKING LIQUID. POUR
COOKING LIQUID INTO A SAUCEPAN. IN A SMALL BOWL,
COMBINE CORNSTARCH AND WATER UNTIL SMOOTH. STIR
CORNSTARCH MIXTURE INTO PAN AND BRING TO A BOIL;
REDUCE HEAT AND SIMMER, STIRRING, FOR 5 MINUTES,

UNTIL THICKENED AND GLOSSY. SLICE MEAT THINLY ACROSS THE GRAIN AND SERVE TOPPED WITH SAUCE. SERVES 6 TO 8.

TIP: JARS OF RED PEPPER JELLY CAN OFTEN BE FOUND IN THE DELI SECTION OF THE SUPERMARKET. YOU CAN SUBSTITUTE RED CURRANT JELLY (LOOK IN THE JAM SECTION) AND ADD A PINCH OF HOT PEPPER FLAKES.

MAKE AHEAD: BRISKET IS EXCELLENT, BUT VERY FATTY. FOR BEST RESULTS, BRAISE A DAY AHEAD. TRANSFER THE COOKED BRISKET AND SAUCE TO SEPARATE AIRTIGHT CONTAINERS, LET COOL AND REFRIGERATE OVERNIGHT OR FOR UP TO 2 DAYS. ONCE THE SAUCE IS CHILLED, YOU CAN SCRAPE THE HARDENED FAT OFF THE SURFACE. SLICE THE BRISKET THINLY ACROSS THE GRAIN. REHEAT THE SLICED MEAT AND SAUCE IN A COVERED CASSEROLE DISH AT 350°F (180°C) FOR ABOUT 45 MINUTES, UNTIL HEATED THROUGH.

RED WINE-BRAISED BRISKET

BRISKET BECOMES FALL-APART TENDER AND JUICY IN THE SLOW COOKER. USE LEFTOVERS TO MAKE HOT CHEESY BEEF SANDWICHES (PAGE 122) OR REMNANT RAGÙ (PAGE 123).

4 to 5 LB	DOUBLE BEEF BRISKET (SEE TIP, OPPOSITE)	2 to 2.5 KG
	SALT AND PEPPER	
2 TBSP	VEGETABLE OIL, DIVIDED	30 ML
1 CUP	DRY RED WINE	250 ML
3	ONIONS, THINLY SLICED	3
6	CLOVES GARLIC, MINCED	6
1 TBSP	PACKED BROWN SUGAR	15 ML
2 TBSP	TOMATO PASTE	30 ML
2	BAY LEAVES	2
1 CUP	BEEF BROTH	250 ML
1/4 CUP	SOUR CREAM (OR TO TASTE)	60 ML
	CHOPPED FRESH PARSLEY OR DILL	

USE A 5- TO 6-QUART SLOW COOKER. SEASON BEEF WELL WITH SALT AND PEPPER. IN A SKILLET, HEAT HALF THE OIL OVER MEDIUM-HIGH HEAT. BROWN BRISKET ON BOTH SIDES. TRANSFER TO SLOW COOKER. REMOVE SKILLET FROM HEAT AND POUR OFF FAT. POUR WINE INTO SKILLET AND STIR TO SCRAPE UP BROWN BITS FROM BOTTOM OF PAN. POUR OVER BRISKET. WIPE OUT SKILLET WITH PAPER TOWEL. ADD REMAINING OIL TO SKILLET AND HEAT OVER MEDIUM HEAT. ADD ONIONS, GARLIC, BROWN SUGAR, 1 TSP (5 ML) SALT, 1/4 TSP (1 ML) PEPPER AND TOMATO PASTE; COOK, STIRRING OCCASIONALLY, FOR 5 MINUTES. SCRAPE ONION MIXTURE OVER BRISKET. ADD BAY LEAVES AND

BROTH. COVER AND COOK ON LOW FOR 8 TO 10 HOURS OR ON HIGH FOR 4 TO 5 HOURS, UNTIL BRISKET IS VERY TENDER. TRANSFER BRISKET TO A CUTTING BOARD, COVER LOOSELY WITH FOIL AND LET REST FOR 10 MINUTES. USING A SPOON, REMOVE EXCESS FAT FROM SURFACE OF GRAVY. DISCARD BAY LEAVES. POUR COOKING LIQUID INTO A SAUCEPAN AND BRING TO A BOIL. REDUCE HEAT AND SIMMER FOR 10 MINUTES, UNTIL SLIGHTLY REDUCED. IN A SMALL BOWL, COMBINE SOUR CREAM AND $\frac{1}{4}$ CUP (60 ML) OF THE COOKING LIQUID, THEN WHISK BACK INTO SAUCEPAN. ADJUST SEASONING WITH SALT AND PEPPER, IF DESIRED. STIR IN PARSLEY. SLICE MEAT THINLY ACROSS THE GRAIN AND SERVE TOPPED WITH GRAVY. SERVES 6 TO 8.

TIP: BRISKET IS A LARGE AND TOUGH CUT OF BEEF. A WHOLE BRISKET CAN WEIGH UP TO 15 LBS (7.5 KG), SO THEY ARE TYPICALLY SOLD CUT IN HALF. A BRISKET HAS A THICK END AND A THIN END; FOR THIS RECIPE, BUY THE THICK END, CALLED THE DOUBLE, POINT OR DECKLE. MAKE SURE TO BUY FRESH BRISKET, NOT CORNED BEEF BRISKET. YOU MAY HAVE TO CUT THE BRISKET IN HALF TO FIT IT IN THE SLOW COOKER. IF SO, LAY ONE PIECE ON TOP OF THE OTHER AND FLIP THE TWO PIECES HALFWAY THROUGH COOKING TO ENSURE EVEN BRAISING.

MAKE AHEAD: SEE PAGE 119.

HOT CHEESY BEEF SANDWICHES

LEFTOVERS NEVER TASTED SO GOOD. USE THINLY SLICED BEEF AND THE SAUCE FROM RED WINE-BRAISED BRISKET (PAGE 120) OR ANOTHER POT ROAST TO MAKE THIS JUICY SUPPER SANDWICH. SERVE WITH A GREEN SALAD AND PLENTY OF NAPKINS!

I TBSP	VEGETABLE OIL	15 ML
I	ONION, THINLY SLICED	I
1/2 CUP	LEFTOVER BEEF BRISKET JUICES OR OTHER BEEF GRAVY	125 ML
6 OZ	THINLY SLICED LEFTOVER COOKED BEEF BRISKET OR OTHER BEEF	175 G
2/3 CUP	SHREDDED MOZZARELLA CHEESE	150 ML
2	6-INCH (15 CM) SUBMARINE ROLLS, SPLIT HORIZONTALLY AND WARMED	2
2 TBSP	DIJON MUSTARD (OPTIONAL)	30 ML

IN A SKILLET, HEAT OIL OVER MEDIUM HEAT. ADD ONION AND COOK, STIRRING OCCASIONALLY, FOR ABOUT 7 MINUTES, UNTIL GOLDEN. TRANSFER TO A BOWL, COVER AND KEEP WARM. POUR BRISKET JUICES INTO SKILLET AND HEAT UNTIL BUBBLING. ADD BRISKET AND TURN TO COAT IN JUICES. REDUCE HEAT, COVER AND SIMMER FOR 5 TO 7 MINUTES, UNTIL HEATED THROUGH. REMOVE FROM HEAT, SPRINKLE CHEESE OVER MEAT, COVER AND LET STAND UNTIL CHEESE MELTS, ABOUT I MINUTE. SPREAD ROLLS WITH MUSTARD (IF USING). MAKE SANDWICHES WITH THE MEAT MIXTURE AND RESERVED ONIONS, POURING JUICES OVER THE FILLING. SERVES 2.

REMNANT RAGÙ

THE VERY THING FOR LEFTOVER RED WINE-BRAISED BRISKET (PAGE 120).

1 TBSP	VEGETABLE OIL	15 ML
3 CUPS	SLICED CREMINI MUSHROOMS	750 ML
2	CLOVES GARLIC, MINCED	2
1/2 TSP	DRIED OREGANO	2 ML
1 TBSP	BRANDY (OPTIONAL)	15 ML
3 CUPS	CHOPPED LEFTOVER BRAISED BEEF BRISKET	750 ML
2 CUPS	LEFTOVER BEEF BRISKET GRAVY (SEE TIP, BELOW)	500 ML
1 CUP	CANNED WHOLE TOMATOES, WITH JUICE	250 ML
	SALT AND PEPPER (OPTIONAL)	
1/4 CUP	CHOPPED FRESH PARSLEY	60 ML
	HOT COOKED PASTA	
	GRATED PARMESAN CHEESE	

IN A LARGE SAUCEPAN, HEAT OIL OVER MEDIUM HEAT. ADD MUSHROOMS AND COOK, STIRRING OFTEN, FOR 5 MINUTES. ADD GARLIC AND OREGANO; COOK, STIRRING, FOR 15 SECONDS. STIR IN BRANDY (IF USING). ADD BRISKET, GRAVY AND TOMATOES, BREAKING TOMATOES UP WITH A SPOON; BRING TO A BOIL. REDUCE HEAT AND SIMMER FOR 15 TO 25 MINUTES, UNTIL SAUCE IS THICK ENOUGH TO HEAP ON A SPOON. SEASON TO TASTE WITH SALT AND PEPPER, IF DESIRED. STIR IN PARSLEY. SERVED LADLED OVER HOT PASTA AND SPRINKLED WITH PARMESAN. SERVES 4.

TIP: IF YOU HAVE LESS THAN 2 CUPS (500 ML) LEFTOVER GRAVY, USE MORE CANNED TOMATOES.

SPANISH BRAISED STEAK AND ONIONS

THE SLOW COOKER WORKS LIKE A DREAM WITH CHEAPER CUTS OF MEAT, SUCH AS SIMMERING STEAKS. GREAT GRAVY. SERVE WITH FLUFFY MASHED POTATOES.

2 LBS	BONELESS SIMMERING BEEF STEAK, SUCH AS CROSS RIB, BLADE OR ROUND	1 KG
	SALT AND PEPPER	
2 TBSP	VEGETABLE OIL, DIVIDED	30 ML
2	LARGE ONIONS, THINLY SLICED	2
1/4 CUP	BALSAMIC VINEGAR	60 ML
3	CLOVES GARLIC, MINCED	3
1 TBSP	TOMATO PASTE	15 ML
2	BAY LEAVES	2
1	CAN (14 OZ/398 ML) WHOLE TOMATOES, WITH JUICE	1
2 TSP	SWEET PAPRIKA	10 ML
2 TSP	FRESHLY SQUEEZED LEMON JUICE	10 ML

USE A 5- TO 6-QUART SLOW COOKER. CUT BEEF INTO 6 TO 8 CHUNKS, IF DESIRED. SEASON BEEF WELL WITH SALT AND PEPPER. IN A LARGE SKILLET, HEAT HALF THE OIL OVER MEDIUM-HIGH HEAT. BROWN STEAK ON BOTH SIDES, IN BATCHES IF NECESSARY. TRANSFER TO SLOW COOKER. REDUCE HEAT TO MEDIUM AND ADD REMAINING OIL TO PAN. ADD ONIONS AND VINEGAR; COOK, STIRRING OFTEN, FOR 5 TO 7 MINUTES, UNTIL SOFTENED AND DARK BROWN. ADD GARLIC, 1 TSP (5 ML) SALT, 1/4 TSP (1 ML) PEPPER AND TOMATO PASTE; COOK, STIRRING, FOR 15 SECONDS. STIR IN BAY LEAVES AND TOMATOES, BREAKING TOMATOES UP WITH A SPOON AND SCRAPING UP BROWN BITS FROM

BOTTOM OF PAN. POUR OVER BEEF; STIR. COVER AND COOK ON LOW FOR ABOUT 8 HOURS OR ON HIGH FOR ABOUT 4 HOURS, UNTIL BEEF IS TENDER. IN A SMALL BOWL, COMBINE PAPRIKA AND LEMON JUICE UNTIL SMOOTH. STIR INTO SLOW COOKER. COVER AND COOK ON HIGH FOR 15 MINUTES TO BLEND THE FLAVORS. DISCARD BAY LEAVES. ADJUST SEASONING WITH SALT AND PEPPER, IF DESIRED. SERVES 4.

TIP: SIMMERING STEAKS ARE TOUGHER CUTS OF BEEF THAT BECOME TASTY AND TENDER WHEN BRAISED, MUCH LIKE A POT ROAST. THIS MAKES THEM PERFECT FOR THE SLOW COOKER. DON'T BE MISLED BY THE WORD "STEAK" — THIS CUT OF MEAT IS NOT GOOD FOR THE GRILL!

ROCKIN' ROULADEN

CUSTOM-MADE FOR THE SLOW COOKER. MAKE IT
ON THE WEEKEND AND IMPRESS YOUR GUESTS.
SERVE OVER BUTTERED NOODLES.

3 TBSP	VEGETABLE OIL, DIVIDED	45 ML
2 CUPS	FINELY CHOPPED ONIONS, DIVIDED	500 ML
1 1/2 CUPS	SLICED MUSHROOMS	375 ML
3	CLOVES GARLIC, MINCED	3
1/2 CUP	FRESH BREAD CRUMBS	125 ML
	SALT AND PEPPER	
4	THIN SLICES BONELESS BEEF ROUND STEAK (ABOUT I LB/500 G TOTAL)	4
2 TBSP	DIJON MUSTARD	30 ML
4	SLICES BACON	4
1/4 CUP	ALL-PURPOSE FLOUR	60 ML
I TBSP	TOMATO PASTE	15 ML
I CUP	BEEF BROTH	250 ML
I TBSP	CORNSTARCH	15 ML
I TSP	PAPRIKA	5 ML
I TBSP	COLD WATER	15 ML
I TBSP	FINELY CHOPPED DILL PICKLE	15 ML
1/4 CUP	SOUR CREAM	60 ML
	CHOPPED FRESH DILL (OPTIONAL)	

USE A 3 1/2- TO 4-QUART SLOW COOKER. IN A SKILLET,
HEAT I TBSP (15 ML) OIL OVER MEDIUM HEAT. ADD I CUP
(250 ML) ONIONS, MUSHROOMS AND GARLIC; COOK,
STIRRING OCCASIONALLY, FOR 5 MINUTES. STIR IN BREAD
CRUMBS, 1/2 TSP (2 ML) SALT AND 1/8 TSP (0.5 ML)
PEPPER. TRANSFER TO A BOWL AND LET COOL SLIGHTLY.
LAY BEEF ON A WORK SURFACE. SPREAD MUSTARD OVER

BEEF SLICES AND TOP EACH WITH A SLICE OF BACON. DIVIDE ONION MIXTURE AMONG BEEF SLICES, SPREADING TO EDGES. STARTING AT A SHORT END, ROLL UP BEEF. SECURE EACH ROLL WITH TWO PIECES OF KITCHEN STRING. PLACE FLOUR IN A DISH AND SEASON TO TASTE WITH SALT AND PEPPER. DREDGE BEEF ROLLS IN FLOUR MIXTURE, SHAKING OFF AND DISCARDING EXCESS. IN A CLEAN SKILLET, HEAT REMAINING OIL OVER MEDIUM-HIGH HEAT. BROWN BEEF ROLLS ON ALL SIDES. TRANSFER TO SLOW COOKER. REDUCE HEAT TO MEDIUM. ADD REMAINING ONIONS AND TOMATO PASTE TO SKILLET; COOK, STIRRING OCCASIONALLY, FOR 3 MINUTES. WHISK IN BROTH AND BRING TO A BOIL. POUR OVER BEEF ROLLS. COVER AND COOK ON LOW FOR ABOUT 6 HOURS OR ON HIGH FOR ABOUT 3 HOURS, UNTIL BEEF IS TENDER. USING TONGS, REMOVE BEEF ROLLS TO A PLATE. IN A SMALL BOWL, COMBINE CORNSTARCH, PAPRIKA AND WATER UNTIL SMOOTH. STIR INTO SLOW COOKER, ALONG WITH PICKLE AND SOUR CREAM. RETURN BEEF AND ACCUMULATED JUICES TO SLOW COOKER. COVER AND COOK ON HIGH FOR ABOUT 20 MINUTES, UNTIL SAUCE IS PIPING HOT. REMOVE STRING FROM ROLLS AND SPRINKLE WITH DILL (IF USING). SERVE IMMEDIATELY. SERVES 4.

TIP: CHECK YOUR SUPERMARKET FOR PACKAGES OF THINLY SLICED TOP OR INSIDE ROUND BEEF, WHICH MAY BE HELPFULLY LABELED "ROULADEN." IF YOU CAN'T FIND ROULADEN, BUY THIN-CUT SIRLOIN BEEF STEAKS AND POUND THEM BETWEEN TWO SHEETS OF PLASTIC WRAP TO A THICKNESS OF $1/4$ INCH (0.5 CM).

STAY-ABED STEW

PREPARE THE VEGETABLES THE NIGHT BEFORE. IN THE MORNING, ASSEMBLE THE RECIPE IN THE SLOW COOKER, THEN HEAD BACK TO BED — OR WORK, IF YOU MUST! SERVE WITH MASHED POTATOES.

3 LB	BONELESS BEEF CHUCK, BLADE OR CROSS RIB ROAST, CUT INTO 1-INCH (2.5 CM) CUBES	1.5 KG
3	LARGE CARROTS, THICKLY SLICED	3
3	STALKS CELERY, THINLY SLICED	3
1	LARGE PARSNIP, THICKLY SLICED	1
2	BAY LEAVES	2
1 TBSP	VEGETABLE OIL	15 ML
2	ONIONS, THINLY SLICED	2
4	CLOVES GARLIC, MINCED	4
	SALT AND PEPPER	
2 TBSP	ALL-PURPOSE FLOUR	30 ML
1 1/2 CUPS	BEEF BROTH	375 ML
1/2 CUP	TOMATO-BASED CHILI SAUCE	125 ML
1 TBSP	WORCESTERSHIRE SAUCE	15 ML
1 CUP	FROZEN BABY PEAS (NO NEED TO THAW)	250 ML
1/4 CUP	CHOPPED FRESH PARSLEY	60 ML

PLACE BEEF, CARROTS, CELERY, PARSNIP AND BAY LEAVES IN A 5- TO 6-QUART SLOW COOKER. IN A SKILLET, HEAT OIL OVER MEDIUM HEAT. ADD ONIONS, GARLIC, 1 TSP (5 ML) SALT AND 1/4 TSP (1 ML) PEPPER; COOK, STIRRING OCCASIONALLY, FOR 5 MINUTES. STIR IN FLOUR. WHISK IN BROTH, CHILI SAUCE AND WORCESTERSHIRE SAUCE; BRING TO A BOIL. POUR OVER BEEF MIXTURE AND STIR WELL. COVER AND COOK ON LOW FOR ABOUT 8 HOURS OR ON

HIGH FOR ABOUT 4 HOURS, UNTIL BEEF IS TENDER. STIR IN PEAS. COVER AND COOK ON HIGH FOR 15 MINUTES, UNTIL PEAS ARE HOT. DISCARD BAY LEAVES. ADJUST SEASONING WITH SALT AND PEPPER, IF DESIRED. SPRINKLE WITH PARSLEY. SERVES 6.

TIP: WORCESTERSHIRE SAUCE (PRONOUNCED *WOOS-TUHR-SHEER*) IS A DARK BROWN SAUCE WITH A PIQUANT, SPICY FLAVOR THAT WAS DEVELOPED FOR BRITISH COLONIALS IN INDIA. IT TAKES ITS NAME FROM WORCESTER, ENGLAND, WHERE IT WAS FIRST BOTTLED. THE SAUCE IS USED TO SEASON MEATS, SAUCES AND SOUPS, AND IS AN ESSENTIAL INGREDIENT IN A BLOODY MARY COCKTAIL. ONCE OPENED, IT KEEPS FOR SEVERAL MONTHS IN THE REFRIGERATOR.

BEEF MUSHROOM STEW WITH HORSERADISH DUMPLINGS

OMG — SOOO GOOD!

2 TBSP	VEGETABLE OIL, DIVIDED	30 ML
2 LB	BONELESS BEEF CHUCK, BLADE OR CROSS RIB ROAST, CUT INTO 1-INCH (2.5 CM) CUBES	1 KG
2	ONIONS, CHOPPED	2
4 CUPS	QUARTERED MUSHROOMS	1 L
4	CLOVES GARLIC, MINCED	4
1 TSP	DRIED THYME	5 ML
	SALT AND PEPPER	
1 TBSP	TOMATO PASTE	15 ML
2 TBSP	ALL-PURPOSE FLOUR	30 ML
1 1/2 CUPS	BEEF BROTH	375 ML
1 TBSP	BALSAMIC VINEGAR	15 ML

DUMPLINGS

1 1/2 CUPS	ALL-PURPOSE FLOUR	375 ML
2 TSP	BAKING POWDER	10 ML
1/2 TSP	SALT	2 ML
2 TBSP	CHOPPED FRESH PARSLEY	30 ML
1	EGG, LIGHTLY BEATEN	1
2/3 CUP	2% OR WHOLE MILK	150 ML
2 TBSP	VEGETABLE OIL	30 ML
2 TBSP	PREPARED HORSERADISH	30 ML

USE A 3 1/2- TO 4-QUART SLOW COOKER. IN A SKILLET, HEAT HALF THE OIL OVER MEDIUM-HIGH HEAT. BROWN BEEF, IN TWO BATCHES. TRANSFER TO SLOW COOKER. REDUCE HEAT TO MEDIUM AND ADD REMAINING OIL TO

SKILLET. ADD ONIONS, MUSHROOMS, GARLIC, THYME, $\frac{1}{2}$ TSP (2 ML) SALT, $\frac{1}{4}$ TSP (1 ML) PEPPER AND TOMATO PASTE; COOK, STIRRING OCCASIONALLY, FOR 5 MINUTES. STIR IN FLOUR. WHISK IN BROTH AND VINEGAR, SCRAPING UP BROWN BITS FROM BOTTOM OF PAN; BRING TO A BOIL. POUR OVER BEEF AND STIR WELL. COVER AND COOK ON LOW FOR ABOUT 8 HOURS OR ON HIGH FOR ABOUT 4 HOURS, UNTIL BEEF IS TENDER.

DUMPLINGS: ABOUT 30 MINUTES BEFORE SERVING, IN A LARGE BOWL, WHISK TOGETHER FLOUR, BAKING POWDER AND SALT. IN ANOTHER BOWL, COMBINE PARSLEY, EGG, MILK, OIL AND HORSERADISH. POUR OVER FLOUR MIXTURE AND STIR UNTIL JUST COMBINED. DROP BATTER BY HEAPING TABLESPOONFULS (15 ML) ONTO STEW. COVER AND COOK ON HIGH FOR ABOUT 20 MINUTES, UNTIL DUMPLINGS ARE NO LONGER DOUGHY ON THE BOTTOM. SERVE IMMEDIATELY. SERVES 4.

BEEF BOURGUIGNON

A SPECIAL BEEF STEW WORTHY OF YOUR BEST FRIENDS.
SERVE WITH BEST-EVER GARLIC MASHED POTATOES
(PAGE 288) OR BUTTERED NOODLES.

4	SLICES BACON, CHOPPED	4
2 TBSP	VEGETABLE OIL (APPROX.)	30 ML
3 LB	BONELESS BEEF CHUCK, BLADE OR CROSS RIB ROAST, CUT INTO 1-INCH (2.5 CM) CUBES	1.5 KG
2	LARGE ONIONS, CHOPPED	2
1	LARGE CARROT, CHOPPED	1
4	CLOVES GARLIC, MINCED	4
1/2 TSP	DRIED THYME	2 ML
	SALT AND PEPPER	
2 TBSP	TOMATO PASTE	30 ML
1/4 CUP	ALL-PURPOSE FLOUR	60 ML
1 1/2 CUPS	DRY RED WINE	375 ML
1/2 CUP	BEEF BROTH	125 ML
2	BAY LEAVES	2
2 CUPS	PEARL ONIONS	500 ML
1 TBSP	BUTTER	15 ML
3 CUPS	SMALL WHOLE MUSHROOMS	750 ML
1/4 CUP	CHOPPED FRESH PARSLEY	60 ML

USE A 5- TO 6-QUART SLOW COOKER. IN A SKILLET, COOK
BACON OVER MEDIUM-HIGH HEAT UNTIL CRISPY. USING
A SLOTTED SPOON, TRANSFER TO SLOW COOKER. IF
NECESSARY, ADD ENOUGH OIL TO FAT IN SKILLET TO MAKE
1 TBSP (15 ML). BROWN BEEF, IN TWO BATCHES. TRANSFER
TO SLOW COOKER. REDUCE HEAT TO MEDIUM AND ADD
1 TBSP (15 ML) OIL TO SKILLET. ADD CHOPPED ONIONS,

CARROT, GARLIC, THYME, 1/2 TSP (2 ML) SALT, 1/4 TSP
(1 ML) PEPPER AND TOMATO PASTE; COOK, STIRRING
OCCASIONALLY, FOR 7 MINUTES. STIR IN FLOUR. WHISK
IN WINE AND BROTH, SCRAPING UP BROWN BITS FROM
BOTTOM OF PAN; BRING TO A BOIL. POUR OVER BEEF AND
STIR WELL. ADD BAY LEAVES. COVER AND COOK ON LOW
FOR ABOUT 8 HOURS OR ON HIGH FOR ABOUT 4 HOURS,
UNTIL BEEF IS TENDER. MEANWHILE, IN A POT OF BOILING
WATER, BOIL PEARL ONIONS FOR 1 MINUTE; RINSE UNDER
COLD WATER. PEEL AND TRIM, LEAVING ROOTS INTACT.
IN A SKILLET, MELT BUTTER OVER MEDIUM HEAT. ADD
PEARL ONIONS AND MUSHROOMS; COOK, STIRRING FOR
6 TO 8 MINUTES, UNTIL BROWNED. WHEN BEEF IS COOKED,
STIR ONION MIXTURE INTO SLOW COOKER. COVER AND
COOK ON HIGH FOR 15 MINUTES TO BLEND THE FLAVORS.
DISCARD BAY LEAVES. SERVE SPRINKLED WITH PARSLEY.
SERVES 6 TO 8.

BEEF GOULASH

WHAT'S NOT TO LOVE! SERVE WITH BUTTERED NOODLES.

3 LB	BONELESS BEEF CHUCK, BLADE OR CROSS RIB ROAST, CUT INTO 1-INCH (2.5 CM) CUBES	1.5 KG
1 TBSP	VEGETABLE OIL	15 ML
3	ONIONS, THINLY SLICED	3
4	CLOVES GARLIC, MINCED	4
1 TSP	DRIED MARJORAM OR OREGANO	5 ML
1 TSP	CARAWAY SEEDS (OPTIONAL)	5 ML
	SALT AND PEPPER	
2 TBSP	TOMATO PASTE	30 ML
1/4 CUP	ALL-PURPOSE FLOUR	60 ML
1 1/2 CUPS	BEEF BROTH	375 ML
1/4 CUP	TOMATO-BASED CHILI SAUCE	60 ML
1 TBSP	SWEET PAPRIKA	15 ML
1 TBSP	FRESHLY SQUEEZED LEMON JUICE	15 ML
1	RED BELL PEPPER, THINLY SLICED	1
2 TBSP	CHOPPED FRESH DILL OR PARSLEY	30 ML
	SOUR CREAM	

PLACE BEEF IN A 5- TO 6-QUART SLOW COOKER. IN A SKILLET, HEAT OIL OVER MEDIUM HEAT. ADD ONIONS, GARLIC, MARJORAM, CARAWAY SEEDS (IF USING), 1 TSP (5 ML) SALT, 1/4 ML (1 ML) PEPPER AND TOMATO PASTE; COOK, STIRRING OCCASIONALLY, FOR 5 MINUTES. STIR IN FLOUR. WHISK IN BROTH AND CHILI SAUCE, SCRAPING UP BROWN BITS FROM BOTTOM OF PAN; BRING TO A BOIL. POUR OVER BEEF AND STIR WELL. COVER AND COOK ON LOW FOR ABOUT 8 HOURS OR ON HIGH FOR ABOUT

4 HOURS, UNTIL BEEF IS TENDER. IN A SMALL BOWL, COMBINE PAPRIKA AND LEMON JUICE UNTIL SMOOTH. STIR INTO SLOW COOKER, ALONG WITH RED PEPPER. COVER AND COOK ON HIGH FOR 20 MINUTES, UNTIL RED PEPPER IS TENDER. STIR IN DILL. SERVE GARNISHED WITH A DOLLOP OF SOUR CREAM. SERVES 6.

TIP: WE USE TOMATO PASTE IN MANY OF OUR SLOW COOKER RECIPES BECAUSE IT GREATLY BOOSTS FLAVOR AND RICHNESS. THE LONG, MOIST COOKING DULLS OTHER AROMATIC INGREDIENTS, SUCH AS ONIONS, GARLIC AND HERBS. MICROWAVING OR BROWNING A DOLLOP OR TWO OF TOMATO PASTE WITH THESE INGREDIENTS MAKES ALL THE DIFFERENCE.

DELECTABLE BEEF DAUBE

A SUPERB COLD-WEATHER CASSEROLE. DON'T BE AFRAID OF THE ALL THE GARLIC — THE CLOVES ARE BRAISED WHOLE TO PRODUCE A RICH MELLOWNESS.

3 LB	BONELESS BEEF CHUCK, BLADE OR CROSS RIB ROAST, CUT INTO 1-INCH (2.5 CM) CUBES)	1.5 KG
1 TBSP	VEGETABLE OIL	15 ML
3	ONIONS, THINLY SLICED	3
3	LARGE CARROTS, THINLY SLICED	3
8	CLOVES GARLIC, LIGHTLY CRUSHED	8
1/2 TSP	DRIED THYME	2 ML
1/2 TSP	DRIED MARJORAM	2 ML
	SALT AND PEPPER	
2 TBSP	TOMATO PASTE	30 ML
2 TBSP	ALL-PURPOSE FLOUR	30 ML
1 1/2 CUPS	DRY RED WINE	375 ML
1/2 CUP	BEEF BROTH	125 ML
2	2-INCH (5 CM) STRIPS ORANGE ZEST	2
2	BAY LEAVES	2

PLACE BEEF IN A 5- TO 6-QUART SLOW COOKER. IN A SKILLET, HEAT OIL OVER MEDIUM HEAT. ADD ONIONS, CARROTS, GARLIC, THYME, MARJORAM, 1 TSP (5 ML) SALT, 1/4 TSP (1 ML) PEPPER AND TOMATO PASTE; COOK, STIRRING OCCASIONALLY, FOR 7 MINUTES. STIR IN FLOUR. WHISK IN WINE AND BROTH, SCRAPING UP BROWN BITS FROM BOTTOM OF PAN; BRING TO A BOIL. POUR OVER BEEF AND STIR WELL. STIR IN ORANGE ZEST AND BAY LEAVES. COVER AND COOK ON LOW FOR ABOUT 8 HOURS OR ON HIGH FOR ABOUT 4 HOURS, UNTIL BEEF IS TENDER. DISCARD ORANGE ZEST AND BAY LEAVES. ADJUST SEASONING WITH SALT AND PEPPER, IF DESIRED.

SERVES 6.

BEEF MADRAS

A JAR OF INDIAN CURRY PASTE WORKS WONDERS. THIS
CURRY IS MEATY AND MID-POINT ON THE "HEAT" DIAL.
SERVE WITH STEAMED BASMATI RICE AND SQUASH
AND CHICKPEA COCONUT CURRY (PAGE 260).

I TBSP	VEGETABLE OIL	15 ML
2	ONIONS, THINLY SLICED	2
4	CLOVES GARLIC, MINCED	4
1/4 CUP	MADRAS OR OTHER MEDIUM INDIAN CURRY PASTE	60 ML
2 LBS	STEWING BEEF, CUT INTO I-INCH (2.5 CM) CUBES	I KG
1 1/2 CUPS	CANNED DICED TOMATOES, WITH JUICE	375 ML
1/2 CUP	WATER	125 ML

USE A 3 1/2- TO 4-QUART SLOW COOKER. IN A SKILLET,
HEAT OIL OVER MEDIUM HEAT. ADD ONIONS, GARLIC AND
CURRY PASTE; COOK, STIRRING OCCASIONALLY, FOR 5
MINUTES. ADD BEEF AND STIR TO COAT WITH SPICE
MIXTURE. STIR IN TOMATOES AND WATER, SCRAPING UP
BROWN BITS FROM BOTTOM OF PAN; BRING TO A BOIL.
TRANSFER TO SLOW COOKER. COVER AND COOK ON LOW
FOR ABOUT 8 HOURS OR ON HIGH FOR ABOUT 4 HOURS,
UNTIL BEEF IS TENDER. SERVES 4.

TIP: MOST SUPERMARKETS SELL PACKAGES OF CUBED
BEEF LABELED AS "STEWING BEEF." ALTERNATIVELY, LOOK
FOR OTHER BRAISING BEEF CUTS SUCH AS BONELESS
CROSS RIB, BLADE OR CHUCK IN THE FORM OF STEAKS
OR POT ROASTS. TRIM OFF EXCESS FAT AND CUT INTO
DESIRED-SIZED PIECES.

HOISIN GINGER BEEF STEW

THE SWEET AND SPICY FLAVORS OF GINGER, GARLIC AND HOISIN SAUCE ADD A LIVELY KICK TO THIS BEEF STEW. SERVE WITH BUTTERY NOODLES OR MASHED SWEET POTATO.

3 LB	BONELESS BEEF CHUCK, BLADE OR CROSS RIB ROAST, CUT INTO 1-INCH (2.5 CM) CUBES	1.5 KG
2 TBSP	SOY SAUCE	30 ML
1 TBSP	VEGETABLE OIL	15 ML
3	LARGE CARROTS, THINLY SLICED	3
2	ONIONS, THINLY SLICED	2
2	STALKS CELERY, THINLY SLICED	2
4	CLOVES GARLIC, MINCED	4
1 TBSP	FINELY CHOPPED GINGERROOT	15 ML
2 TBSP	ALL-PURPOSE FLOUR	30 ML
1 1/2 CUPS	BEEF BROTH	375 ML
1/3 CUP	HOISIN SAUCE	75 ML
1 TBSP	RICE VINEGAR OR CIDER VINEGAR	15 ML
8 OZ	SUGAR SNAP PEAS, TRIMMED	250 G
1 TSP	ASIAN CHILI PASTE (SEE TIP, OPPOSITE)	5 ML

PLACE BEEF IN A 5- TO 6-QUART SLOW COOKER. SPRINKLE WITH SOY SAUCE; TOSS TO COMBINE. IN A SKILLET, HEAT OIL OVER MEDIUM HEAT. ADD CARROTS, ONIONS, CELERY, GARLIC AND GINGER; COOK, STIRRING OCCASIONALLY, FOR 5 MINUTES. STIR IN FLOUR. WHISK IN BROTH, HOISIN SAUCE AND VINEGAR, SCRAPING UP BROWN BITS FROM BOTTOM OF PAN; BRING TO A BOIL. POUR OVER BEEF AND STIR WELL. COVER AND COOK ON LOW FOR ABOUT 8 HOURS OR ON HIGH FOR ABOUT 4 HOURS, UNTIL BEEF

IS TENDER. STIR IN PEAS AND CHILI PASTE. COVER AND COOK ON HIGH FOR 15 MINUTES, UNTIL PEAS ARE TENDER-CRISP. SERVE IMMEDIATELY. SERVES 6.

TIP: ASIAN CHILI PASTE, NOT TO BE CONFUSED WITH SWEET CHILI DIPPING SAUCE, IS A MIX OF GROUND HOT CHILE PEPPERS AND OTHER SEASONINGS. IT'S A GREAT WAY TO ADD HEAT TO YOUR COOKING. OUR FAVORITE VERSION IS LABELED "SAMBAL OELEK." THE JARS ARE USUALLY FOUND IN THE ASIAN FOODS AISLE OF THE SUPERMARKET. A GOOD SUBSTITUTE IS HOT PEPPER FLAKES, ADDED TO TASTE.

WESTERN BEEF AND BEAN HOTPOT

A QUICK-ASSEMBLY CASSEROLE FOR A WINTER DAY.
SERVE IN BOWLS, WITH CRUSTY DINNER ROLLS.

2 LBS	STEWING BEEF, CUT INTO 1-INCH (2.5 CM) CUBES	1 KG
3	LARGE POTATOES, PEELED AND CUT INTO 1-INCH (2.5 CM) CUBES	3
2	LARGE CARROTS, QUARTERED LENGTHWISE AND CHOPPED	2
1 TBSP	VEGETABLE OIL	15 ML
2	LARGE ONIONS, CHOPPED	2
4	CLOVES GARLIC, MINCED	4
2	CANS (EACH 14 OZ/398 ML) BEANS IN TOMATO SAUCE (SEE TIP, BELOW)	2
1 CUP	BEEF BROTH	250 ML
1/4 CUP	STEAK SAUCE	60 ML
1/4 CUP	BALSAMIC VINEGAR, DIVIDED	60 ML
	SALT AND PEPPER	

IN A 4- TO 6-QUART SLOW COOKER, COMBINE BEEF, POTATOES AND CARROTS. IN A SKILLET, HEAT OIL OVER MEDIUM HEAT. ADD ONIONS AND GARLIC; COOK, STIRRING OCCASIONALLY, FOR 5 MINUTES. STIR IN BEANS, BROTH, STEAK SAUCE, HALF THE VINEGAR, $1/2$ TSP (2 ML) SALT AND $1/4$ TSP (1 ML) PEPPER. POUR OVER BEEF MIXTURE AND STIR WELL. COVER AND COOK ON LOW FOR ABOUT 8 HOURS OR ON HIGH FOR ABOUT 4 HOURS, UNTIL BEEF IS TENDER. STIR IN REMAINING VINEGAR. ADJUST SEASONING WITH SALT AND PEPPER, IF DESIRED. SERVES 4.

TIP: CANS OF BEANS ARE SOMETIMES LABELED "DEEP-BROWNED" BEANS IN TOMATO SAUCE. WHATEVER THEY ARE CALLED, THAT'S WHAT YOU WANT!

SIMPLY SAUERBRATEN

GINGERSNAP COOKIES LEND A SWEET AND TANGY
APPEAL TO THIS GERMAN BEEF STEW. SERVE WITH
MASHED POTATOES AND QUICK COLESLAW (PAGE 176).

2 LBS	STEWING BEEF, CUT INTO 1-INCH (2.5 CM) CUBES	1 KG
2	BAY LEAVES	2
2	WHOLE CLOVES	2
1 TBSP	VEGETABLE OIL	15 ML
2	ONIONS, CHOPPED	2
1 TBSP	ALL-PURPOSE FLOUR	15 ML
$1\frac{1}{2}$ CUPS	BEEF BROTH	375 ML
$\frac{1}{4}$ CUP	RED WINE VINEGAR	60 ML
1 TBSP	WORCESTERSHIRE SAUCE	15 ML
	SALT AND PEPPER	
$\frac{1}{2}$ CUP	CRUSHED GINGERSNAP COOKIES	125 ML
1 TBSP	FRESHLY SQUEEZED LEMON JUICE (OPTIONAL)	15 ML

PLACE BEEF, BAY LEAVES AND CLOVES IN A $3\frac{1}{2}$- TO 4-QUART
SLOW COOKER. IN A SKILLET, HEAT OIL OVER MEDIUM
HEAT. ADD ONIONS AND COOK, STIRRING OCCASIONALLY,
FOR 5 MINUTES. STIR IN FLOUR. WHISK IN BROTH, VINEGAR,
WORCESTERSHIRE SAUCE, $\frac{1}{2}$ TSP (2 ML) SALT AND $\frac{1}{4}$ TSP
(1 ML) PEPPER; BRING TO A BOIL. POUR OVER BEEF MIXTURE
AND STIR WELL. COVER AND COOK ON LOW FOR ABOUT
8 HOURS OR ON HIGH FOR ABOUT 4 HOURS, UNTIL BEEF
IS TENDER. STIR IN GINGERSNAPS. COVER AND COOK ON
HIGH FOR ABOUT 20 MINUTES, UNTIL SAUCE IS THICKENED.
DISCARD BAY LEAVES AND CLOVES. ADJUST SEASONING
WITH SALT, PEPPER AND LEMON JUICE, IF DESIRED. SERVES 4.

SHEPHERD'S PIE

THE SLOW COOKER TAKES CARE OF DINNER WHILE YOU TEND TO YOUR FLOCK.

FILLING

1 LB	LEAN GROUND BEEF	500 G
1 TBSP	VEGETABLE OIL	15 ML
2	ONIONS, FINELY CHOPPED	2
1	LARGE CARROT, FINELY CHOPPED	1
3	CLOVES GARLIC, MINCED	3
1 TSP	DRIED OREGANO	5 ML
	SALT AND PEPPER	
3 TBSP	TOMATO KETCHUP	45 ML
1	ENVELOPE (4.5 G) BEEF BOUILLON POWDER	1
2 TBSP	ALL-PURPOSE FLOUR	30 ML
1 CUP	BEEF BROTH	250 ML
1 TBSP	WORCESTERSHIRE SAUCE	15 ML
1 CUP	FROZEN PEAS (NO NEED TO THAW)	250 ML

TOPPING

1 LB	SWEET POTATOES, PEELED AND CUBED	500 G
1 LB	YELLOW-FLESHED POTATOES (SUCH AS YUKON GOLD), PEELED AND CUBED	500 G
1/2 to 3/4 CUP	MILK, WARMED	125 to 175 ML
2 TBSP	BUTTER	30 ML
1/8 TSP	GROUND NUTMEG	0.5 ML
	SALT AND PEPPER	

FILLING: USE A 3½- TO 4-QUART SLOW COOKER. IN A SKILLET, OVER MEDIUM-HIGH HEAT, BROWN BEEF, BREAKING IT UP WITH A SPOON. USING A SLOTTED SPOON,

TRANSFER TO SLOW COOKER. DRAIN FAT FROM SKILLET. REDUCE HEAT TO MEDIUM AND ADD OIL TO SKILLET. ADD ONIONS, CARROT, GARLIC, OREGANO, $\frac{1}{4}$ TSP (1 ML) SALT, $\frac{1}{4}$ TSP (1 ML) PEPPER AND KETCHUP; COOK, STIRRING OFTEN, FOR 5 MINUTES. STIR IN BOUILLON POWDER AND FLOUR. WHISK IN BROTH AND WORCESTERSHIRE SAUCE, SCRAPING UP BROWN BITS FROM BOTTOM OF PAN; BRING TO A BOIL. POUR OVER BEEF AND STIR WELL. COVER AND COOK ON LOW FOR 4 TO 6 HOURS OR ON HIGH FOR 2 TO 3 HOURS, UNTIL MIXTURE IS BUBBLING. STIR IN PEAS. ADJUST SEASONING WITH SALT AND PEPPER, IF DESIRED.

TOPPING: MEANWHILE, IN A LARGE POT OF BOILING SALTED WATER, COOK SWEET POTATOES AND POTATOES FOR 20 TO 25 MINUTES, UNTIL TENDER. DRAIN AND RETURN TO PAN. ADD $\frac{1}{2}$ CUP (125 ML) MILK, BUTTER AND NUTMEG; MASH WELL. ADD ADDITIONAL MILK TO REACH DESIRED CONSISTENCY. SEASON TO TASTE WITH SALT AND PEPPER, IF DESIRED. SPREAD OVER MEAT MIXTURE. COVER AND COOK ON HIGH FOR 1 HOUR, UNTIL BUBBLING. SERVES 4.

TIP: YUKON GOLD AND OTHER YELLOW-FLESHED POTATOES RESULT IN VERY CREAMY MASHED POTATOES — BUT YOU COULD SUBSTITUTE RUSSETS OR ANOTHER WHITE-FLESHED VARIETY. WHEN IT COMES TO MASHING SPUDS, DON'T USE A FOOD PROCESSOR OR ELECTRIC MIXER — THE POTATOES WILL TURN GLUEY. FOR VERY SMOOTH MASHED POTATOES, USE A POTATO RICER OR FOOD MILL.

MAKE AHEAD: PREPARE THE TOPPING. LET COOL, TRANSFER TO AN AIRTIGHT CONTAINER AND REFRIGERATE FOR UP TO 3 DAYS. FREEZING IS NOT RECOMMENDED.

THE BEST DARN CHILI AROUND

MAKE A DAY OR SO AHEAD — THE FLAVOR IMPROVES AND SO DO THE REVIEWS!

I TBSP	VEGETABLE OIL	15 ML
3	HOT ITALIAN SAUSAGES, CASINGS REMOVED, PINCHED INTO BITE-SIZE PIECES	3
I LB	LEAN GROUND BEEF	500 G
2 CUPS	FINELY CHOPPED ONIONS	500 ML
4	CLOVES GARLIC, MINCED	4
I TBSP	GROUND CUMIN	15 ML
2 TSP	DRIED OREGANO	10 ML
	SALT AND PEPPER	
2 TBSP	TOMATO PASTE	30 ML
2 TBSP	PACKED BROWN SUGAR	30 ML
I	CAN (28 OZ/796 ML) DICED TOMATOES, WITH JUICE	I
I CUP	BEEF BROTH	250 ML
2	CANS (EACH 14 TO 19 OZ/398 TO 540 ML) RED KIDNEY BEANS, DRAINED AND RINSED (SEE TIP, OPPOSITE)	2
2 TBSP	CHILI POWDER	30 ML
2 TBSP	FRESHLY SQUEEZED LEMON JUICE	30 ML
I	RED BELL PEPPER, CHOPPED	I
I	JALAPEÑO PEPPER, SEEDED AND FINELY CHOPPED	I

USE A 5- TO 6-QUART SLOW COOKER. IN A SKILLET, HEAT OIL OVER MEDIUM-HIGH HEAT. BROWN SAUSAGES. USING A SLOTTED SPOON, TRANSFER TO SLOW COOKER. ADD BEEF TO SKILLET AND BROWN, BREAKING IT UP WITH A SPOON. USING A SLOTTED SPOON, TRANSFER TO SLOW COOKER.

DRAIN ALL BUT I TBSP (15 ML) FAT FROM SKILLET. REDUCE HEAT TO MEDIUM. ADD ONIONS, GARLIC, CUMIN, OREGANO, $\frac{1}{2}$ TSP (2 ML) SALT, $\frac{1}{4}$ TSP (I ML) PEPPER AND TOMATO PASTE; COOK, STIRRING OCCASIONALLY, FOR 3 MINUTES. STIR IN BROWN SUGAR, TOMATOES AND BROTH, SCRAPING UP BROWN BITS FROM BOTTOM OF PAN; BRING TO A BOIL. POUR OVER SAUSAGE MIXTURE. ADD BEANS AND STIR WELL. COVER AND COOK ON LOW FOR 6 TO 8 HOURS OR ON HIGH FOR 3 TO 4 HOURS, UNTIL BUBBLING. IN A SMALL BOWL, COMBINE CHILI POWDER AND LEMON JUICE. STIR INTO SLOW COOKER, ALONG WITH RED PEPPER AND JALAPEÑO. COVER AND COOK ON HIGH FOR ABOUT 20 MINUTES, UNTIL PEPPERS ARE TENDER. ADJUST SEASONING WITH SALT AND PEPPER, IF DESIRED. SERVES 6 TO 8.

TIP: IF YOU PREFER TO USE COOKED DRIED BEANS INSTEAD OF CANNED, SEE BASIC BEANS (PAGE 282). YOU'LL NEED 2 CUPS (500 ML) COOKED BEANS FOR THIS RECIPE.

EASY BEEF CHILI

A SIMPLE BUT EXCELLENT CHILI. SERVE EASY CORNBREAD (PAGE 33) OR TEX-MEX CORNBREAD (PAGE 34) ON THE SIDE.

I LB	LEAN GROUND BEEF	500 G
I	LARGE ONION, FINELY CHOPPED	I
3	CLOVES GARLIC, MINCED	3
2 TSP	GROUND CUMIN	IO ML
I TSP	DRIED OREGANO	5 ML
	SALT AND PEPPER	
I	CAN (14 OZ/398 ML) DICED TOMATOES, WITH JUICE	I
I	CAN (14 TO 19 OZ/398 TO 540 ML) RED KIDNEY BEANS, DRAINED AND RINSED (SEE TIP, PAGE 145)	I
I	$1\frac{1}{2}$-INCH (4 CM) CINNAMON STICK	I
$\frac{1}{2}$ CUP	TOMATO-BASED CHILI SAUCE	125 ML
I	CAN ($4\frac{1}{2}$ OZ/127 ML) DICED MILD GREEN CHILES	I
I	JALAPEÑO PEPPER, SEEDED AND FINELY CHOPPED (OPTIONAL)	I

USE A 4- TO 6-QUART SLOW COOKER. IN A SKILLET, OVER MEDIUM-HIGH HEAT, COOK BEEF, ONION, GARLIC, CUMIN, OREGANO, $\frac{1}{2}$ TSP (2 ML) SALT AND $\frac{1}{4}$ TSP (I ML) PEPPER, BREAKING BEEF UP WITH A SPOON, UNTIL BEEF IS BROWNED. DRAIN OFF EXCESS FAT. STIR IN TOMATOES AND BRING TO A BOIL. TRANSFER TO SLOW COOKER. ADD BEANS, CINNAMON STICK AND CHILI SAUCE; STIR WELL. COVER AND COOK ON LOW FOR ABOUT 6 HOURS OR ON HIGH FOR ABOUT 3 HOURS, UNTIL BUBBLING. DISCARD CINNAMON STICK. STIR IN GREEN CHILES AND JALAPEÑO (IF USING). COVER AND COOK ON

HIGH FOR 15 MINUTES TO BLEND THE FLAVORS. ADJUST SEASONING WITH SALT, IF DESIRED. SERVES 4 TO 6.

TIP: WE GO EASY ON THE SALT WHEN ASSEMBLING THIS RECIPE, AS THE CHILI SAUCE ADDS A FAIR BIT OF SALTINESS. YOU CAN ALWAYS ADD MORE JUST BEFORE SERVING.

FRESH TOMATO SALSA

THE SLOW COOKER IS TAKING CARE OF THE CHILI, SO USE THE FREE TIME TO MAKE A BOWL OF THIS FRESH TOMATO SALSA TO GO WITH IT.

2	GREEN ONIONS, CHOPPED	2
1	JALAPEÑO PEPPER, SEEDED AND FINELY CHOPPED	1
1	CLOVE GARLIC, MINCED	1
2 CUPS	GRAPE TOMATOES, HALVED	500 ML
2 TBSP	CHOPPED FRESH CILANTRO	30 ML
	SALT AND PEPPER	

IN A BOWL, COMBINE GREEN ONIONS, JALAPEÑO, GARLIC, TOMATOES AND CILANTRO. SEASON TO TASTE WITH SALT AND PEPPER. COVER AND REFRIGERATE FOR AT LEAST 30 MINUTES, TO BLEND THE FLAVORS, OR FOR UP TO 4 HOURS. MAKES ABOUT $2\frac{1}{4}$ CUPS (550 ML).

TIP: WE LIKE THE SWEET TASTE OF GRAPE TOMATOES, ESPECIALLY IN THE WINTER, WHEN RIPE GLOBE TOMATOES ARE HARD TO FIND. YOU CAN USE QUARTERED CHERRY TOMATOES IF YOU PREFER. OR USE 3 RIPE GLOBE TOMATOES, SEEDED AND CHOPPED.

CHUNKY BEEF AND SAUSAGE CHILI

*GREAT WINTER FARE. SERVE WITH A WEDGE OF
TEX-MEX CORNBREAD (PAGE 34).*

2 TBSP	VEGETABLE OIL (APPROX.), DIVIDED	30 ML
4	FRESH CHORIZO OR HOT ITALIAN SAUSAGES	4
1 1/2 LB	BONELESS BEEF CHUCK, BLADE OR CROSS RIB ROAST, CUT INTO 1-INCH (2.5 CM) CUBES	750 G
2	ONIONS, CHOPPED	2
6	CLOVES GARLIC, MINCED	6
1 TBSP	PACKED BROWN SUGAR	15 ML
2 TSP	GROUND CUMIN	10 ML
1 TSP	DRIED OREGANO	5 ML
	SALT AND PEPPER	
2 TBSP	TOMATO PASTE	30 ML
1	CAN (14 OZ/398 ML) DICED TOMATOES, WITH JUICE	1
1/2 CUP	DRY RED WINE	125 ML
1/2 CUP	BEEF BROTH	125 ML
1	CAN (14 TO 19 OZ/398 TO 540 ML) RED KIDNEY BEANS, DRAINED AND RINSED (SEE TIP, PAGE 145)	1
1/4 CUP	CHOPPED FRESH CILANTRO	60 ML
2 TSP	CHIPOTLE CHILE POWDER	10 ML
	SOUR CREAM, CHOPPED TOMATO, SHREDDED CHEDDAR CHEESE	

USE A 4- TO 6-QUART SLOW COOKER. IN A SKILLET, HEAT
HALF THE OIL OVER MEDIUM HEAT. ADD SAUSAGES AND
BROWN ON ALL SIDES. (DON'T WORRY IF THEY ARE NOT
COOKED THROUGH.) TRANSFER SAUSAGES TO A CUTTING
BOARD AND LET COOL FOR 5 MINUTES. CUT EACH SAUSAGE

INTO 4 TO 6 PIECES. TRANSFER TO SLOW COOKER. ADD BEEF TO SKILLET AND BROWN. USING A SLOTTED SPOON, TRANSFER TO SLOW COOKER. REDUCE HEAT TO MEDIUM AND ADD ENOUGH OF THE REMAINING OIL TO THE SKILLET TO MAKE I TBSP (15 ML). ADD ONIONS, GARLIC, BROWN SUGAR, CUMIN, OREGANO, $\frac{1}{2}$ TSP (2 ML) SALT, $\frac{1}{4}$ TSP (I ML) PEPPER AND TOMATO PASTE; COOK, STIRRING OCCASIONALLY, FOR 5 MINUTES. ADD TOMATOES, WINE AND BROTH, SCRAPING UP BROWN BITS FROM BOTTOM OF PAN; BRING TO A BOIL. POUR OVER SAUSAGE MIXTURE. ADD BEANS AND STIR WELL. COVER AND COOK ON LOW FOR ABOUT 8 HOURS OR ON HIGH FOR ABOUT 4 HOURS, UNTIL BEEF IS TENDER. STIR IN CILANTRO AND CHIPOTLE CHILE POWDER. COVER AND COOK ON HIGH FOR 15 MINUTES TO BLEND THE FLAVORS. LADLE INTO BOWLS AND PASS SOUR CREAM, TOMATO AND CHEESE FOR GARNISHING. SERVES 4.

TIP: JARS OF CHIPOTLE CHILE POWDER ARE AVAILABLE IN MOST SUPERMARKETS. THE REDDISH-BROWN POWDER IS MADE FROM DRIED SMOKED JALAPEÑO PEPPERS. IT LENDS AN AUTHENTIC MEXICAN TOUCH TO SOUPS, STEWS AND CHILIS. REGULAR CHILI POWDER CAN BE SUBSTITUTED IF YOU PREFER TO NOT HAVE A SMOKY FLAVOR.

MEDITERRANEAN MEATLOAF

OPA! HERE'S DINNER. SERVE WITH GREEK SALAD
AND WARMED PITA BREAD.

1/2 CUP	FRESH BREAD CRUMBS	125 ML
1/2 CUP	MILK	125 ML
1 TBSP	VEGETABLE OIL	15 ML
1	LARGE ONION, FINELY CHOPPED	1
4	CLOVES GARLIC, MINCED	4
1 TSP	DRIED OREGANO	5 ML
	SALT AND PEPPER	
1/2 CUP	CHOPPED FRESH PARSLEY, DIVIDED	125 ML
2	EGGS, LIGHTLY BEATEN	2
1 CUP	CRUMBLED FETA CHEESE, DIVIDED	250 ML
1/4 CUP	CHOPPED DRAINED OIL-PACKED SUN-DRIED TOMATOES	60 ML
	GRATED ZEST OF 1 LEMON	
1 LB	LEAN GROUND BEEF	500 G
1 LB	LEAN GROUND PORK	500 G
1/3 CUP	CHOPPED PITTED KALAMATA OLIVES	75 ML

USE A 5- TO 6-QUART SLOW COOKER. FOLD A 2-FOOT
(60 CM) PIECE OF FOIL IN HALF LENGTHWISE. PLACE
LENGTHWISE ALONG BOTTOM OF SLOW COOKER,
BRINGING ENDS UP THE SIDES AND OVER THE RIM. IN
A BOWL, COMBINE BREAD CRUMBS AND MILK; LET SOAK
FOR 5 MINUTES. MEANWHILE, IN A SKILLET, HEAT OIL
OVER MEDIUM HEAT. ADD ONION, GARLIC, OREGANO, 1 TSP
(5 ML) SALT AND 1/4 TSP (1 ML) PEPPER; COOK, STIRRING
OCCASIONALLY, FOR 3 MINUTES. LET COOL SLIGHTLY,
THEN SCRAPE INTO BREAD CRUMB MIXTURE. STIR IN
HALF THE PARSLEY, EGGS, HALF THE FETA, SUN-DRIED

TOMATOES AND LEMON ZEST. ADD BEEF AND PORK; MIX WELL. TRANSFER MEAT MIXTURE TO MIDDLE OF FOIL IN PREPARED SLOW COOKER AND, USING A SPATULA, SHAPE INTO A LOAF. COVER, TUCKING FOIL ENDS UNDER LID, AND COOK ON LOW FOR 8 TO 10 HOURS OR ON HIGH FOR 4 TO 5 HOURS, UNTIL AN INSTANT-READ THERMOMETER INSERTED IN THE CENTER REGISTERS 160°F (71°C) AND JUICES RUN CLEAR WHEN MEATLOAF IS PIERCED. SPRINKLE MEATLOAF WITH OLIVES AND REMAINING FETA. COVER AND COOK ON HIGH FOR 15 MINUTES, UNTIL TOPPINGS ARE HOT. GRASP FOIL ENDS AND LIFT OUT MEATLOAF, DRAINING OFF ACCUMULATED FAT. TRANSFER TO A CUTTING BOARD AND LET REST FOR 10 MINUTES BEFORE SLICING. SERVE SPRINKLED WITH REMAINING PARSLEY. SERVES 6 TO 8.

TIP: BUY OLIVES FROM THE REFRIGERATED OR DELI SECTION OF THE SUPERMARKET, RATHER THAN BUYING CANNED. THE CANNED ONES HAVE AN UNDESIRABLE TEXTURE AND LITTLE FLAVOR.

MIDWEEK MEATBALLS IN TOMATO SAUCE

A JAR OF PASTA SAUCE AND DRIED ONIONS SPEED UP THE PREP TIME. SERVE WITH PASTA OR MASHED POTATOES, OR LADLED OVER TOASTED BUNS.

1/4 CUP	QUICK-COOKING ROLLED OATS OR DRY BREAD CRUMBS	60 ML
1/4 CUP	MILK	60 ML
1 LB	LEAN GROUND BEEF (OR A MIXTURE OF BEEF AND PORK)	500 G
2 TBSP	CHOPPED FRESH PARSLEY	30 ML
1 TSP	DRIED ITALIAN SEASONING	5 ML
	SALT AND PEPPER	
1	EGG, LIGHTLY BEATEN	1
1 TBSP	VEGETABLE OIL	15 ML
2 TBSP	DEHYDRATED CHOPPED ONION	30 ML
1/4 TSP	GROUND NUTMEG	1 ML
1	JAR (24 TO 26 OZ/650 TO 700 ML) TOMATO PASTA SAUCE	1
1 TBSP	BALSAMIC VINEGAR	15 ML
	GRATED PARMESAN CHEESE	

USE A 3 1/2- TO 4-QUART SLOW COOKER. IN A BOWL, COMBINE OATS AND MILK; LET SOAK FOR 5 MINUTES. ADD BEEF, PARSLEY, ITALIAN SEASONING, 1 TSP (5 ML) SALT, 1/4 TSP (1 ML) PEPPER AND EGG; MIX WELL. SCOOP TABLESPOONFULS (15 ML) OF MEAT MIXTURE AND ROLL INTO MEATBALLS. IN A SKILLET, HEAT OIL OVER MEDIUM-HIGH HEAT. BROWN MEATBALLS, IN BATCHES IF NECESSARY. TRANSFER TO SLOW COOKER. ADD DEHYDRATED ONION, NUTMEG AND PASTA SAUCE. STIR

TO COAT MEATBALLS. COVER AND COOK ON LOW FOR ABOUT 6 HOURS OR ON HIGH FOR ABOUT 3 HOURS, UNTIL MEATBALLS ARE NO LONGER PINK INSIDE. STIR IN VINEGAR. ADJUST SEASONING WITH SALT AND PEPPER, IF DESIRED. SERVE MEATBALLS AND SAUCE SPRINKLED WITH PARMESAN. MAKES ABOUT 20 MEATBALLS; SERVES 4 TO 6.

TIP: DEHYDRATED CHOPPED ONIONS ARE A HANDY ITEM TO KEEP IN THE PANTRY. LOOK FOR THEM ALONGSIDE THE DRIED HERBS AND SPICES AT YOUR SUPERMARKET. A QUARTER CUP (60 ML) DEHYDRATED ONION IS EQUIVALENT TO ABOUT 1 CUP (250 ML) CHOPPED FRESH ONION.

TIP: IT'S EASY TO CHECK WHETHER YOU HAVE CORRECTLY SEASONED THE MEAT MIXTURE FOR MEATBALLS, MEATLOAF OR BURGERS. HEAT A SMALL SKILLET OVER MEDIUM-HIGH HEAT AND FRY 1 TSP (5 ML) OF THE MIXTURE FOR 2 TO 3 MINUTES, UNTIL NO LONGER PINK INSIDE. TASTE THE COOKED SAMPLE. IF DESIRED, ADJUST THE SEASONING IN THE REMAINING MIXTURE BEFORE SHAPING IT.

BIG-BATCH BOLOGNESE SAUCE

THE PERFECT MEAT SAUCE FOR YOUR FAVORITE PASTA.
JUST SPRINKLE GENEROUSLY WITH PARMESAN CHEESE.
FREEZES WELL.

I LB	LEAN GROUND BEEF	500 G
I LB	LEAN GROUND PORK	500 G
I TBSP	VEGETABLE OIL	15 ML
2	LARGE ONIONS, FINELY CHOPPED	2
2	STALKS CELERY, THINLY SLICED	2
I	LARGE CARROT, FINELY CHOPPED	I
4	CLOVES GARLIC, MINCED	4
2 TSP	DRIED ITALIAN SEASONING	10 ML
	SALT AND PEPPER	
2 TBSP	TOMATO PASTE	30 ML
$1/2$ CUP	2% OR WHOLE MILK	125 ML
I	CAN (28 OZ/796 ML) CRUSHED TOMATOES	I
2 TBSP	BALSAMIC VINEGAR	30 ML

USE A 5- TO 6-QUART SLOW COOKER. IN A SKILLET, OVER
MEDIUM-HIGH HEAT, BROWN BEEF AND PORK, BREAKING
MEAT UP WITH A SPOON. USING A SLOTTED SPOON,
TRANSFER TO SLOW COOKER. DISCARD FAT FROM SKILLET.
REDUCE HEAT TO MEDIUM AND ADD OIL TO SKILLET. ADD
ONIONS, CELERY, CARROT, GARLIC, ITALIAN SEASONING,
I TSP (5 ML) SALT, $1/4$ TSP (I ML) PEPPER AND TOMATO
PASTE; COOK, STIRRING OCCASIONALLY, FOR 5 MINUTES.
ADD MILK AND BRING TO A SIMMER; SIMMER, STIRRING,
FOR 4 TO 5 MINUTES, UNTIL ALMOST EVAPORATED. ADD
TOMATOES AND VINEGAR; BRING TO A BOIL. POUR INTO
SLOW COOKER AND STIR WELL. COVER AND COOK ON LOW

FOR ABOUT 6 HOURS OR ON HIGH FOR ABOUT 3 HOURS, UNTIL VEGETABLES ARE TENDER AND SAUCE IS THICK ENOUGH TO MOUND ON A SPOON. ADJUST SEASONING WITH SALT AND PEPPER, IF DESIRED. SERVES 8.

TIP: WE USE TOMATO PASTE IN MANY OF OUR SLOW COOKER RECIPES BECAUSE IT GREATLY BOOSTS FLAVOR AND RICHNESS. THE LONG, MOIST COOKING DULLS OTHER AROMATIC INGREDIENTS, SUCH AS ONIONS, GARLIC AND HERBS. MICROWAVING OR BROWNING A DOLLOP OR TWO OF TOMATO PASTE WITH THESE INGREDIENTS MAKES ALL THE DIFFERENCE.

VARIATION: WE LIKE THE RICH COMBINED FLAVORS OF BEEF AND PORK IN THIS MEAT SAUCE. USE ALL BEEF IF YOU PREFER.

I'D RATHER BE FIFTY THAN PREGNANT.

OSSO BUCO MILANESE

*CLASSIC ITALIAN FARE — A SHOWOFF DISH OF VEAL
SHANKS BRAISED IN A RICH BROTH, GARNISHED WITH A
ZINGY BLEND OF PARSLEY, LEMON ZEST AND GARLIC.*

4	SLICED VEAL SHANKS (SEE TIP, OPPOSITE)	4
	SALT AND PEPPER	
2 TBSP	VEGETABLE OIL, DIVIDED	30 ML
3/4 CUP	DRY WHITE WINE	175 ML
1	LARGE ONION, FINELY CHOPPED	1
1	CARROT, FINELY CHOPPED	1
1	STALK CELERY, THINLY SLICED	1
4	CLOVES GARLIC, MINCED	4
1 CUP	CHOPPED DRAINED CANNED TOMATOES	250 ML
1/2 CUP	CHICKEN BROTH	125 ML

GREMOLATA

1	CLOVE GARLIC, MINCED	1
1/2 CUP	CHOPPED FRESH PARSLEY	125 ML
	GRATED ZEST OF 1/2 LEMON	

USE A 5- TO 6-QUART SLOW COOKER. SEASON VEAL WELL
WITH SALT AND PEPPER. IN A SKILLET, HEAT HALF THE
OIL OVER MEDIUM HEAT. ADD VEAL, IN TWO BATCHES, AND
BROWN ON BOTH SIDES. TRANSFER TO SLOW COOKER.
REMOVE SKILLET FROM HEAT. ADD WINE, STIRRING TO
SCRAPE UP BROWN BITS FROM BOTTOM OF PAN. POUR
OVER VEAL. ADD REMAINING OIL TO SKILLET AND HEAT
OVER MEDIUM HEAT. ADD ONION, CARROT AND CELERY;
COOK, STIRRING OCCASIONALLY, FOR 5 MINUTES. ADD
GARLIC AND COOK, STIRRING, FOR 15 SECONDS. STIR IN
TOMATOES AND BROTH. POUR OVER VEAL. COVER AND

COOK ON LOW FOR ABOUT 8 HOURS OR ON HIGH FOR ABOUT 4 HOURS, UNTIL VEAL IS VERY TENDER.

GREMOLATA: IN A BOWL, COMBINE GARLIC, PARSLEY AND LEMON ZEST. SERVE VEAL WITH SOME OF THE BRAISING BROTH LADLED OVER TOP. SPRINKLE WITH GREMOLATA. SERVES 4.

TIP: VEAL SLICES FOR OSSO BUCO ARE GENERALLY CUT CROSSWISE FROM THE UPPER PART OF THE HIND LEG. FOR BEST RESULTS, LOOK FOR VEAL SHANK SLICES THAT ARE ABOUT $1\frac{1}{2}$ INCHES (4 CM) THICK AND WEIGH 8 TO 10 OZ (250 TO 300 G), INCLUDING THE BONE. ALLOW ONE SLICE PER PERSON. IF YOUR LOCAL SUPERMARKET DOESN'T CARRY VEAL SHANKS, CHECK WITH A BUTCHER. IT'S WORTH THE EFFORT!

BISTRO BRAISED LAMB CHOPS

LAMB LOVERS TAKE NOTE: THIS IS OUTSTANDING!
SERVE WITH MASHED POTATOES AND A STEAMED
GREEN VEGETABLE.

8	LAMB SHOULDER CHOPS	8
	SALT AND PEPPER	
2 TBSP	VEGETABLE OIL, DIVIDED	30 ML
2	LARGE ONIONS, THINLY SLICED	2
4	CLOVES GARLIC, MINCED	4
1 TBSP	TOMATO PASTE	15 ML
1	CAN (14 OZ/398 ML) WHOLE TOMATOES, WITH JUICE	1
1/3 CUP	BEEF BROTH	75 ML
2 TBSP	BALSAMIC VINEGAR	30 ML
2	ZUCCHINI, CHOPPED	2
1/3 CUP	CHOPPED PITTED BLACK OLIVES (OPTIONAL)	75 ML
1 TSP	DRIED ROSEMARY	5 ML

USE A 5- TO 6-QUART SLOW COOKER. SEASON LAMB WELL
WITH SALT AND PEPPER. IN A SKILLET, HEAT HALF THE
OIL OVER MEDIUM-HIGH HEAT. ADD LAMB, IN BATCHES IF
NECESSARY, AND BROWN ON BOTH SIDES. TRANSFER
TO SLOW COOKER. REDUCE HEAT TO MEDIUM AND ADD
REMAINING OIL TO SKILLET. ADD ONIONS, GARLIC, 1 TSP
(5 ML) SALT, 1/4 TSP (1 ML) PEPPER AND TOMATO PASTE;
COOK, STIRRING OCCASIONALLY, FOR 5 MINUTES. STIR IN
TOMATOES, BROTH AND VINEGAR, BREAKING TOMATOES
UP WITH A SPOON AND SCRAPING UP BROWN BITS FROM
BOTTOM OF PAN; BRING TO A BOIL. POUR OVER LAMB.
COVER AND COOK ON LOW FOR 6 TO 8 HOURS OR ON

HIGH FOR 3 TO 4 HOURS, UNTIL LAMB IS VERY TENDER. STIR IN ZUCCHINI, OLIVES (IF USING) AND ROSEMARY. COVER AND COOK ON HIGH FOR ABOUT 30 MINUTES, UNTIL ZUCCHINI IS TENDER-CRISP. SERVES 4 TO 6.

TIP: LAMB SHOULDER CHOPS ARE AN ECONOMICAL CHOICE, AND THEY BRAISE BEAUTIFULLY IN THE SLOW COOKER. THEY ARE WIDER AND THINNER THAN LOIN CHOPS, BUT VERY MEATY. IF YOU CAN'T FIND FRESH LAMB SHOULDER CHOPS, CHECK THE FROZEN MEATS SECTION.

TIP: FOR THIS RECIPE, WE PREFER TO USE CANNED WHOLE PLUM (ROMA) TOMATOES IN JUICE, WITH NO ADDED SALT OR SEASONINGS. THESE ARE THE CLOSEST TO FRESH TOMATOES IN TASTE AND TEXTURE. FOR STEWS AND CHILIS, WE GENERALLY USE CANNED DICED TOMATOES BECAUSE THEY HOLD THEIR SHAPE QUITE WELL. CRUSHED TOMATOES LEND BODY AND FLAVOR TO A DISH. STEWED TOMATOES, WITH VARIOUS FLAVORINGS, PROVIDE SHORTCUTS BUT MAY BE QUITE SALTY.

BRAISED LAMB SHANKS WITH LENTILS

A RUSTIC FRENCH COMBINATION. DEEP, EARTHY LENTILS PAIR PERFECTLY WITH LAMB. A STEAMED LEAFY GREEN VEGETABLE ROUNDS OUT THE DISH.

6	LAMB SHANKS (ABOUT 4 LBS/2 KG)	6
	SALT AND PEPPER	
1 TBSP	VEGETABLE OIL	15 ML
3	LARGE ONIONS, THINLY SLICED	3
4	CLOVES GARLIC, MINCED	4
2 TBSP	PACKED BROWN SUGAR	30 ML
1/4 CUP	TOMATO PASTE	60 ML
1 CUP	DRY RED WINE	250 ML
1 CUP	DRIED BROWN OR GREEN LENTILS, RINSED	250 ML
2 CUPS	BEEF BROTH	500 ML
2 TBSP	WORCESTERSHIRE SAUCE	30 ML
2 TSP	DRIED ROSEMARY	10 ML
1 TBSP	RED WINE VINEGAR	15 ML

USE A 5- TO 6-QUART SLOW COOKER. SEASON LAMB SHANKS WELL WITH SALT AND PEPPER. IN A SKILLET, HEAT OIL OVER MEDIUM-HIGH HEAT. ADD LAMB, IN BATCHES IF NECESSARY, AND BROWN ON ALL SIDES. TRANSFER TO SLOW COOKER. DRAIN OFF ALL BUT 1 TBSP (15 ML) FAT FROM THE PAN. REDUCE HEAT TO MEDIUM. ADD ONIONS, GARLIC, BROWN SUGAR AND TOMATO PASTE TO SKILLET AND COOK, STIRRING OCCASIONALLY, FOR 5 MINUTES. STIR IN WINE, SCRAPING UP BROWN BITS FROM BOTTOM OF PAN. STIR IN LENTILS, BROTH AND WORCESTERSHIRE SAUCE; BRING TO A BOIL. POUR OVER LAMB. COVER AND

CONTINUED ON PAGE 161...

Beef Goulash (page 134)

Hoisin Ginger Beef Stew (page 138)

Pulled Pork on a Bun (page 174)

Flamenco Stew (page 180)

COOK ON LOW FOR ABOUT 8 HOURS OR ON HIGH FOR ABOUT 4 HOURS, UNTIL MEAT IS FALLING OFF THE BONE AND LENTILS ARE VERY TENDER. STIR ROSEMARY AND VINEGAR INTO SAUCE AROUND LAMB. COVER AND COOK ON HIGH FOR 15 MINUTES TO BLEND THE FLAVORS. ADJUST SEASONING WITH SALT AND PEPPER, IF DESIRED. SERVES 6.

TIP: WORCESTERSHIRE SAUCE (PRONOUNCED *WOOS-TUHR-SHEER*) IS A DARK BROWN SAUCE WITH A PIQUANT, SPICY FLAVOR THAT WAS DEVELOPED FOR BRITISH COLONIALS IN INDIA. IT TAKES ITS NAME FROM WORCESTER, ENGLAND, WHERE IT WAS FIRST BOTTLED. THE SAUCE IS USED TO SEASON MEATS, SAUCES AND SOUPS, AND IS AN ESSENTIAL INGREDIENT IN A BLOODY MARY COCKTAIL. ONCE OPENED, IT KEEPS FOR SEVERAL MONTHS IN THE REFRIGERATOR.

BEST-EVER BRAISED SHORT RIBS

FRED FLINTSTONE WOULD APPROVE! SERVE WITH MUSHROOM PARMESAN POLENTA (PAGE 298) OR PARSNIP BUTTERMILK CHIVE PURÉE (PAGE 276).

4 to 5 LBS	BEEF SHORT RIBS	2 to 2.5 KG
	SALT AND PEPPER	
I TBSP	VEGETABLE OIL	15 ML
2	ONIONS, CHOPPED	2
2	STALKS CELERY, SLICED	2
I	LARGE CARROT, CHOPPED	I
4	CLOVES GARLIC, MINCED	4
1/2 TSP	DRIED THYME	2 ML
2 TBSP	TOMATO PASTE	30 ML
1/4 CUP	BALSAMIC VINEGAR	60 ML
I CUP	BEEF BROTH	250 ML
2	BAY LEAVES	2
I TBSP	FRESHLY SQUEEZED LEMON JUICE	15 ML
2 TBSP	CHOPPED FRESH PARSLEY	30 ML

USE A 5- TO 6-QUART SLOW COOKER. SEASON RIBS WELL WITH SALT AND PEPPER. IN A LARGE SKILLET, HEAT OIL OVER MEDIUM HEAT. ADD RIBS, IN BATCHES, AND BROWN ON ALL SIDES. TRANSFER TO SLOW COOKER. DRAIN ALL BUT I TBSP (15 ML) FAT FROM SKILLET. ADD ONIONS, CELERY AND CARROT TO SKILLET AND COOK, STIRRING OCCASIONALLY, UNTIL TENDER AND LIGHTLY BROWNED, ABOUT 6 MINUTES. ADD GARLIC, THYME AND TOMATO PASTE; COOK, STIRRING, FOR 30 SECONDS. STIR IN VINEGAR (IT WILL EVAPORATE ALMOST IMMEDIATELY). STIR IN BROTH AND BAY LEAVES. POUR OVER RIBS. COVER

AND COOK ON LOW FOR ABOUT 8 HOURS OR ON HIGH FOR ABOUT 4 HOURS, UNTIL RIBS ARE VERY TENDER. (THE MEAT MIGHT FALL OFF THE BONES BEFORE THE END OF THE COOKING TIME, BUT THIS DOESN'T MEAN THE RIBS ARE FULLY TENDER.) TRANSFER RIBS TO A PLATE, DISCARDING LOOSE BONES IF NECESSARY. DISCARD BAY LEAVES. USING A SPOON, REMOVE AS MUCH FAT FROM THE SURFACE OF THE SAUCE AS POSSIBLE. STIR IN LEMON JUICE. ADJUST SEASONING WITH SALT AND PEPPER, IF DESIRED. SERVE RIBS TOPPED WITH SAUCE AND SPRINKLED WITH PARSLEY. SERVES 4 TO 6.

MAKE AHEAD: SHORT RIBS ARE SUPERB, BUT VERY FATTY. FOR BEST RESULTS, BRAISE A DAY AHEAD. TRANSFER THE COOKED RIBS AND SAUCE TO SEPARATE CONTAINERS, LET COOL AND REFRIGERATE OVERNIGHT OR FOR UP TO 2 DAYS. ONCE THE SAUCE IS CHILLED, YOU CAN SCRAPE THE HARDENED FAT OFF THE SURFACE. REHEAT THE RIBS AND SAUCE IN A COVERED CASSEROLE DISH AT 350°F (180°C) FOR ABOUT 45 MINUTES, UNTIL HEATED THROUGH.

BARBECUE-BRAISED SHORT RIBS

THESE ARE AMAZING!

4 to 5 LBS	BEEF SHORT RIBS	2 to 2.5 KG
	SALT AND PEPPER	
I TBSP	VEGETABLE OIL	15 ML
2	LARGE ONIONS, CHOPPED	2
2 TBSP	PACKED DARK BROWN SUGAR	30 ML
1/2 CUP	BARBECUE SAUCE	125 ML
1/2 CUP	TOMATO SAUCE	125 ML
1/4 CUP	WATER	60 ML
2 TBSP	CIDER VINEGAR	30 ML
I TBSP	FRESHLY SQUEEZED LEMON JUICE (OPTIONAL)	15 ML

USE A 5- TO 6-QUART SLOW COOKER. SEASON RIBS WELL WITH SALT AND PEPPER. IN A LARGE SKILLET, HEAT OIL OVER MEDIUM HEAT. ADD RIBS, IN BATCHES, AND BROWN ON ALL SIDES. TRANSFER TO SLOW COOKER. ARRANGE ONIONS ON TOP. IN A BOWL, WHISK TOGETHER BROWN SUGAR, BARBECUE SAUCE, TOMATO SAUCE, WATER AND VINEGAR. COVER AND COOK ON LOW FOR ABOUT 8 HOURS OR ON HIGH FOR ABOUT 4 HOURS, UNTIL RIBS ARE VERY TENDER. (THE MEAT MIGHT FALL OFF THE BONES BEFORE THE END OF THE COOKING TIME, BUT THIS DOESN'T MEAN THE RIBS ARE FULLY TENDER.) TRANSFER RIBS TO A PLATE, DISCARDING LOOSE BONES IF NECESSARY. USING A SPOON, REMOVE AS MUCH FAT FROM THE SURFACE OF THE SAUCE AS POSSIBLE. ADJUST SEASONING WITH SALT, PEPPER AND LEMON JUICE, IF DESIRED. SERVE RIBS TOPPED WITH SAUCE AND SPRINKLED WITH PARSLEY. SERVES 4 TO 6.

MAKE AHEAD: SEE PAGE 163.

PORK

CREAMY HAM AND MUSHROOM LASAGNA

LASAGNA IN THE SLOW COOKER? DELIGHTFUL!
SERVE WITH A CRUNCHY GREEN SALAD AND
WARM BREADSTICKS.

2 TBSP	VEGETABLE OIL, DIVIDED	30 ML
1	LARGE LEEK (WHITE TO MEDIUM GREEN PARTS ONLY), THINLY SLICED	1
3 CUPS	SLICED MUSHROOMS	750 ML
2	CLOVES GARLIC, MINCED	2
1	EGG, LIGHTLY BEATEN	1
6 OZ	HAM, CHOPPED	175 G
1 CUP	RICOTTA CHEESE	250 ML
1/2 CUP	GRATED PARMESAN CHEESE	125 ML
1/8 TSP	PEPPER	0.5 ML
1	JAR (14 OZ/410 ML) ALFREDO PASTA SAUCE	1
1 CUP	WATER	250 ML
9	OVEN-READY LASAGNA NOODLES (APPROX.)	9
1 CUP	SHREDDED MOZZARELLA CHEESE	250 ML
2 TBSP	CHOPPED FRESH PARSLEY	30 ML

GREASE THE INSERT OF A 3½- TO 4-QUART SLOW
COOKER. IN A SKILLET, HEAT HALF THE OIL OVER MEDIUM
HEAT. STIR IN LEEK AND REDUCE HEAT TO LOW. COVER
AND COOK, STIRRING OCCASIONALLY, UNTIL SOFTENED
BUT NOT BROWNED, ABOUT 10 MINUTES. TRANSFER
TO A LARGE BOWL. INCREASE HEAT TO MEDIUM AND
ADD REMAINING OIL TO SKILLET. ADD MUSHROOMS AND
COOK, STIRRING, FOR 5 MINUTES. ADD GARLIC AND COOK,
STIRRING, FOR 15 SECONDS. SCRAPE INTO BOWL WITH

LEEK AND LET COOL SLIGHTLY. ADD EGG, HAM, RICOTTA, PARMESAN AND PEPPER; MIX WELL. IN ANOTHER BOWL, COMBINE ALFREDO SAUCE AND WATER. COVER BOTTOM OF PREPARED SLOW COOKER WITH 2 TO 3 NOODLES, BREAKING TO FIT AS NECESSARY. SPREAD WITH ONE-THIRD OF THE EGG MIXTURE AND ONE-QUARTER OF THE SAUCE MIXTURE. REPEAT LAYERS TWICE. TOP WITH REMAINING NOODLES. POUR REMAINING SAUCE MIXTURE OVER TOP. SPRINKLE WITH MOZZARELLA. COVER AND COOK ON LOW FOR ABOUT 6 HOURS OR ON HIGH FOR ABOUT 3 HOURS, UNTIL BUBBLING. SPRINKLE WITH PARSLEY. SERVES 4.

TIP: BE SURE TO USE OVEN-READY LASAGNA NOODLES FOR THIS RECIPE. THEY STAND UP BETTER THAN FRESH OR REGULAR DRIED PASTA TO THE LONG, MOIST COOKING. AND THEY SAVE TIME.

PORK STEAKS WITH APPLE MUSTARD GRAVY

A WINNING COMBINATION! SERVE WITH STEAMED BROCCOLI AND MASHED SWEET POTATO.

3 LBS	BONE-IN PORK SHOULDER BLADE STEAKS (ABOUT 3)	1.5 KG
	SALT AND PEPPER	
2 TBSP	VEGETABLE OIL, DIVIDED	30 ML
2	BAY LEAVES	2
1 1/4 CUPS	PACKED DRIED APPLE SLICES	300 ML
2	ONIONS, THINLY SLICED	2
4	CLOVES GARLIC, MINCED	4
3 TBSP	ALL-PURPOSE FLOUR	45 ML
1 1/4 CUPS	UNSWEETENED APPLE JUICE	300 ML
2 TBSP	CIDER VINEGAR	30 ML
1/3 CUP	PLAIN YOGURT (PREFERABLY GREEK-STYLE)	75 ML
1 1/2 TBSP	DIJON MUSTARD	22 ML
1/4 CUP	CHOPPED FRESH PARSLEY	60 ML

USE A 5- TO 6-QUART SLOW COOKER. SEASON PORK WELL WITH SALT AND PEPPER. IN A SKILLET, HEAT HALF THE OIL OVER MEDIUM-HIGH HEAT. BROWN PORK ON BOTH SIDES, IN BATCHES IF NECESSARY. TRANSFER TO SLOW COOKER. ARRANGE BAY LEAVES AND APPLES ON TOP OF PORK. REDUCE HEAT TO MEDIUM AND ADD REMAINING OIL TO SKILLET. ADD ONIONS AND GARLIC; COOK, STIRRING OCCASIONALLY, FOR 5 MINUTES. STIR IN FLOUR. WHISK IN APPLE JUICE, VINEGAR, 1 TSP (5 ML) SALT AND 1/4 TSP (1 ML) PEPPER, SCRAPING UP BROWN BITS FROM BOTTOM OF PAN. POUR OVER PORK. COVER AND COOK ON LOW FOR

6 TO 8 HOURS OR ON HIGH FOR 3 TO 4 HOURS, UNTIL PORK IS TENDER. TRANSFER PORK TO A CUTTING BOARD, PULL MEAT INTO CHUNKS AND DISCARD BONES. IN A BOWL, COMBINE YOGURT, MUSTARD AND $\frac{1}{2}$ CUP (125 ML) COOKING LIQUID. STIR INTO SLOW COOKER. RETURN PORK TO SLOW COOKER. COVER AND COOK ON HIGH FOR 15 MINUTES, UNTIL HOT. ADJUST SEASONING WITH SALT AND PEPPER, IF DESIRED. DISCARD BAY LEAVES. STIR IN PARSLEY. SERVES 4 TO 6.

TIP: DRIED APPLE SLICES HAVE LOTS OF FLAVOR. UNLIKE FRESH APPLES, THEY SOFTEN WITHOUT TURNING MUSHY DURING LONG COOKING TIMES. DRIED APPLE SLICES ARE READILY AVAILABLE IN MAJOR SUPERMARKETS AND IN BULK BIN STORES.

PARTY PORK TACOS

*FUN FOOD FOR FRIENDS. SET OUT THE SLOW COOKER,
ALONG WITH WARM CORN TORTILLAS OR TACO SHELLS
AND YOUR FAVORITE TACO TOPPINGS.*

3 LBS	BONE-IN PORK SHOULDER BLADE STEAKS (ABOUT 3)	1.5 KG
	SALT AND PEPPER	
2 TBSP	VEGETABLE OIL, DIVIDED	30 ML
1	LARGE ONION, CHOPPED	1
3	CLOVES GARLIC, MINCED	3
1½ TSP	GROUND CUMIN	7 ML
1 TSP	GROUND CORIANDER	5 ML
1½ CUPS	TOMATILLO SALSA	375 ML
2 TBSP	CHOPPED FRESH CILANTRO	30 ML

USE A 5- TO 6-QUART SLOW COOKER. SEASON PORK WELL
WITH SALT AND PEPPER. IN A SKILLET, HEAT HALF THE OIL
OVER MEDIUM-HIGH HEAT. BROWN PORK ON BOTH SIDES,
IN BATCHES IF NECESSARY. TRANSFER TO SLOW COOKER.
REDUCE HEAT TO MEDIUM AND ADD REMAINING OIL TO
SKILLET. ADD ONION, GARLIC, CUMIN AND CORIANDER; COOK,
STIRRING OCCASIONALLY, FOR 5 MINUTES. ADD SALSA
AND BRING TO A BOIL, SCRAPING UP BROWN BITS FROM
BOTTOM OF PAN. POUR OVER PORK. COVER AND COOK ON
LOW FOR 6 TO 8 HOURS OR ON HIGH FOR 3 TO 4 HOURS,
UNTIL PORK IS PULL-APART TENDER. TRANSFER PORK TO
A CUTTING BOARD AND, USING TWO FORKS, SHRED MEAT.
DISCARD BONES. USING A SPOON, REMOVE EXCESS FAT
FROM SURFACE OF COOKING LIQUID, IF DESIRED. RETURN
PORK TO SLOW COOKER. COVER AND COOK ON HIGH FOR
ABOUT 20 MINUTES, UNTIL STEAMING. STIR IN CILANTRO.

ADJUST SEASONING WITH SALT AND PEPPER, IF DESIRED. SERVES 6.

TIP: TOMATILLOS RESEMBLE SMALL GREEN TOMATOES AND LEND A CITRUS-HERB TANG TO MEXICAN COOKING. TOMATILLO SALSA IS SOMETIMES LABELED "SALSA VERDE" OR "GREEN SALSA." LOOK FOR IT IN THE MEXICAN FOODS SECTION OF THE SUPERMARKET.

VARIATION: WE USE PORK SHOULDER STEAKS FOR SHREDDED PORK RATHER THAN THE TYPICAL BONELESS PORK SHOULDER ROAST. THE STEAKS ABSORB MORE FLAVOR FROM THE SAUCE AND ARE EASIER TO HANDLE. BUT USE A 3-LB (1.5 KG) BONELESS PORK SHOULDER ROAST IF YOU PREFER.

LEMON AND HERB PORK POT ROAST

DON'T EVEN THINK OF SKIPPING THE ZINGY PARSLEY AND LEMON ZEST GARNISH — IT'S WHAT MAKES THIS DISH WORK!

3 LB	BONELESS PORK SHOULDER BLADE ROAST	1.5 KG
	SALT AND PEPPER	
1 TBSP	VEGETABLE OIL	15 ML
1	LARGE SWEET POTATO, PEELED AND CUT INTO 2-INCH (5 CM) CHUNKS	1
3	ONIONS, THINLY SLICED	3
4	CLOVES GARLIC, MINCED	4
1 TBSP	CRUMBLED DRIED SAGE	15 ML
1 TBSP	GRANULATED SUGAR	15 ML
2 TBSP	TOMATO PASTE	30 ML
2 TBSP	ALL-PURPOSE FLOUR	30 ML
1/2 CUP	DRY WHITE WINE	125 ML
1/2 CUP	CHICKEN BROTH	125 ML
1/4 CUP	FRESHLY SQUEEZED LEMON JUICE	60 ML
1/4 CUP	CHOPPED FRESH PARSLEY	60 ML
	GRATED ZEST OF 1 LEMON	

USE A 5- TO 6-QUART SLOW COOKER. SEASON PORK WELL WITH SALT AND PEPPER. IN A SKILLET, HEAT OIL OVER MEDIUM-HIGH HEAT. ADD PORK AND BROWN ON ALL SIDES. TRANSFER TO SLOW COOKER. ARRANGE SWEET POTATO AROUND PORK. REDUCE HEAT TO MEDIUM. ADD ONIONS, GARLIC, SAGE, SUGAR AND TOMATO PASTE TO SKILLET; COOK, STIRRING OCCASIONALLY, UNTIL ONIONS ARE GOLDEN BROWN, ABOUT 7 MINUTES. STIR IN FLOUR. WHISK IN WINE AND COOK, SCRAPING UP BROWN BITS FROM

BOTTOM OF PAN. STIR IN BROTH AND LEMON JUICE. POUR OVER PORK. COVER AND COOK ON LOW FOR 6 TO 8 HOURS OR ON HIGH FOR 3 TO 4 HOURS, UNTIL PORK IS TENDER. TRANSFER PORK TO A CUTTING BOARD, COVER LOOSELY WITH FOIL AND LET REST FOR 10 MINUTES. USING A SPOON, REMOVE EXCESS FAT FROM SURFACE OF COOKING LIQUID. ADJUST SEASONING WITH SALT AND PEPPER. IN A BOWL, COMBINE PARSLEY AND LEMON ZEST. SLICE PORK ACROSS THE GRAIN OR PULL APART INTO CHUNKS. SERVE TOPPED WITH SAUCE AND SPRINKLED WITH PARSLEY MIXTURE. SERVES 6.

TIP: BE SURE TO USE CRUMBLED DRIED SAGE AND NOT GROUND DRIED SAGE, WHICH HAS AN INTENSE AND OVERPOWERING FLAVOR.

PULLED PORK ON A BUN

*SHREDDED, OR "PULLED," PORK IS THE PERFECT
SLOW COOKER FOOD.*

4 TBSP	PACKED BROWN SUGAR, DIVIDED	60 ML
3 TBSP	PAPRIKA	45 ML
1 TBSP	CHILI POWDER	15 ML
1 TBSP	DRY MUSTARD	15 ML
1 TSP	SALT	5 ML
3 LB	BONELESS PORK SHOULDER BLADE ROAST, CUT INTO 4 CHUNKS	1.5 KG
1	ENVELOPE (1.4 OZ/38.5 G) ONION SOUP MIX	1
1½ CUPS	CHICKEN BROTH	375 ML
¼ TSP	CAYENNE PEPPER	1 ML
1½ CUPS	TOMATO-BASED CHILI SAUCE	375 ML
3 TBSP	CIDER VINEGAR	45 ML
1 TBSP	SOY SAUCE	15 ML
	KAISER BUNS, WARMED	
	QUICK COLESLAW (PAGE 176)	

USE A 5- TO 6-QUART SLOW COOKER. IN A BOWL, COMBINE
1 TBSP (15 ML) BROWN SUGAR, PAPRIKA, CHILI POWDER,
MUSTARD AND SALT. RUB OVER ALL SIDES OF PORK. COVER
AND REFRIGERATE FOR AT LEAST 2 HOURS OR OVERNIGHT.
PLACE PORK IN SLOW COOKER. WHISK TOGETHER SOUP MIX
AND BROTH; POUR OVER PORK. COVER AND COOK ON LOW
FOR 8 TO 10 HOURS OR ON HIGH FOR 4 TO 5 HOURS, UNTIL
PORK SHREDS EASILY WITH A FORK. TRANSFER PORK TO A
PLATE AND LET COOL SLIGHTLY. USING A SPOON, REMOVE
EXCESS FAT FROM SURFACE OF SAUCE. POUR SAUCE INTO
A LARGE SAUCEPAN AND BRING TO A BOIL. REDUCE HEAT

AND SIMMER FOR ABOUT 20 MINUTES, UNTIL SYRUPY. STIR IN REMAINING BROWN SUGAR, CAYENNE, CHILI SAUCE, VINEGAR AND SOY SAUCE; SIMMER FOR 10 MINUTES TO BLEND THE FLAVORS. ADJUST SEASONING WITH SALT AND CAYENNE, IF DESIRED. MEANWHILE, TRANSFER PORK TO A CUTTING BOARD AND ADD ACCUMULATED JUICES TO SAUCE. USING TWO FORKS, SHRED PORK, PLACING IT IN A SERVING BOWL. (THIS IS A SUPER-MESSY JOB BUT WORTH THE EFFORT!) POUR 1 CUP (250 ML) SAUCE OVER SHREDDED MEAT, TURNING PORK TO ABSORB SAUCE. SERVE PORK ON WARMED BUNS, TOPPED WITH COLESLAW, WITH EXTRA SAUCE FOR DIPPING. SERVES 8.

QUICK COLESLAW

THIS LIGHT AND PRETTY COLESLAW IS THE PERFECT SIDE DISH FOR PULLED PORK ON A BUN (PAGE 174), AS WELL AS AT BUFFETS, BARBECUES AND PICNICS.

2	PACKAGES (EACH 12 OZ/340 G) COLESLAW MIX	2
	ICE WATER	
2 TBSP	GRANULATED SUGAR	30 ML
1 TSP	CELERY SALT	5 ML
1/2 CUP	VEGETABLE OIL	125 ML
1/4 CUP	CIDER VINEGAR	60 ML
2 TSP	DIJON MUSTARD	10 ML

PLACE COLESLAW MIX IN A BOWL, COVER WITH ICE WATER AND LET SOAK FOR 10 MINUTES. (THIS WILL HELP MAKE IT CRUNCHIER.) DRAIN AND DRY IN A SALAD SPINNER OR WRAP IN A CLEAN DISH TOWEL AND GENTLY PRESS TO REMOVE EXCESS WATER. PLACE COLESLAW MIX IN A LARGE SALAD BOWL. IN A SAUCEPAN, COMBINE SUGAR, CELERY SALT, OIL, VINEGAR AND MUSTARD; BRING TO A BOIL. BOIL, WITHOUT STIRRING, FOR 1 MINUTE, UNTIL SLIGHTLY SYRUPY. REMOVE FROM HEAT AND IMMEDIATELY TOSS WITH COLESLAW MIX, COATING EVENLY. REFRIGERATE FOR 30 TO 60 MINUTES BEFORE SERVING. SERVES 8.

BARBECUE PORK AND BEANS STEW

A HEARTY ONE-POT DINNER. SERVE WITH CRUSTY BREAD
AND A GREEN SALAD.

2 LBS	BONELESS PORK SHOULDER BLADE, TRIMMED AND CUT INTO 1-INCH (2.5 CM) CUBES	1 KG
4	CLOVES GARLIC, MINCED	4
2	ONIONS, CHOPPED	2
1	LARGE SWEET POTATO, PEELED, QUARTERED LENGTHWISE AND CUT INTO 3/4-INCH (2 CM) THICK SLICES	1
1	CAN (14 TO 19 OZ/398 TO 540 ML) SMALL WHITE BEANS, DRAINED AND RINSED (SEE TIP, PAGE 199)	1
1 CUP	BARBECUE SAUCE	250 ML
1 CUP	BEEF BROTH	250 ML
3 CUPS	PACKED, THINLY SLICED STEMMED KALE	750 ML

IN A 5- TO 6- QUART SLOW COOKER, COMBINE PORK,
GARLIC, ONIONS, SWEET POTATO AND BEANS. IN A SMALL
BOWL, WHISK TOGETHER BARBECUE SAUCE AND BROTH.
POUR OVER PORK MIXTURE. COVER AND COOK ON LOW FOR
6 TO 8 HOURS OR ON HIGH FOR 3 TO 4 HOURS, UNTIL PORK
IS TENDER. STIR IN KALE. COVER AND COOK ON HIGH FOR
ABOUT 15 MINUTES, UNTIL KALE IS TENDER. SERVES 4 TO 6.

TIP: EITHER A MILD OR A SPICY BARBECUE SAUCE WILL
WORK IN THIS RECIPE. HEAT SEEKERS WILL LOVE IT MADE
WITH A HOT AND SPICY BARBECUE SAUCE THAT INCLUDES
JALAPEÑO AND CHIPOTLE PEPPERS. IF YOU CAN'T FIND
ONE LIKE THAT, ADD 1 TSP (5 ML) CHIPOTLE CHILE POWDER
OR REGULAR CHILI POWDER WITH THE KALE.

PORK ADOBO

A PHILIPPINE STEW, WITH A TOUCH OF
SWEET AND SOUR. SERVE WITH RICE.

2 TBSP	VEGETABLE OIL, DIVIDED	30 ML
3 LBS	BONELESS PORK SHOULDER BLADE, TRIMMED AND CUT INTO 1-INCH (2.5 CM) CUBES	1.5 KG
6	CARROTS, CUT INTO THICK SLICES	6
2	LARGE ONIONS, CHOPPED	2
4	CLOVES GARLIC, MINCED	4
1 TBSP	FINELY CHOPPED GINGERROOT	15 ML
1/2 CUP	CIDER VINEGAR	125 ML
1/4 CUP	SOY SAUCE	60 ML
3	BAY LEAVES	3
1	WHOLE CLOVE	1
1	2-INCH (5 CM) CINNAMON STICK	1
1/2 TSP	COARSELY GROUND BLACK PEPPER	2 ML
2 TBSP	BUTTER	30 ML
2 CUPS	PEARL ONIONS, PEELED	500 ML
1 TBSP	CORNSTARCH	15 ML
2 TBSP	COLD WATER	30 ML

USE A 5- TO 6-QUART SLOW COOKER. IN A SKILLET, HEAT HALF THE OIL OVER MEDIUM-HIGH HEAT. BROWN PORK, IN BATCHES. TRANSFER TO SLOW COOKER. REDUCE HEAT TO MEDIUM AND ADD REMAINING OIL TO SKILLET. ADD CARROTS AND ONIONS; COOK, STIRRING OCCASIONALLY, FOR 5 MINUTES. ADD GARLIC AND GINGER; COOK, STIRRING, FOR 15 SECONDS. STIR IN VINEGAR AND SOY SAUCE, SCRAPING UP BROWN BITS FROM BOTTOM OF PAN. POUR OVER PORK. ADD BAY LEAVES, CLOVE, CINNAMON

STICK AND PEPPER. COVER AND COOK ON LOW FOR 6 TO 8 HOURS OR ON HIGH FOR 3 TO 4 HOURS, UNTIL PORK IS TENDER. DISCARD BAY LEAVES, CLOVES AND CINNAMON STICK. MEANWHILE, IN A SKILLET, MELT BUTTER OVER MEDIUM HEAT. COOK PEARL ONIONS, STIRRING OFTEN, UNTIL GOLDEN, ABOUT 5 MINUTES. STIR INTO SLOW COOKER. IN A SMALL BOWL, COMBINE CORNSTARCH AND COLD WATER. STIR INTO SLOW COOKER. COVER AND COOK ON HIGH FOR ABOUT 20 MINUTES, UNTIL SAUCE IS THICKENED. SERVES 6 TO 8.

TIP: TO SAVE TIME, YOU CAN USE FROZEN READY-PEELED PEARL ONIONS. THAW AND PAT THEM DRY BEFORE COOKING IN BUTTER.

FLAMENCO STEW

*TASTES OF SPAIN! SERVE WITH ROASTED GARLIC
POTATOES AND STEAMED BROCCOLI.*

2	FRESH CHORIZO SAUSAGES (EACH ABOUT 4 OZ/125 G), CASINGS REMOVED, PINCHED INTO BITE-SIZE PIECES	2
2 TBSP	OLIVE OIL (APPROX.), DIVIDED	30 ML
1 1/2 LBS	BONELESS PORK SHOULDER BLADE, TRIMMED AND CUT INTO 1-INCH (2.5 CM) CUBES	750 G
1	LARGE ONION, THINLY SLICED	1
1	FENNEL BULB, TRIMMED AND THINLY SLICED	1
4	CLOVES GARLIC, MINCED	4
1 TBSP	TOMATO PASTE	15 ML
3 TBSP	SHERRY VINEGAR	45 ML
2 TBSP	ALL-PURPOSE FLOUR	30 ML
1/2 CUP	CHICKEN BROTH	125 ML
2	2-INCH (5 CM) STRIPS LEMON ZEST	2
1	CAN (14 OZ/398 ML) WHOLE TOMATOES, WITH JUICE	1
	SALT AND PEPPER (OPTIONAL)	
1/3 CUP	CHOPPED FRESH PARSLEY	75 ML
	GRATED ZEST OF 1 LEMON	

USE A 3 1/2- TO 4-QUART SLOW COOKER. IN A SKILLET,
OVER MEDIUM-HIGH HEAT, BROWN SAUSAGE. USING
A SLOTTED SPOON, TRANSFER TO SLOW COOKER.
ADD 1 TBSP (15 ML) OIL TO SKILLET. BROWN PORK, IN
BATCHES. USING A SLOTTED SPOON, TRANSFER TO SLOW
COOKER. REDUCE HEAT TO MEDIUM AND ADD ENOUGH
OF THE REMAINING OIL TO SKILLET TO MAKE 1 TBSP

(15 ML), IF NECESSARY. ADD ONION, FENNEL, GARLIC AND TOMATO PASTE; COOK, STIRRING OCCASIONALLY, FOR 5 MINUTES. STIR IN VINEGAR (IT WILL EVAPORATE ALMOST IMMEDIATELY). STIR IN FLOUR. WHISK IN BROTH, SCRAPING UP BROWN BITS FROM BOTTOM OF PAN. STIR IN LEMON ZEST STRIPS AND TOMATOES, BREAKING TOMATOES UP WITH A SPOON; BRING TO A BOIL. POUR OVER SAUSAGE MIXTURE. COVER AND COOK ON LOW FOR 6 TO 8 HOURS OR ON HIGH FOR 3 TO 4 HOURS, UNTIL PORK IS TENDER. SEASON TO TASTE WITH SALT AND PEPPER, IF DESIRED. DISCARD LEMON ZEST STRIPS. IN A SMALL BOWL, COMBINE PARSLEY AND GRATED LEMON ZEST. SERVE STEW SPRINKLED WITH PARSLEY MIXTURE. SERVES 4.

TIP: CHORIZO IS A SPICY PORK SAUSAGE SEASONED WITH PAPRIKA THAT'S USED IN A LOT OF SPANISH, MEXICAN AND PORTUGUESE DISHES. IT IS WIDELY AVAILABLE IN SUPERMARKETS. FOR THIS RECIPE, USE FRESH CHORIZO RATHER THAN THE CURED VERSION. HOT ITALIAN SAUSAGE IS A GOOD SUBSTITUTE FOR CHORIZO.

SWEET-AND-SOUR PORK

A FOREVER AND FOR ALWAYS FAVORITE. SERVE WITH RICE.

1	CAN (14 OZ/398 ML) PINEAPPLE CHUNKS IN JUICE	1
2 TBSP	VEGETABLE OIL, DIVIDED	30 ML
1½ LBS	BONELESS PORK SHOULDER BLADE, TRIMMED AND CUT INTO 1-INCH (2.5 CM) CUBES	750 G
1	LARGE ONION, CHOPPED	1
3	CLOVES GARLIC, MINCED	3
2 CUPS	SLICED MUSHROOMS	500 ML
2 TBSP	TOMATO PASTE	30 ML
1	LARGE CARROT, THINLY SLICED	1
1	STALK CELERY, THINLY SLICED	1
¼ CUP	PACKED BROWN SUGAR	60 ML
¼ CUP	CHICKEN BROTH	60 ML
¼ CUP	CIDER VINEGAR	60 ML
1 TBSP	SOY SAUCE	15 ML
2 TBSP	CORNSTARCH	30 ML
3 TBSP	COLD WATER	45 ML
1	RED BELL PEPPER, CHOPPED	1
	SALT (OPTIONAL)	

USE A 3½- TO 4-QUART SLOW COOKER. DRAIN PINEAPPLE, RESERVING JUICE. SET BOTH ASIDE. IN A SKILLET, HEAT HALF THE OIL OVER MEDIUM-HIGH HEAT. BROWN PORK, IN BATCHES. USING A SLOTTED SPOON, TRANSFER TO SLOW COOKER. REDUCE HEAT TO MEDIUM AND ADD REMAINING OIL TO SKILLET. ADD ONION, GARLIC, MUSHROOMS AND TOMATO PASTE; COOK, STIRRING OCCASIONALLY, FOR 5 MINUTES. STIR IN PINEAPPLE JUICE, SCRAPING UP BROWN

BITS FROM BOTTOM OF PAN. POUR OVER PORK. STIR IN CARROT, CELERY, BROWN SUGAR, BROTH, VINEGAR AND SOY SAUCE. COVER AND COOK ON LOW FOR 6 TO 8 HOURS OR ON HIGH FOR 3 TO 4 HOURS, UNTIL PORK IS TENDER. IN A SMALL BOWL, COMBINE CORNSTARCH AND COLD WATER. STIR INTO SLOW COOKER. STIR IN RED PEPPER AND RESERVED PINEAPPLE. COVER AND COOK ON HIGH FOR ABOUT 20 MINUTES, UNTIL THICKENED AND STEAMING. ADJUST SEASONING WITH SALT, IF DESIRED. SERVES 4.

TIP: WE USE TOMATO PASTE IN MANY OF OUR SLOW COOKER RECIPES BECAUSE IT GREATLY BOOSTS FLAVOR AND RICHNESS. THE LONG, MOIST COOKING DULLS OTHER AROMATIC INGREDIENTS, SUCH AS ONIONS, GARLIC AND HERBS. MICROWAVING OR BROWNING A DOLLOP OR TWO OF TOMATO PASTE WITH THESE INGREDIENTS MAKES ALL THE DIFFERENCE.

PORK VINDALOO

SOME LIKE IT HOT! SERVE WITH RED LENTIL AND VEGETABLE CURRY (PAGE 258), STEAMED BASMATI RICE AND A DOLLOP OF PLAIN YOGURT.

1 TBSP	VEGETABLE OIL	15 ML
2	ONIONS, THINLY SLICED	2
6	CLOVES GARLIC, MINCED	6
1 TBSP	FINELY CHOPPED GINGERROOT	15 ML
1/4 CUP	VINDALOO OR OTHER HOT INDIAN CURRY PASTE (SEE TIP, PAGE 235)	60 ML
2 LBS	BONELESS PORK SHOULDER BLADE, TRIMMED AND CUT INTO 1-INCH (2.5 CM) CUBES	1 KG
2	BAY LEAVES	2
1	CAN (14 OZ/398 ML) WHOLE TOMATOES, WITH JUICE	1
1 TSP	GRANULATED SUGAR	5 ML
2 TBSP	RED WINE VINEGAR	30 ML
2 TBSP	CHOPPED FRESH CILANTRO	30 ML
	SALT AND PEPPER (OPTIONAL)	

USE A 3½- TO 4-QUART SLOW COOKER. IN A LARGE SKILLET, HEAT OIL OVER MEDIUM HEAT. ADD ONIONS, GARLIC, GINGER AND CURRY PASTE; COOK, STIRRING, FOR 5 MINUTES. ADD PORK AND STIR TO COAT WITH SPICE MIXTURE. STIR IN BAY LEAVES, TOMATOES, SUGAR AND VINEGAR, BREAKING TOMATOES UP WITH A SPOON. TRANSFER TO SLOW COOKER. COVER AND COOK ON LOW FOR 6 TO 8 HOURS OR ON HIGH FOR 3 TO 4 HOURS, UNTIL PORK IS TENDER. DISCARD BAY LEAVES. STIR IN CILANTRO. ADJUST SEASONING WITH SALT AND PEPPER, IF DESIRED. SERVES 4.

BARBECUE-BRAISED RIBS

A DOWN-HOME DINNER. SERVE WITH BEST-EVER GARLIC MASHED POTATOES (PAGE 288) AND A CAESAR SALAD.

3 LBS	BONE-IN COUNTRY-STYLE PORK RIBS, CUT INTO INDIVIDUAL RIBS	1.5 KG
	SALT AND PEPPER	
1 TBSP	VEGETABLE OIL	15 ML
2	ONIONS, FINELY CHOPPED	2
4	CLOVES GARLIC, MINCED	4
2 TBSP	PACKED BROWN SUGAR	30 ML
1 TBSP	DRY MUSTARD	15 ML
1 CUP	TOMATO-BASED CHILI SAUCE	250 ML
$1/2$ CUP	CHICKEN BROTH	125 ML
1 TBSP	WORCESTERSHIRE SAUCE	15 ML
4	GREEN ONIONS, CHOPPED	4

USE A 5- TO 6-QUART SLOW COOKER. SEASON RIBS WELL WITH SALT AND PEPPER. IN A SKILLET, HEAT OIL OVER MEDIUM-HIGH HEAT. BROWN RIBS ON ALL SIDES, IN BATCHES IF NECESSARY. TRANSFER TO SLOW COOKER. REDUCE HEAT TO MEDIUM. ADD ONIONS AND GARLIC TO SKILLET; COOK, STIRRING OCCASIONALLY, FOR 3 MINUTES. STIR IN BROWN SUGAR, MUSTARD, CHILI SAUCE, BROTH AND WORCESTERSHIRE SAUCE. POUR OVER RIBS. COVER AND COOK ON LOW FOR 5 TO 6 HOURS OR ON HIGH FOR $2\frac{1}{2}$ TO 3 HOURS, UNTIL RIBS ARE TENDER. USING A SPOON, REMOVE EXCESS FAT FROM SURFACE OF SAUCE, IF NECESSARY. SERVE RIBS TOPPED WITH SAUCE AND SPRINKLED WITH GREEN ONIONS. SERVES 4 TO 6.

CRANBERRY HERB BONELESS RIBS

THICK AND MEATY RIBS, WITH A YUMMY SAUCE. SERVE WITH BUTTERY BAKED POTATOES AND STEAMED GREEN CABBAGE.

2 LBS	BONELESS COUNTRY-STYLE PORK RIBS, CUT INTO 1-INCH (2.5 CM) THICK SLICES	1 KG
	SALT AND PEPPER	
1 TBSP	VEGETABLE OIL	15 ML
1	APPLE (UNPEELED), GRATED	1
1	LARGE ONION, THINLY SLICED	1
4	CLOVES GARLIC, MINCED	4
2 TSP	CRUMBLED DRIED SAGE	10 ML
3/4 CUP	CANNED WHOLE CRANBERRY SAUCE	175 ML
1 TBSP	BALSAMIC VINEGAR	15 ML
1 TSP	DIJON MUSTARD (APPROX.)	5 ML

USE A 4- TO 6-QUART SLOW COOKER. SEASON RIBS WELL WITH SALT AND PEPPER. IN A SKILLET, HEAT OIL OVER MEDIUM-HIGH HEAT. BROWN RIBS ON ALL SIDES, IN BATCHES IF NECESSARY. TRANSFER TO SLOW COOKER AND SPRINKLE WITH APPLE. REDUCE HEAT TO MEDIUM. ADD ONION, GARLIC, SAGE, 1/2 TSP (2 ML) SALT AND 1/4 TSP (1 ML) PEPPER TO SKILLET; COOK, STIRRING OCCASIONALLY, FOR 5 MINUTES. STIR IN CRANBERRY SAUCE AND VINEGAR; BRING TO A BOIL. POUR OVER RIBS. COVER AND COOK ON LOW FOR 5 TO 6 HOURS OR ON HIGH FOR 2 1/2 TO 3 HOURS, UNTIL RIBS ARE TENDER. USING A SPOON, REMOVE EXCESS FAT FROM SURFACE OF SAUCE, IF NECESSARY. STIR MUSTARD INTO SAUCE.

ADJUST SEASONING WITH SALT, PEPPER AND ADDITIONAL MUSTARD, IF DESIRED. SERVE RIBS TOPPED WITH SAUCE. SERVES 4.

TIP: COUNTRY-STYLE RIBS ARE MEATIER AND MORE MARBLED WITH FAT THAN BABY BACK RIBS OR SPARERIBS. AS SUCH, THEY ARE WELL SUITED TO BRAISING IN THE SLOW COOKER. THEY ARE AVAILABLE BONE-IN OR BONELESS, AND THESE ARE INTERCHANGEABLE IN THE RIB RECIPES IN THIS CHAPTER. IF THE RECIPE CALLS FOR 2 LBS (1 KG) BONELESS RIBS AND YOU WANT TO USE BONE-IN, INCREASE THE QUANTITY TO 3 LBS (1.5 KG) — AND VICE VERSA.

DON'T CONFUSE MY TOLERANCE
WITH HOSPITALITY.

SWEET-AND-SPICY PORK RIBS

AN EASY WEEKEND SUPPER. SERVE WITH RICE AND LEAFY GREENS, SUCH AS STEAMED BOK CHOY.

3 LBS	BONE-IN COUNTRY-STYLE PORK RIBS, CUT INTO INDIVIDUAL RIBS	1.5 KG
	SALT AND PEPPER	
I TBSP	VEGETABLE OIL	15 ML
I	ONION, FINELY CHOPPED	I
4	CLOVES GARLIC, MINCED	4
I TBSP	FINELY CHOPPED GINGERROOT	15 ML
6 TBSP	PACKED BROWN SUGAR	90 ML
3 TSP	GRATED ORANGE ZEST, DIVIDED	15 ML
1/4 CUP	SOY SAUCE	60 ML
1/4 CUP	HOISIN SAUCE	60 ML
I TBSP	CORNSTARCH	15 ML
I TBSP	CIDER VINEGAR	15 ML
I TSP	ASIAN CHILI PASTE	5 ML

USE A 5- TO 6-QUART SLOW COOKER. SEASON RIBS WELL WITH SALT AND PEPPER. IN A SKILLET, HEAT OIL OVER MEDIUM-HIGH HEAT. BROWN RIBS ON ALL SIDES, IN BATCHES IF NECESSARY. TRANSFER TO SLOW COOKER. REDUCE HEAT TO MEDIUM. ADD ONION, GARLIC AND GINGER TO SKILLET; COOK, STIRRING OCCASIONALLY, FOR 3 MINUTES. SCRAPE OVER RIBS. IN A BOWL, COMBINE BROWN SUGAR, 2 TSP (10 ML) ORANGE ZEST, SOY SAUCE AND HOISIN SAUCE. POUR OVER RIBS, TURNING TO COAT. COVER AND COOK ON LOW FOR 5 TO 6 HOURS OR ON HIGH FOR $2^{1}/_{2}$ TO 3 HOURS, UNTIL RIBS ARE TENDER. USING A SPOON, REMOVE EXCESS FAT FROM SURFACE OF SAUCE, IF NECESSARY. IN A SMALL BOWL, COMBINE CORNSTARCH, VINEGAR AND CHILI PASTE. STIR INTO

SLOW COOKER. STIR IN REMAINING ORANGE ZEST. COVER AND
COOK ON HIGH FOR 15 MINUTES, UNTIL SAUCE IS THICKENED.
SERVE RIBS TOPPED WITH SAUCE. SERVES 4 TO 6.

RUSH HOUR WRAPS

USE LEFTOVERS FROM CHINESE PORK RIBS IN MUSHROOM
SAUCE (PAGE 190) OR SWEET-AND-SPICY PORK RIBS
(OPPOSITE) TO MAKE THESE QUICK AND DELICIOUS WRAPS.

1 CUP	CHOPPED LEFTOVER COOKED PORK	250 ML
1 CUP	LEFTOVER SAUCE	250 ML
2 TBSP	SWEET CHILI DIPPING SAUCE	30 ML
2	9-INCH (23 CM) FLOUR TORTILLAS, WARMED	2
	BABY SPINACH	
	FRESH BEAN SPROUTS	
	SHREDDED CARROT	

IN A SAUCEPAN, COMBINE PORK, SAUCE AND CHILI SAUCE.
COOK OVER MEDIUM HEAT, STIRRING, UNTIL BUBBLING. LAY
TORTILLAS ON A WORK SURFACE. SPOON PORK MIXTURE
DOWN THE CENTER OF EACH TORTILLA, DIVIDING EVENLY.
TOP WITH SPINACH, BEAN SPROUTS AND CARROT. FOLD
RIGHT SIDE OF TORTILLA OVER FILLING. FOLD BOTTOM OF
TORTILLA UP, THEN FOLD LEFT SIDE OVER AND ROLL UNTIL
FILLING IS ENCLOSED. SERVES 2.

TIP: TO WARM TORTILLAS, WRAP THEM IN PAPER TOWELS
AND MICROWAVE ON HIGH FOR ABOUT 30 SECONDS. FOR
LARGE QUANTITIES, STACK TORTILLAS, THEN WRAP THEM
IN FOIL AND HEAT IN A 350°F (180°C) OVEN FOR ABOUT
20 MINUTES.

CHINESE PORK RIBS IN MUSHROOM SAUCE

FOR A FRESH PRESENTATION, LADLE THE RIBS AND SAUCE OVER A BED OF STEAMED RICE, FRESH BABY SPINACH AND CRUNCHY BEAN SPROUTS. USE LEFTOVERS TO MAKE RUSH HOUR WRAPS (PAGE 189).

I	PACKAGE ($1/2$ OZ/I4 G) DRIED SHIITAKE MUSHROOMS	I
I CUP	BOILING WATER	250 ML
2 LBS	BONELESS COUNTRY-STYLE PORK RIBS, CUT INTO I-INCH (2.5 CM) THICK SLICES	I KG
2 TBSP	VEGETABLE OIL, DIVIDED	30 ML
2	ONIONS, CHOPPED	2
4	CLOVES GARLIC, MINCED	4
I TBSP	FINELY CHOPPED GINGERROOT	I5 ML
3 CUPS	SLICED CREMINI MUSHROOMS	750 ML
2 TBSP	RICE WINE (SEE TIP, OPPOSITE)	30 ML
I CUP	BEEF BROTH	250 ML
$1/4$ CUP	SOY SAUCE	60 ML
2 TBSP	OYSTER SAUCE	30 ML
2 TBSP	HOISIN SAUCE	30 ML
I TBSP	CORNSTARCH	I5 ML
I TSP	ASIAN CHILI PASTE	5 ML
I TBSP	RICE OR CIDER VINEGAR	I5 ML
	CHOPPED GREEN ONIONS	

USE A 5- TO 6-QUART SLOW COOKER. IN A SMALL BOWL, SOAK SHIITAKE MUSHROOMS IN BOILING WATER FOR 30 MINUTES. STRAIN THROUGH A COFFEE FILTER SET OVER A STRAINER, RESERVING SOAKING LIQUID. CHOP MUSHROOMS AND SET ASIDE. PLACE RIBS IN SLOW

COOKER. IN A SKILLET, HEAT HALF THE OIL OVER MEDIUM HEAT. ADD ONIONS, GARLIC AND GINGER; COOK, STIRRING OCCASIONALLY, FOR 5 MINUTES. SCRAPE OVER RIBS. ADD REMAINING OIL TO SKILLET. ADD CREMINI MUSHROOMS AND RESERVED SHIITAKE MUSHROOMS AND COOK, STIRRING, FOR 5 MINUTES. ADD RICE WINE AND COOK, STIRRING, FOR 15 SECONDS. ADD RESERVED MUSHROOM LIQUID, BROTH, SOY SAUCE, OYSTER SAUCE AND HOISIN SAUCE; BRING TO A BOIL. POUR OVER RIBS. COVER AND COOK ON LOW FOR 5 TO 6 HOURS OR ON HIGH FOR $2\frac{1}{2}$ TO 3 HOURS, UNTIL RIBS ARE TENDER. SKIM EXCESS FAT FROM SURFACE OF SAUCE, IF DESIRED. IN A SMALL BOWL, COMBINE CORNSTARCH, CHILI PASTE AND VINEGAR. STIR INTO SAUCE. COVER AND COOK ON HIGH FOR 15 MINUTES, UNTIL SAUCE IS THICKENED. SERVE RIBS TOPPED WITH SAUCE AND SPRINKLED WITH GREEN ONIONS. SERVES 4 TO 6.

TIP: RICE WINE, A.K.A. SAKE, IS A JAPANESE ALCOHOLIC DRINK THAT'S OFTEN FEATURED IN ASIAN COOKING. MOST LIQUOR STORES CARRY IT. BUY A BOTTLE (IT'S RELATIVELY INEXPENSIVE) AND ENJOY THE THRILL WHEN EVERYONE TELLS YOU HOW AUTHENTIC YOUR ASIAN-STYLE DISHES TASTE. DRY SHERRY OR DRY VERMOUTH ARE GOOD SUBSTITUTES FOR RICE WINE, OR YOU CAN OMIT IT FROM THE RECIPE. BUT THAT WOULD BE A SHAME.

SAUSAGE MUSHROOM RAGÙ

HEARTY FARE FOR A FAMILY SUPPER. A CHUNKY PASTA,
SUCH AS RIGATONI, IS THE IDEAL ACCOMPANIMENT.

2 TBSP	VEGETABLE OIL, DIVIDED	30 ML
1 LB	FRESH CHORIZO OR HOT ITALIAN SAUSAGES, CASINGS REMOVED, PINCHED INTO BITE-SIZED PIECES	500 G
2	ONIONS, FINELY CHOPPED	2
4	CLOVES GARLIC, MINCED	4
1	FENNEL BULB, TRIMMED AND THINLY SLICED	1
3 CUPS	SLICED MUSHROOMS	750 ML
1 TSP	DRIED MARJORAM OR ITALIAN SEASONING	5 ML
	SALT AND PEPPER	
1/2 CUP	DRY RED WINE	125 ML
2	BAY LEAVES	2
1	CAN (14 OZ/398 ML) DICED TOMATOES, WITH JUICE	1
1 TSP	SWEET PAPRIKA	5 ML
1 TBSP	FRESHLY SQUEEZED LEMON JUICE	15 ML
1/4 CUP	CHOPPED FRESH PARSLEY	60 ML

USE A 3½- TO 4-QUART SLOW COOKER. IN A SKILLET,
HEAT HALF THE OIL OVER MEDIUM HEAT. BROWN
SAUSAGES. USING A SLOTTED SPOON, TRANSFER TO SLOW
COOKER. ADD REMAINING OIL TO SKILLET. ADD ONIONS,
GARLIC, FENNEL, MUSHROOMS, MARJORAM, 1/2 TSP (2 ML)
SALT AND 1/4 TSP (1 ML) PEPPER; COOK, STIRRING, FOR
7 MINUTES. STIR IN WINE, SCRAPING UP BROWN BITS
FROM BOTTOM OF PAN. POUR OVER SAUSAGES. STIR IN
BAY LEAVES AND TOMATOES. COVER AND COOK ON LOW

CONTINUED ON PAGE 193...

Southwestern Pork Chili (page 198)

Hoisin Orange Chicken (page 218)

Friday Fiesta Chicken Stew (page 220)

Easy Chicken Curry (page 234)

FOR 6 TO 8 HOURS OR ON HIGH FOR 3 TO 4 HOURS, UNTIL BUBBLING. DISCARD BAY LEAVES. IN A BOWL, COMBINE PAPRIKA AND LEMON JUICE. STIR INTO SLOW COOKER. COVER AND COOK ON HIGH FOR 15 MINUTES TO BLEND THE FLAVORS. STIR IN PARSLEY. ADJUST SEASONING WITH SALT AND PEPPER, IF DESIRED. SERVES 4.

TIP: FENNEL BULB IS LABELED "ANISE" IN SOME SUPERMARKETS. IF IT HAS FEATHERY STALKS ATTACHED, TRIM THEM OFF ABOUT 1 INCH (2.5 CM) ABOVE THE BULB. CUT THE BULB IN HALF VERTICALLY AND REMOVE THE WOODY CORE FROM EACH HALF. CUT EACH HALF CROSSWISE INTO VERY THIN STRIPS.

VARIATION: IF YOU PREFER TO OMIT THE WINE, ADD $\frac{1}{2}$ CUP (125 ML) CHICKEN BROTH AND 1 TBSP (15 ML) BALSAMIC VINEGAR WITH THE TOMATOES.

HEARTY SAUSAGE LENTIL STEW

SAUSAGES AND LENTILS ARE A CLASSIC ITALIAN
COMBINATION. SERVE OVER CHUNKY PASTA.

2 TBSP	VEGETABLE OIL, DIVIDED	30 ML
I LB	MILD OR HOT ITALIAN PORK SAUSAGES	500 G
2	ONIONS, FINELY CHOPPED	2
2	CARROTS, QUARTERED LENGTHWISE AND CHOPPED	2
2	STALKS CELERY, THINLY SLICED	2
4	CLOVES GARLIC, MINCED	4
I TSP	DRIED ITALIAN SEASONING	5 ML
	SALT AND PEPPER	
1/2 CUP	DRY WHITE WINE	125 ML
2	BAY LEAVES	2
I	CAN (14 OZ/398 ML) DICED TOMATOES, WITH JUICE	I
1/2 CUP	DRIED GREEN OR BROWN LENTILS, RINSED	125 ML
I CUP	CHICKEN BROTH	250 ML
	CHOPPED FRESH PARSLEY (OPTIONAL)	

USE A 4- TO 6-QUART SLOW COOKER. IN A SKILLET, HEAT
HALF THE OIL OVER MEDIUM HEAT. BROWN SAUSAGES.
TRANSFER TO A CUTTING BOARD AND LET COOL SLIGHTLY.
CUT EACH SAUSAGE INTO 4 TO 6 PIECES (THEY WON'T BE
COOKED ALL THE WAY THROUGH) AND TRANSFER TO SLOW
COOKER. ADD REMAINING OIL TO SKILLET. ADD ONIONS,
CARROTS, CELERY, GARLIC, ITALIAN SEASONING, 1/2 TSP
(2 ML) SALT AND PEPPER TO TASTE; COOK, STIRRING
OCCASIONALLY, FOR 5 MINUTES. STIR IN WINE, SCRAPING
UP BROWN BITS FROM BOTTOM OF PAN. POUR OVER

SAUSAGES. STIR IN BAY LEAVES, TOMATOES, LENTILS AND
BROTH. COVER AND COOK ON LOW FOR 6 TO 8 HOURS OR
ON HIGH FOR 3 TO 4 HOURS, UNTIL LENTILS ARE TENDER.
DISCARD BAY LEAVES. SERVE SPRINKLED WITH PARSLEY
(IF USING). SERVES 4.

TIP: WE LIKE THE LARGE CHUNKS OF SAUSAGE IN THIS
RECIPE, BUT IF YOU PREFER, YOU CAN REMOVE THE
SAUSAGES FROM THEIR CASINGS AND USE YOUR FINGERS
TO PINCH OFF SMALL PIECES BEFORE BROWNING.

VARIATION: IF YOU OMIT THE WINE, INCREASE THE
CHICKEN BROTH TO $1\frac{1}{4}$ CUPS (300 ML) AND ADD 1 TBSP
(15 ML) LEMON JUICE.

PERFECT PORK CHILI

A SATISFYING AND CHUNKY CHILI.

4	SLICES BACON, CHOPPED	4
2 TBSP	VEGETABLE OIL (APPROX.), DIVIDED	30 ML
2 LBS	BONELESS PORK SHOULDER BLADE, CUT INTO 1-INCH (2.5 CM) CUBES	I KG
2	ONIONS, CHOPPED	2
I	CARROT, CHOPPED	I
4	CLOVES GARLIC, MINCED	4
I TBSP	GROUND CUMIN	15 ML
1½ TSP	DRIED OREGANO	7 ML
	SALT AND PEPPER	
2 TBSP	TOMATO PASTE	30 ML
I	CAN (14 OZ/398 ML) DICED TOMATOES	I
I	CAN (14 TO 19 OZ/398 TO 540 ML) RED KIDNEY BEANS, DRAINED AND RINSED (SEE TIP, PAGE 199)	I
2 TSP	PACKED BROWN SUGAR	10 ML
¾ CUP	CHICKEN BROTH	175 ML
2	JALAPEÑO PEPPERS, FINELY CHOPPED	2
¼ TSP	CAYENNE PEPPER, OR TO TASTE	I ML
I TSP	CIDER VINEGAR	5 ML
	SOUR CREAM, CHOPPED GREEN ONIONS AND SLICED RADISHES	

USE A 4- TO 6-QUART SLOW COOKER. IN A SKILLET, COOK BACON OVER MEDIUM-HIGH HEAT UNTIL CRISPY. USING A SLOTTED SPOON, TRANSFER TO SLOW COOKER. ADD ENOUGH OIL TO SKILLET TO MAKE I TBSP (15 ML) FAT, IF NECESSARY. BROWN PORK, IN BATCHES. TRANSFER TO SLOW COOKER. REDUCE HEAT TO MEDIUM AND ADD I TBSP (15 ML) OIL TO SKILLET. ADD ONIONS, CARROT, GARLIC,

CUMIN, OREGANO, 1/2 TSP (2 ML) SALT, 1/4 TSP (1 ML) PEPPER AND TOMATO PASTE; COOK, STIRRING OCCASIONALLY, FOR 5 MINUTES. STIR IN TOMATOES AND BRING TO A BOIL. POUR OVER PORK MIXTURE. STIR IN BEANS, BROWN SUGAR AND BROTH. COVER AND COOK ON LOW FOR 6 TO 8 HOURS OR ON HIGH FOR 3 TO 4 HOURS, UNTIL PORK IS TENDER. STIR IN JALAPEÑOS, CAYENNE AND VINEGAR. COVER AND COOK ON HIGH FOR 20 MINUTES. LADLE INTO BOWLS AND PASS SOUR CREAM, GREEN ONIONS AND RADISHES FOR GARNISHING. SERVES 4 TO 6.

PAPAYA SALSA

THE BEST CHILI IS MADE BETTER WHEN ACCOMPANIED BY A TERRIFIC HOMEMADE SALSA. THIS ONE IS ESPECIALLY GOOD WITH PERFECT PORK CHILI (OPPOSITE).

1	JALAPEÑO PEPPER, SEEDED AND FINELY CHOPPED	1
2 CUPS	DICED PAPAYA	500 ML
1/4 CUP	FINELY CHOPPED RED ONION	60 ML
1 TBSP	CHOPPED FRESH CILANTRO	15 ML
2 TBSP	FRESHLY SQUEEZED LIME JUICE	30 ML
1 TSP	LIQUID HONEY	5 ML
	SALT AND PEPPER	

IN A BOWL, COMBINE JALAPEÑO, PAPAYA, RED ONION, CILANTRO, LIME JUICE AND HONEY. SEASON TO TASTE WITH SALT AND PEPPER. STIR GENTLY. COVER AND REFRIGERATE FOR AT LEAST 30 MINUTES OR UP TO 4 HOURS TO BLEND THE FLAVORS. MAKES ABOUT 2 1/4 CUPS (550 ML).

SOUTHWESTERN PORK CHILI

A RICH CHILI WITH A SMOKY BACON FLAVOR AND COLORFUL VEGGIES. SERVE WITH TEX-MEX CORNBREAD (PAGE 34).

1 TBSP	VEGETABLE OIL	15 ML
1 LB	LEAN GROUND PORK	500 G
2	ONIONS, FINELY CHOPPED	2
2	STALKS CELERY, FINELY CHOPPED	2
1	LARGE CARROT, FINELY CHOPPED	1
3	CLOVES GARLIC, MINCED	3
2 TSP	GROUND CUMIN	10 ML
1 TSP	DRIED OREGANO	5 ML
	SALT AND PEPPER	
1	CAN (14 OZ/398 ML) TOMATO SAUCE	1
1	CAN (14 TO 19 OZ/398 TO 540 ML) BLACK BEANS, DRAINED AND RINSED (SEE TIP, OPPOSITE)	1
1 CUP	FROZEN CORN KERNELS (NO NEED TO THAW)	250 ML
2 TBSP	PACKED BROWN SUGAR	30 ML
1 CUP	CHICKEN BROTH	250 ML
1	RED BELL PEPPER, CHOPPED	1
2 TBSP	CHOPPED FRESH CILANTRO	30 ML
2 TSP	CHOPPED CHIPOTLE PEPPERS IN ADOBO SAUCE	10 ML
1 TBSP	FRESHLY SQUEEZED LIME JUICE (APPROX.)	15 ML
	SOUR CREAM, SHREDDED CHEDDAR CHEESE, DICED AVOCADO	

USE A 4- TO 6-QUART SLOW COOKER. IN A SKILLET, HEAT OIL OVER MEDIUM-HIGH HEAT. BROWN PORK, BREAKING IT

UP WITH A SPOON. USING A SLOTTED SPOON, TRANSFER
TO SLOW COOKER. DRAIN ALL BUT I TBSP (15 ML) FAT FROM
SKILLET. REDUCE HEAT TO MEDIUM. ADD ONIONS, CELERY,
CARROT, GARLIC, CUMIN, OREGANO, I TSP (5 ML) SALT AND
$1/4$ TSP (I ML) PEPPER; COOK, STIRRING OCCASIONALLY, FOR
5 MINUTES. STIR IN TOMATO SAUCE AND BRING TO A BOIL.
POUR OVER PORK. STIR IN BEANS, CORN, BROWN SUGAR
AND BROTH. COVER AND COOK ON LOW FOR 6 TO 8 HOURS
OR ON HIGH FOR 3 TO 4 HOURS, UNTIL BUBBLING. STIR IN
RED PEPPER, CILANTRO, CHIPOTLE PEPPERS AND I TBSP
(15 ML) LIME JUICE. COVER AND COOK ON HIGH FOR ABOUT
20 MINUTES, UNTIL RED PEPPER IS TENDER. ADJUST
SEASONING WITH SALT, PEPPER AND ADDITIONAL LIME
JUICE, IF DESIRED. LADLE INTO BOWLS AND PASS SOUR
CREAM, CHEESE AND AVOCADO FOR GARNISHING. SERVES 6.

TIP: IF YOU PREFER TO USE COOKED DRIED BEANS
INSTEAD OF CANNED, SEE BASIC BEANS (PAGE 282). YOU'LL
NEED 2 CUPS (500 ML) COOKED BEANS FOR THIS RECIPE.

DINNER PARTY MEATBALLS

MEATBALLS GO UPSCALE! SERVE WITH NO-FUSS
WILD RICE MEDLEY (PAGE 289) OR EGG NOODLES.

1/4 CUP	QUICK-COOKING ROLLED OATS	60 ML
1/4 CUP	MILK	60 ML
1 LB	LEAN GROUND PORK	500 G
1 TSP	DRIED OREGANO	5 ML
1 TSP	FENNEL SEEDS, CRACKED (SEE TIP, OPPOSITE)	5 ML
3/4 TSP	GRATED LEMON ZEST, DIVIDED	3 ML
	SALT AND PEPPER	
1	EGG, LIGHTLY BEATEN	1
1 TBSP	VEGETABLE OIL	15 ML
2	ONIONS, THINLY SLICED	2
1	FENNEL BULB, TRIMMED AND THINLY SLICED	1
3	CLOVES GARLIC, MINCED	3
1/4 CUP	TOMATO PASTE	60 ML
1 CUP	CHICKEN BROTH	250 ML
1/2 CUP	TOMATO SAUCE	125 ML
1/4 CUP	CHOPPED FRESH PARSLEY	60 ML

USE A 3 1/2 - TO 4-QUART SLOW COOKER. IN A BOWL,
COMBINE OATS AND MILK; LET SOAK FOR 5 MINUTES. ADD
PORK, OREGANO, FENNEL SEEDS, 1/4 TSP (1 ML) LEMON
ZEST, 1 TSP (5 ML) SALT, 1/4 TSP (1 ML) PEPPER AND EGG;
MIX WELL. SCOOP TABLESPOONFULS (15 ML) OF MEAT
MIXTURE AND ROLL INTO MEATBALLS. IN A SKILLET, HEAT
OIL OVER MEDIUM-HIGH HEAT. BROWN MEATBALLS, IN
BATCHES IF NECESSARY. TRANSFER TO SLOW COOKER.
REDUCE HEAT TO MEDIUM. ADD ONIONS, SLICED FENNEL,

GARLIC, 1/2 TSP (2 ML) SALT, 1/4 TSP (1 ML) PEPPER AND TOMATO PASTE TO SKILLET AND COOK, STIRRING OCCASIONALLY, FOR 5 MINUTES. STIR IN BROTH AND TOMATO SAUCE; BRING TO A BOIL, SCRAPING UP BROWN BITS FROM BOTTOM OF PAN. POUR OVER MEATBALLS. COVER AND COOK ON LOW FOR ABOUT 6 HOURS OR ON HIGH FOR ABOUT 3 HOURS, UNTIL MEATBALLS ARE NO LONGER PINK INSIDE AND SAUCE IS BUBBLING. STIR IN PARSLEY AND REMAINING LEMON ZEST. ADJUST SEASONING WITH SALT AND PEPPER, IF DESIRED. MAKES ABOUT 20 MEATBALLS; SERVES 4 TO 6.

TIP: FENNEL SEEDS ARE A COMMON INGREDIENT IN ITALIAN COOKING, ESPECIALLY IN PORK DISHES. TO CRACK FENNEL SEEDS, PLACE THEM IN A SMALL PLASTIC BAG. LAY THE BAG ON A FLAT SURFACE AND ROLL A ROLLING PIN FIRMLY OVER TOP. ALTERNATIVELY, PRESS THE BACK OF A LARGE SPOON FIRMLY AGAINST THE SEEDS, USING A ROCKING MOTION.

PORK AND APPLE MEATBALLS

A FRESH SPIN ON SWEET-AND-SOUR MEATBALLS! SERVE WITH STEAMED RICE AND CRISPY SPRING ROLLS ON THE SIDE.

I	APPLE, PEELED AND GRATED	I
1/4 CUP	QUICK-COOKING ROLLED OATS	60 ML
1/4 CUP	MILK	60 ML
I LB	LEAN GROUND PORK	500 G
2	CLOVES GARLIC, MINCED	2
1/2 TSP	CRUMBLED DRIED SAGE	2 ML
	SALT AND PEPPER	
I TBSP	VEGETABLE OIL	15 ML
I	LARGE ONION, FINELY CHOPPED	I
I TSP	GROUND CINNAMON	5 ML
1/2 CUP	APPLE JELLY	125 ML
3 TBSP	CIDER VINEGAR	45 ML
I	RED BELL PEPPER, CHOPPED	I
I CUP	FROZEN COOKED SHELLED EDAMAME	250 ML

USE A 3 1/2- TO 4-QUART SLOW COOKER. WORKING OVER A BOWL AND USING YOUR HANDS, SQUEEZE JUICE FROM GRATED APPLE. ADD ENOUGH WATER TO JUICE TO MAKE 1/4 CUP (60 ML); SET ASIDE. PLACE GRATED APPLE IN ANOTHER BOWL. ADD OATS AND MILK; LET SOAK FOR 5 MINUTES. ADD PORK, GARLIC, SAGE, I TSP (5 ML) SALT AND 1/4 TSP (I ML) PEPPER; MIX WELL. SCOOP TABLESPOONFULS (15 ML) OF MEAT MIXTURE AND ROLL INTO MEATBALLS. IN A SKILLET, HEAT OIL OVER MEDIUM-HIGH HEAT. BROWN MEATBALLS, IN BATCHES IF NECESSARY. TRANSFER TO SLOW COOKER. REDUCE HEAT TO MEDIUM. ADD ONION TO SKILLET AND COOK, STIRRING OCCASIONALLY, FOR

3 MINUTES. STIR IN CINNAMON, APPLE JELLY, RESERVED APPLE JUICE AND VINEGAR; COOK, STIRRING, UNTIL APPLE JELLY IS DISSOLVED. POUR OVER MEATBALLS. COVER AND COOK ON LOW FOR ABOUT 6 HOURS OR ON HIGH FOR ABOUT 3 HOURS, UNTIL MEATBALLS ARE NO LONGER PINK INSIDE. STIR IN RED PEPPER AND EDAMAME. COVER AND COOK ON HIGH FOR ABOUT 20 MINUTES, UNTIL VEGETABLES ARE TENDER-CRISP. MAKES ABOUT 20 MEATBALLS; SERVES 4 TO 6.

TIP: APPLE JELLY CAN USUALLY BE FOUND NEAR THE JAMS AND OTHER PRESERVES IN THE SUPERMARKET. YOU CAN SUBSTITUTE APRICOT, PINEAPPLE OR PEACH JAM.

TIP: LOOK FOR COOKED SHELLED EDAMAME (ALSO KNOWN AS GREEN SOYBEANS) IN THE FREEZER SECTION OF THE SUPERMARKET. EDAMAME BEANS, WHICH RESEMBLE SMALL LIMA BEANS, ARE DELICIOUS AND NUTRITIOUS. THEY'RE IDEAL FOR ADDING TO STIR-FRIES, AS THEY ONLY REQUIRE REHEATING.

SWEET CHILI PORK MEATLOAF

TOO GOOD TO BE MEATLOAF!

1/2 CUP	FRESH BREAD CRUMBS	125 ML
1/2 CUP	MILK	125 ML
4	CLOVES GARLIC, MINCED	4
2 TBSP	FINELY CHOPPED GINGERROOT	30 ML
2	EGGS, LIGHTLY BEATEN	2
1/4 CUP	HOISIN SAUCE	60 ML
2 TSP	ASIAN CHILI PASTE	10 ML
2 LBS	LEAN GROUND PORK	1 KG
1/4 CUP	SWEET CHILI DIPPING SAUCE	60 ML
6	GREEN ONIONS, CHOPPED	6

USE A 5- TO 6-QUART SLOW COOKER. FOLD A 2-FOOT (60 CM) PIECE OF FOIL IN HALF LENGTHWISE. PLACE LENGTHWISE ALONG BOTTOM OF SLOW COOKER, BRINGING ENDS UP THE SIDES AND OVER THE RIM. IN A BOWL, COMBINE BREAD CRUMBS AND MILK; LET SOAK FOR 5 MINUTES. STIR IN GARLIC, GINGER, EGGS, HOISIN SAUCE AND CHILI PASTE. ADD PORK AND MIX WELL. TRANSFER MIXTURE TO MIDDLE OF FOIL IN PREPARED SLOW COOKER AND, USING A SPATULA, SHAPE INTO A LOAF. COVER, TUCKING FOIL ENDS UNDER LID, AND COOK ON LOW FOR 8 TO 10 HOURS OR ON HIGH FOR 4 TO 5 HOURS, UNTIL AN INSTANT-READ THERMOMETER INSERTED IN THE CENTER REGISTERS 160°F (71°C) AND JUICES RUN CLEAR WHEN MEATLOAF IS PIERCED. BRUSH TOP OF MEATLOAF WITH SWEET CHILI SAUCE. COVER AND COOK ON HIGH FOR 15 MINUTES. GRASP FOIL ENDS AND LIFT OUT MEATLOAF, DRAINING OFF ACCUMULATED FAT. TRANSFER TO A CUTTING BOARD AND LET REST FOR 10 MINUTES BEFORE SLICING. SPRINKLE WITH GREEN ONIONS. SERVES 6 TO 8.

TURKEY AND CHICKEN

CRANBERRY-GLAZED TURKEY MEATLOAF

MEATLOAF IS ENJOYING A REVIVAL. THIS GUEST-WORTHY VERSION IS ADAPTED FROM A RECIPE BY BRANDON BOONE OF FLAVOURS MAGAZINE. SERVE WITH MASHED MAPLE GINGER SQUASH (PAGE 277) AND A STEAMED GREEN VEGETABLE.

4 TBSP	CANNED JELLIED CRANBERRY SAUCE, DIVIDED	60 ML
I TSP	CHOPPED CHIPOTLE PEPPER IN ADOBO SAUCE	5 ML
I CUP	FRESH BREAD CRUMBS	250 ML
1/2 CUP	MILK	125 ML
I TBSP	VEGETABLE OIL	15 ML
I CUP	FINELY CHOPPED ONION	250 ML
I	SMALL CARROT, GRATED	I
4	CLOVES GARLIC, MINCED	4
1/2 TSP	SALT	2 ML
1/4 TSP	PEPPER	I ML
1/4 CUP	CHOPPED FRESH PARSLEY	60 ML
I	EGG, LIGHTLY BEATEN	I
I TBSP	SOY SAUCE	15 ML
2 LBS	LEAN GROUND TURKEY	I KG
4 OZ	BACK BACON (CANADIAN BACON) OR GOOD-QUALITY HAM, CHOPPED	125 G

USE A 5- TO 6-QUART SLOW COOKER. FOLD A 2-FOOT (60 CM) LENGTH OF FOIL IN HALF LENGTHWISE. PLACE LENGTHWISE ALONG BOTTOM OF SLOW COOKER, BRINGING ENDS UP THE SIDES AND OVER THE RIM. IN A BOWL, COMBINE 3 TBSP (45 ML) CRANBERRY SAUCE AND CHIPOTLE PEPPER; COVER AND SET ASIDE. IN ANOTHER

BOWL, COMBINE BREAD CRUMBS AND MILK; LET SOAK FOR 5 MINUTES. MEANWHILE, IN A SKILLET, HEAT OIL OVER MEDIUM HEAT. ADD ONION, CARROT, GARLIC, SALT AND PEPPER; COOK, STIRRING OCCASIONALLY, FOR 3 MINUTES. LET COOL SLIGHTLY, THEN SCRAPE INTO BREAD CRUMB MIXTURE. STIR IN PARSLEY, EGG, SOY SAUCE AND REMAINING CRANBERRY SAUCE. ADD TURKEY AND BACON; MIX WELL. TRANSFER MEAT MIXTURE TO MIDDLE OF FOIL IN PREPARED SLOW COOKER AND, USING A SPATULA, SHAPE INTO A LOAF. COVER, TUCKING FOIL ENDS UNDER LID, AND COOK ON LOW FOR 8 TO 10 HOURS OR ON HIGH FOR 4 TO 5 HOURS, UNTIL AN INSTANT-READ THERMOMETER INSERTED IN THE CENTER REGISTERS 165°F (74°C) AND JUICES RUN CLEAR WHEN MEATLOAF IS PIERCED. BRUSH TOP OF MEATLOAF WITH RESERVED CRANBERRY SAUCE MIXTURE. COVER AND COOK ON HIGH FOR 15 MINUTES. GRASP FOIL ENDS AND LIFT OUT MEATLOAF, DRAINING OFF ACCUMULATED FAT. TRANSFER TO A CUTTING BOARD AND LET REST FOR 10 MINUTES BEFORE SLICING. SERVES 6 TO 8.

TURKEY MEATBALL KORMA

GROUND TURKEY MEATBALLS, COOKED IN A MILDLY SPICED, CREAMY COCONUT SAUCE. DEE-LISH! SERVE OVER STEAMED BASMATI RICE, WITH HOT PEPPER JELLY ON THE SIDE.

1/4 CUP	QUICK-COOKING ROLLED OATS OR DRY BREAD CRUMBS	60 ML
3 TBSP	CHOPPED FRESH CILANTRO, DIVIDED	45 ML
1/2 TSP	FINELY CHOPPED GINGERROOT	2 ML
	SALT	
1	EGG, LIGHTLY BEATEN	1
3 TBSP	MILD OR MEDIUM INDIAN CURRY PASTE, DIVIDED	45 ML
1 LB	LEAN GROUND TURKEY	500 G
1 TBSP	VEGETABLE OIL	15 ML
1	ONION, FINELY CHOPPED	1
1/2 TSP	GRANULATED SUGAR	2 ML
1 CUP	COCONUT MILK	250 ML
1/2 CUP	CHICKEN BROTH	125 ML
16	SUGAR SNAP PEAS, TRIMMED AND HALVED	16
12	GRAPE TOMATOES	12
	TOASTED ALMONDS	

USE A 3 1/2- TO 4-QUART SLOW COOKER. IN A BOWL, COMBINE OATS, 1 TBSP (15 ML) CILANTRO, GINGER, 1/4 TSP (1 ML) SALT, EGG AND 1 TBSP (15 ML) CURRY PASTE; LET STAND FOR 5 MINUTES. ADD TURKEY AND MIX WELL. SCOOP TABLESPOONFULS (15 ML) OF MEAT MIXTURE AND ROLL INTO MEATBALLS. IN A SKILLET, HEAT OIL OVER MEDIUM-HIGH HEAT. BROWN MEATBALLS, IN BATCHES IF NECESSARY. TRANSFER TO SLOW COOKER. REDUCE HEAT

TO MEDIUM. ADD ONION AND REMAINING CURRY PASTE TO SKILLET; COOK, STIRRING OCCASIONALLY, FOR 3 MINUTES. STIR IN SUGAR, COCONUT MILK AND BROTH; BRING TO A BOIL. POUR OVER MEATBALLS. COVER AND COOK ON LOW FOR ABOUT 6 HOURS OR ON HIGH FOR ABOUT 3 HOURS, UNTIL MEATBALLS ARE NO LONGER PINK INSIDE. STIR IN PEAS, TOMATOES AND REMAINING CILANTRO. COVER AND COOK ON HIGH FOR 20 TO 30 MINUTES, UNTIL VEGETABLES ARE HEATED THROUGH. ADJUST SEASONING WITH SALT, IF DESIRED. SERVE SPRINKLED WITH ALMONDS. MAKES ABOUT 20 MEATBALLS; SERVES 4 TO 6.

TIP: IT'S EASY TO CHECK WHETHER YOU HAVE CORRECTLY SEASONED THE MEAT MIXTURE FOR MEATBALLS, MEATLOAF OR BURGERS. HEAT A SMALL SKILLET OVER MEDIUM-HIGH HEAT AND FRY 1 TSP (5 ML) OF THE MIXTURE FOR 2 TO 3 MINUTES, UNTIL NO LONGER PINK INSIDE. TASTE THE COOKED SAMPLE. IF DESIRED, ADJUST THE SEASONING IN THE REMAINING MIXTURE BEFORE SHAPING IT.

EASY CHICKEN CHASSEUR

CHICKEN LEGS ARE CHEAP, SO USE GOOD WINE AND ENJOY THE REST WITH DINNER. SERVE WITH MASHED POTATOES AND BUTTERY STEAMED CARROTS.

4	SKIN-ON BONE-IN CHICKEN LEGS	4
	SALT AND PEPPER	
I TBSP	OLIVE OIL	15 ML
2	ONIONS, CHOPPED	2
4	CLOVES GARLIC, MINCED	4
3 CUPS	WHOLE MUSHROOMS	750 ML
1/2 TSP	DRIED THYME	2 ML
2 TBSP	TOMATO PASTE	30 ML
2 TBSP	ALL-PURPOSE FLOUR	30 ML
I CUP	DRY RED WINE	250 ML
1/2 CUP	CHICKEN BROTH	125 ML
1/4 CUP	CHOPPED FRESH PARSLEY	60 ML

USE A 5- TO 6-QUART SLOW COOKER. SEASON CHICKEN WELL WITH SALT AND PEPPER. IN A SKILLET, HEAT OIL OVER MEDIUM HEAT. BROWN CHICKEN ON BOTH SIDES. TRANSFER TO SLOW COOKER. DRAIN OFF ALL BUT I TBSP (15 ML) FAT FROM SKILLET. ADD ONIONS, GARLIC, MUSHROOMS, THYME, I TSP (5 ML) SALT, 1/4 TSP (I ML) PEPPER AND TOMATO PASTE; COOK, STIRRING, FOR 5 MINUTES. STIR IN FLOUR. WHISK IN WINE AND BROTH, SCRAPING UP BROWN BITS FROM BOTTOM OF PAN; BRING TO A BOIL. POUR OVER CHICKEN. COVER AND COOK ON LOW FOR 5 TO 6 HOURS OR ON HIGH FOR 2 1/2 TO 3 HOURS, UNTIL JUICES RUN CLEAR WHEN CHICKEN IS PIERCED. STIR IN PARSLEY. ADJUST SEASONING WITH SALT AND PEPPER, IF DESIRED. SERVES 4.

BUTTER CHICKEN

A POPULAR INDIAN DISH WITH A HEAVENLY AROMA.

8	SKINLESS BONE-IN CHICKEN THIGHS OR DRUMSTICKS	8
1	2-INCH (5 CM) CINNAMON STICK	1
1/4 CUP	BUTTER	60 ML
2	LARGE ONIONS, FINELY CHOPPED	2
6	CLOVES GARLIC, MINCED	6
2 TBSP	FINELY CHOPPED GINGERROOT	30 ML
2 TBSP	MILD OR MEDIUM INDIAN CURRY PASTE	30 ML
1 TBSP	TOMATO PASTE	15 ML
1	CAN (14 OZ/398 ML) TOMATO SAUCE	1
1 CUP	GRAPE OR CHERRY TOMATOES, HALVED	250 ML
1 CUP	FROZEN BABY PEAS (NO NEED TO THAW)	250 ML
1 CUP	EVAPORATED MILK	250 ML
	SALT (OPTIONAL)	

PLACE CHICKEN AND CINNAMON STICK IN A 5- TO 6-QUART SLOW COOKER. IN A SKILLET, MELT BUTTER OVER MEDIUM HEAT. ADD ONIONS, GARLIC, GINGER, CURRY PASTE AND TOMATO PASTE; COOK, STIRRING OCCASIONALLY, FOR 5 MINUTES. STIR IN TOMATO SAUCE AND BRING TO A BOIL. POUR OVER CHICKEN, TURNING CHICKEN TO COAT. COVER AND COOK ON LOW FOR 5 TO 6 HOURS OR ON HIGH FOR $2\frac{1}{2}$ TO 3 HOURS, UNTIL JUICES RUN CLEAR WHEN CHICKEN IS PIERCED. DISCARD CINNAMON STICK. STIR IN GRAPE TOMATOES, PEAS AND MILK. COVER AND COOK ON HIGH FOR ABOUT 30 MINUTES, UNTIL TOMATOES AND PEAS ARE HOT AND SAUCE IS BUBBLING. ADJUST SEASONING WITH SALT, IF DESIRED. *SERVES 4 TO 6.*

CHICKEN "CATCH-A-TORY"

*THE SLOW COOKER SOLUTION TO OUR OLD FAVORITE.
SERVE LADLED OVER MUSHROOM PARMESAN
POLENTA (PAGE 298).*

8	SKINLESS BONE-IN CHICKEN THIGHS OR DRUMSTICKS	8
4	CLOVES GARLIC, MINCED	4
3	STALKS CELERY, FINELY CHOPPED	3
2	CARROTS, FINELY CHOPPED	2
1	LARGE ONION, FINELY CHOPPED	1
1 1/2 TSP	DRIED ITALIAN SEASONING OR BASIL	7 ML
	SALT AND PEPPER	
2 TBSP	TOMATO PASTE	30 ML
1 TBSP	VEGETABLE OIL	15 ML
3 CUPS	SLICED CREMINI MUSHROOMS	750 ML
1 CUP	TOMATO SAUCE	250 ML
1/2 CUP	CHICKEN BROTH	125 ML
1 TBSP	BALSAMIC VINEGAR	15 ML

PLACE CHICKEN IN A 5- TO 6-QUART SLOW COOKER. IN
A MICROWAVE-SAFE BOWL, COMBINE GARLIC, CELERY,
CARROTS, ONION, ITALIAN SEASONING, 1 TSP (5 ML)
SALT, 1/4 TSP (1 ML) PEPPER, TOMATO PASTE AND
OIL. MICROWAVE ON HIGH FOR 7 MINUTES, STOPPING
THREE TIMES TO STIR. SCRAPE OVER CHICKEN. STIR IN
MUSHROOMS, TOMATO SAUCE AND BROTH, TURNING
CHICKEN TO COAT. COVER AND COOK ON LOW FOR 5 TO
6 HOURS OR ON HIGH FOR 2 1/2 TO 3 HOURS, UNTIL JUICES
RUN CLEAR WHEN CHICKEN IS PIERCED. TRANSFER CHICKEN
TO A SERVING DISH. STIR VINEGAR INTO SAUCE. ADJUST

SEASONING WITH SALT AND PEPPER, IF DESIRED. SERVE CHICKEN TOPPED WITH SAUCE. SERVES 4 TO 6.

TIP: YOU'LL PROBABLY HAVE TO BUY THE BONE-IN CHICKEN THIGHS WITH THE SKIN ON. TO REMOVE THE SKIN, USE A PIECE OF PAPER TOWEL TO GRAB THE SKIN AT ONE END. PULL FIRMLY. THE SKIN SHOULD PEEL RIGHT OFF.

TIP: FOR A THICKER SAUCE, COMBINE 1 TBSP (15 ML) CORNSTARCH AND 2 TBSP (30 ML) COLD WATER. STIR INTO SAUCE AFTER REMOVING THE COOKED CHICKEN. COOK, UNCOVERED AND STIRRING, ON HIGH FOR 5 MINUTES, UNTIL THICKENED, BEFORE ADDING THE VINEGAR.

WARNING: CONSUMPTION OF ALCOHOL MAY
LEAD YOU TO THINK THEY ARE LAUGHING WITH YOU.

BARBECUE CHICKEN CASSEROLE

YEAR-ROUND BARBECUE FLAVORS. SERVE WITH BAKED POTATOES AND STEAMED BROCCOLI. DOUBLE THE RECIPE AND SAVE LEFTOVERS FOR BARBECUE CHICKEN AND PINEAPPLE PIZZA (PAGE 215).

8	SKINLESS BONE-IN CHICKEN THIGHS OR DRUMSTICKS	8
1 TBSP	VEGETABLE OIL	15 ML
2	ONIONS, CHOPPED	2
3	CLOVES GARLIC, MINCED	3
2 TBSP	PACKED BROWN SUGAR	30 ML
1 TBSP	DRY MUSTARD	15 ML
	SALT AND PEPPER	
1 CUP	TOMATO-BASED CHILI SAUCE	250 ML
1/2 CUP	CHICKEN BROTH	125 ML
1 TBSP	WORCESTERSHIRE SAUCE	15 ML
1	RED OR GREEN BELL PEPPER, CHOPPED	1

PLACE CHICKEN IN A 5- TO 6-QUART SLOW COOKER. IN A SKILLET, HEAT OIL OVER MEDIUM HEAT. ADD ONIONS AND GARLIC; COOK, STIRRING OCCASIONALLY, FOR 5 MINUTES. STIR IN BROWN SUGAR, MUSTARD, 1/2 TSP (2 ML) SALT, 1/4 TSP (1 ML) PEPPER, CHILI SAUCE, BROTH AND WORCESTERSHIRE SAUCE; BRING TO A BOIL. POUR OVER CHICKEN. COVER AND COOK ON LOW FOR 5 TO 6 HOURS OR ON HIGH FOR 2 1/2 TO 3 HOURS, UNTIL JUICES RUN CLEAR WHEN CHICKEN IS PIERCED. ADD RED PEPPER. COVER AND COOK ON HIGH FOR ABOUT 20 MINUTES, UNTIL PEPPER IS TENDER. SERVES 4 TO 6.

BARBECUE CHICKEN AND PINEAPPLE PIZZA

A NEW DINNER MADE FROM LEFTOVER BARBECUE CHICKEN CASSEROLE (PAGE 214).

4	LEFTOVER COOKED CHICKEN THIGHS	4
1 CUP	LEFTOVER SAUCE AND VEGETABLES (APPROX.)	250 ML
1	UNBAKED 12- OR 14-INCH (30 OR 35 CM) PIZZA CRUST	1
1	GREEN BELL PEPPER, THINLY SLICED	1
1 CUP	DRAINED CANNED PINEAPPLE CHUNKS	250 ML
1 1/2 CUPS	SHREDDED MOZZARELLA CHEESE	375 ML

PREHEAT OVEN TO 400°F (200°C). LIGHTLY OIL A 12- OR 14-INCH (30 OR 35 CM) PIZZA PAN. PLACE CHICKEN ON A CUTTING BOARD AND SHRED OR SLICE MEAT, DISCARDING BONES. TRANSFER CHICKEN TO A BOWL. ADD SAUCE AND VEGETABLES, TOSSING TO COAT. ADD MORE SAUCE (OR YOUR FAVORITE BOTTLED BARBECUE SAUCE), IF NECESSARY, TO REACH DESIRED CONSISTENCY. PLACE PIZZA CRUST ON PREPARED PAN. SPREAD CHICKEN MIXTURE EVENLY OVER CRUST. ARRANGE GREEN PEPPER AND PINEAPPLE ON TOP. SPRINKLE WITH CHEESE. BAKE FOR 12 TO 15 MINUTES, UNTIL CRUST IS BROWNED AND CHEESE IS BUBBLY. MAKES 8 SLICES.

CHICKEN WITH TOMATOES AND HONEY

THIS AROMATIC STEW HAS A HINT OF MIDDLE EASTERN FLAVORS. SERVE WITH STEAMED COUSCOUS OR MASHED POTATOES AND A STEAMED GREEN VEGETABLE.

8	SKINLESS BONE-IN CHICKEN THIGHS OR DRUMSTICKS	8
I	2-INCH (5 CM) CINNAMON STICK	I
2 TBSP	BUTTER OR OLIVE OIL	30 ML
2	ONIONS, FINELY CHOPPED	2
4	CLOVES GARLIC, MINCED	4
	SALT AND PEPPER	
I	CAN (28 OZ/796 ML) WHOLE TOMATOES, WITH JUICE	I
$1/8$ TSP	CRUSHED SAFFRON THREADS (OPTIONAL)	0.5 ML
2 TBSP	LIQUID HONEY	30 ML
$1/4$ CUP	CHOPPED FRESH PARSLEY	60 ML
I TBSP	FRESHLY SQUEEZED LEMON JUICE	15 ML
2 TBSP	TOASTED SLIVERED OR FLAKED ALMONDS	30 ML
I TBSP	TOASTED SESAME SEEDS	15 ML

PLACE CHICKEN AND CINNAMON STICK IN A 5- TO 6-QUART SLOW COOKER. IN A SKILLET, MELT BUTTER OVER MEDIUM HEAT. ADD ONIONS, GARLIC, I TSP (5 ML) SALT AND $1/4$ TSP (I ML) PEPPER; COOK, STIRRING OCCASIONALLY, FOR 5 MINUTES. STIR IN TOMATOES, SAFFRON (IF USING) AND HONEY, BREAKING TOMATOES UP WITH A SPOON; BRING TO A BOIL. POUR OVER CHICKEN. COVER AND COOK ON LOW FOR 5 TO 6 HOURS OR ON HIGH FOR $2^1/2$ TO 3 HOURS, UNTIL JUICES RUN CLEAR WHEN CHICKEN IS PIERCED.

STIR IN PARSLEY AND LEMON JUICE. ADJUST SEASONING WITH SALT AND PEPPER, IF DESIRED. COVER AND COOK ON HIGH FOR 10 MINUTES TO BLEND THE FLAVORS. SERVE SPRINKLED WITH ALMONDS AND SESAME SEEDS. SERVES 4 TO 6.

TIP: SAFFRON IS A VIVID YELLOW-ORANGE SPICE THAT'S MADE FROM THE DRIED STIGMAS OF A TYPE OF CROCUS. COMMON IN MIDDLE EASTERN COOKING, SAFFRON HAS A UNIQUE, SLIGHTLY BITTER FLAVOR. LEAVE IT OUT IF YOU DON'T HAVE IT, BUT DON'T SUBSTITUTE TURMERIC; ALTHOUGH SIMILAR IN COLOR, TURMERIC TASTES QUITE DIFFERENT.

HOISIN ORANGE CHICKEN

A WEEKNIGHT WINNER. SERVE WITH STEAMED RICE AND WITH SUGAR SNAP PEAS TOSSED WITH BUTTER AND CHOPPED FRESH MINT.

8	SKINLESS BONE-IN CHICKEN THIGHS OR DRUMSTICKS	8
4	GREEN ONIONS	4
3	CLOVES GARLIC, MINCED	3
1 TBSP	MINCED GINGERROOT	15 ML
1/4 CUP	ORANGE JUICE	60 ML
3 TBSP	HOISIN SAUCE	45 ML
2 TBSP	LIQUID HONEY	30 ML
2 TBSP	RICE OR CIDER VINEGAR	30 ML
1 TBSP	CORNSTARCH	15 ML
2 TBSP	COLD WATER	30 ML
1	RED BELL PEPPER, CHOPPED	1
	TOASTED SESAME SEEDS	

PLACE CHICKEN IN A 4- TO 6-QUART SLOW COOKER. CHOP GREEN ONIONS, SEPARATING WHITE AND GREEN PARTS. SPRINKLE WHITE PARTS OVER CHICKEN. COVER AND SET ASIDE GREEN PARTS. IN A BOWL, WHISK TOGETHER GARLIC, GINGER, ORANGE JUICE, HOISIN SAUCE, HONEY AND VINEGAR. POUR OVER CHICKEN, TURNING CHICKEN TO COAT. COVER AND COOK ON LOW FOR 5 TO 6 HOURS OR ON HIGH FOR $2\frac{1}{2}$ TO 3 HOURS, UNTIL JUICES RUN CLEAR WHEN CHICKEN IS PIERCED. IN A BOWL, COMBINE CORNSTARCH AND COLD WATER UNTIL SMOOTH. STIR INTO SLOW COOKER. STIR IN RED PEPPER. COVER AND COOK ON HIGH FOR 20 MINUTES, UNTIL RED PEPPER IS TENDER AND SAUCE IS SLIGHTLY THICKENED. SERVE

CHICKEN TOPPED WITH SAUCE AND SPRINKLED WITH SESAME SEEDS AND RESERVED GREEN ONIONS. SERVES 4 TO 6.

TIP: TOASTED SESAME SEEDS ADD A NICE NUTTY FLAVOR AND TEXTURE TO THE FINISHED DISH. WHITE SESAME SEEDS ARE THE ONES MOST COMMONLY AVAILABLE IN SUPERMARKETS, BUT YOU MAY ALSO FIND YELLOW, BROWN OR BLACK SEEDS. STORE SESAME SEEDS IN AN AIRTIGHT CONTAINER IN THE REFRIGERATOR — THEY HAVE A HIGH OIL CONTENT AND MAY TURN RANCID IF KEPT AT ROOM TEMPERATURE.

FRIDAY FIESTA CHICKEN STEW

SET OUT BOWLS OF CHOPPED FRESH TOMATOES, DICED AVOCADO AND TOASTED PUMPKIN SEEDS AND LET EVERYONE GARNISH THEIR OWN PLATES. SERVE WITH WARM TEX-MEX CORNBREAD (PAGE 34).

8	SKINLESS BONE-IN CHICKEN THIGHS OR DRUMSTICKS	8
1 TBSP	VEGETABLE OIL	15 ML
2	ONIONS, FINELY CHOPPED	2
3	CLOVES GARLIC, MINCED	3
2 TSP	GROUND CUMIN	10 ML
1 TSP	DRIED OREGANO	5 ML
1/4 TSP	PEPPER	1 ML
	SALT	
1	CAN (14 OZ/398 ML) DICED TOMATOES, WITH JUICE	1
2 TSP	PACKED BROWN SUGAR	10 ML
1/2 CUP	CHICKEN BROTH	125 ML
1	RED BELL PEPPER, CHOPPED	1
1 CUP	CORN KERNELS (NO NEED TO THAW IF FROZEN)	250 ML
2 TBSP	CHOPPED FRESH CILANTRO	30 ML
1 to 2 TSP	PURÉED CHIPOTLE PEPPER (SEE TIP, OPPOSITE)	5 to 10 ML
2 TBSP	FRESHLY SQUEEZED LIME JUICE	30 ML

PLACE CHICKEN IN A 5- TO 6-QUART SLOW COOKER. IN A SKILLET, HEAT OIL OVER MEDIUM HEAT. ADD ONIONS, GARLIC, CUMIN, OREGANO, PEPPER AND 1/2 TSP (2 ML) SALT; COOK, STIRRING OCCASIONALLY, FOR 5 MINUTES. STIR IN TOMATOES, BROWN SUGAR AND BROTH; BRING TO A BOIL. POUR OVER CHICKEN, TURNING CHICKEN TO COAT.

COVER AND COOK ON LOW FOR 5 TO 6 HOURS OR ON HIGH FOR $2\frac{1}{2}$ TO 3 HOURS, UNTIL JUICES RUN CLEAR WHEN CHICKEN IS PIERCED. STIR IN RED PEPPER, CORN, CILANTRO, 1 TSP (5 ML) CHIPOTLE PEPPER AND LIME JUICE. COOK ON HIGH FOR ABOUT 20 MINUTES, UNTIL RED PEPPER IS TENDER. ADJUST SEASONING WITH SALT AND ADDITIONAL CHIPOTLE PEPPER, IF DESIRED. SERVES 4 TO 6.

TIP: CHIPOTLE PEPPERS ARE SMOKED JALAPEÑO PEPPERS PACKED IN ADOBO SAUCE, AND ARE TYPICALLY FOUND CANNED IN THE MEXICAN FOOD SECTION OF THE SUPERMARKET. PURÉE THE PEPPERS IN THEIR SAUCE, TRANSFER TO A CLEAN SCREW-TOP JAR AND STORE IN THE REFRIGERATOR FOR SEVERAL WEEKS. CHIPOTLES ARE FIERY LITTLE DEVILS, SO USE IN SMALL QUANTITIES. WASH YOUR HANDS THOROUGHLY AFTER HANDLING CHIPOTLES.

SATURDAY CHICKEN STEW WITH SWEET POTATOES

A WARM WELCOME AFTER A WHIRL OF WEEKEND ERRANDS! SERVE WITH LAZY DAYS BUTTERMILK BISCUITS (PAGE 224) OR A CRISPY BAGUETTE.

I LB	SWEET POTATOES, PEELED AND CUT INTO 2-INCH (5 CM) CHUNKS	500 G
2	CARROTS, CHOPPED	2
2	STALKS CELERY, SLICED	2
2	BAY LEAVES	2
8	SKINLESS BONE-IN CHICKEN THIGHS	8
I TBSP	OLIVE OR VEGETABLE OIL	15 ML
2	ONIONS, CHOPPED	2
4	CLOVES GARLIC, MINCED	4
1/2 TSP	DRIED THYME OR OREGANO	2 ML
	SALT AND PEPPER	
2 TBSP	ALL-PURPOSE FLOUR	30 ML
1 1/4 CUPS	CHICKEN BROTH	300 ML
3/4 CUP	UNSWEETENED APPLE JUICE	175 ML
I CUP	FROZEN PEAS (NO NEED TO THAW)	250 ML
I TBSP	CIDER VINEGAR	15 ML
1/4 CUP	CHOPPED FRESH PARSLEY	60 ML

PLACE SWEET POTATOES, CARROTS, CELERY AND BAY LEAVES A 5- TO 6-QUART SLOW COOKER. ARRANGE CHICKEN ON TOP. IN A SKILLET, HEAT OIL OVER MEDIUM HEAT. ADD ONIONS, GARLIC, THYME, I TSP (5 ML) SALT AND 1/4 TSP (I ML) PEPPER; COOK, STIRRING OCCASIONALLY, FOR 5 MINUTES. STIR IN FLOUR. WHISK IN BROTH AND APPLE JUICE; BRING TO A BOIL. POUR OVER CHICKEN. COVER AND COOK ON LOW FOR 5 TO 6 HOURS OR ON HIGH FOR 2 1/2 TO

3 HOURS, UNTIL JUICES RUN CLEAR WHEN CHICKEN IS PIERCED. STIR IN PEAS AND VINEGAR. ADJUST SEASONING WITH SALT AND PEPPER, IF DESIRED. COVER AND COOK ON HIGH FOR 15 MINUTES, UNTIL PEAS ARE HOT. DISCARD BAY LEAVES. STIR IN PARSLEY. SERVES 4 TO 6.

TIP: YOU'LL PROBABLY HAVE TO BUY THE BONE-IN CHICKEN THIGHS WITH THE SKIN ON. TO REMOVE THE SKIN, USE A PIECE OF PAPER TOWEL TO GRAB THE SKIN AT ONE END. PULL FIRMLY. THE SKIN SHOULD PEEL RIGHT OFF.

JAZZ IS MY FAVORITE COLOR OF MUSIC.
– KATEY, 5 YEARS OLD

LAZY DAYS BUTTERMILK BISCUITS

PERFECT WITH YOUR FAVORITE POT ROAST, STEW OR SOUP.

2 CUPS	ALL-PURPOSE FLOUR	500 ML
2 TSP	BAKING POWDER	10 ML
1 TSP	SALT	5 ML
1/2 TSP	BAKING SODA	2 ML
1/3 CUP	COLD UNSALTED BUTTER, ROUGHLY CUT INTO 6 TO 8 PIECES	75 ML
1 1/2 CUPS	BUTTERMILK	375 ML

PREHEAT OVEN TO 450°F (230°C). LIGHTLY GREASE 2 LARGE BAKING SHEETS OR LINE WITH PARCHMENT PAPER. IN A LARGE BOWL, SIFT TOGETHER FLOUR, BAKING POWDER, SALT AND BAKING SODA. ADD BUTTER AND RUB FLOUR MIXTURE THROUGH YOUR FINGERTIPS UNTIL IT RESEMBLES COARSE CRUMBS ABOUT THE SIZE OF SMALL PEAS. (OR USE A PASTRY BLENDER OR TWO KNIVES TO CUT IN BUTTER.) ADD BUTTERMILK AND, USING A FORK OR SPATULA, STIR JUST UNTIL DRY INGREDIENTS ARE MOISTENED. DO NOT OVERMIX. DROP BY HEAPING DESSERT SPOONFULS (THE KIND IN YOUR CUTLERY DRAWER) ONTO PREPARED BAKING SHEETS, SPACING THEM ABOUT 1 INCH (2.5 CM) APART. BAKE FOR 12 TO 15 MINUTES, UNTIL PUFFY AND LIGHTLY BROWNED. SERVE IMMEDIATELY. MAKES ABOUT 12 BISCUITS.

TIP: DON'T TRY TO REPLACE THE BUTTERMILK — IT'S WHAT MAKES THESE BISCUITS SO GOOD.

TIP: IT'S IMPORTANT TO USE COLD BUTTER AND TO BAKE IMMEDIATELY AFTER MIXING; OTHERWISE, THE DOUGH WILL SPREAD AND WON'T RISE AS WELL.

ALISON'S DAD'S CHICKEN BACON SPECIAL

ALISON'S KIDS LOVE IT — AND SO DO WE! SERVE WITH STEAMED COUSCOUS AND A CAESAR SALAD.

8	SLICES BACON	8
8	SKINLESS BONE-IN CHICKEN THIGHS	8
1	ONION, CHOPPED	1
1	APPLE, PEELED AND GRATED	1
1½ CUPS	BARBECUE SAUCE	375 ML
½ CUP	CHICKEN BROTH OR WATER	125 ML
	CHOPPED GREEN ONION AND TOMATO	

USE A 5- TO 6-QUART SLOW COOKER. WRAP ONE SLICE OF BACON AROUND EACH CHICKEN THIGH. PLACE IN SLOW COOKER. SPRINKLE ONION AND APPLE OVER TOP. POUR IN BARBECUE SAUCE AND BROTH, TURNING CHICKEN TO COAT. COVER AND COOK ON LOW FOR 5 TO 6 HOURS OR ON HIGH FOR 2½ TO 3 HOURS, UNTIL JUICES RUN CLEAR WHEN CHICKEN IS PIERCED. TRANSFER CHICKEN TO SERVING DISH. USING A SPOON, REMOVE EXCESS FAT FROM SURFACE OF SAUCE, IF NECESSARY. SERVE CHICKEN TOPPED WITH SAUCE AND SPRINKLED WITH GREEN ONION AND TOMATO. SERVES 4 TO 6.

TIP: EITHER A MILD OR A SPICY BARBECUE SAUCE WILL WORK IN THIS RECIPE. HEAT SEEKERS WILL LOVE IT MADE WITH A HOT AND SPICY BARBECUE SAUCE THAT INCLUDES JALAPEÑO AND CHIPOTLE PEPPERS. IF YOU CAN'T FIND ONE LIKE THAT, ADD 1 TSP (5 ML) CHIPOTLE CHILE POWDER OR REGULAR CHILI POWDER TO THE SAUCE ONCE THE CHICKEN IS COOKED. COVER AND COOK ON HIGH FOR 15 MINUTES TO BLEND THE FLAVORS.

CHICKEN STEW AND DUMPLINGS

JUST LIKE MOM USED TO MAKE, BUT YOU'RE NOT CHAINED TO THE STOVE.

2	CARROTS, CHOPPED	2
2	STALKS CELERY, CHOPPED	2
2	POTATOES, PEELED AND CUT INTO 1-INCH (2.5 CM) CUBES	2
2	BAY LEAVES	2
8	SKINLESS BONE-IN CHICKEN THIGHS	8
1 TBSP	VEGETABLE OIL	15 ML
2	ONIONS, CHOPPED	2
4	CLOVES GARLIC, MINCED	4
1/2 TSP	DRIED THYME	2 ML
	SALT AND PEPPER	
1 TBSP	CIDER VINEGAR	15 ML
2 TBSP	ALL-PURPOSE FLOUR	30 ML
2 CUPS	CHICKEN BROTH	500 ML

DUMPLINGS

1 1/2 CUPS	ALL-PURPOSE FLOUR	375 ML
2 TSP	BAKING POWDER	10 ML
1/2 TSP	SALT	2 ML
2 TBSP	CHOPPED FRESH PARSLEY	30 ML
1	EGG, LIGHTLY BEATEN	1
2/3 CUP	2% OR WHOLE MILK	150 ML
2 TBSP	VEGETABLE OIL	30 ML

PLACE CARROTS, CELERY, POTATOES AND BAY LEAVES IN A 5- TO 6-QUART SLOW COOKER. ARRANGE CHICKEN ON TOP. IN A SKILLET, HEAT OIL OVER MEDIUM HEAT. ADD ONIONS, GARLIC, THYME, 1 TSP (5 ML) SALT AND 1/4 TSP (1 ML)

PEPPER; COOK, STIRRING, FOR 5 MINUTES. STIR IN VINEGAR AND COOK FOR 15 SECONDS. STIR IN FLOUR. WHISK IN BROTH AND BRING TO A BOIL. POUR OVER CHICKEN. COVER AND COOK ON LOW FOR 5 TO 6 HOURS OR ON HIGH FOR $2\frac{1}{2}$ TO 3 HOURS, UNTIL JUICES RUN CLEAR WHEN CHICKEN IS PIERCED. DISCARD BAY LEAVES.

DUMPLINGS: IN A BOWL, WHISK TOGETHER FLOUR, BAKING POWDER AND SALT. IN ANOTHER BOWL, COMBINE PARSLEY, EGG, MILK AND OIL. POUR OVER FLOUR MIXTURE AND STIR UNTIL JUST COMBINED. DROP BATTER BY HEAPING TABLESPOONFULS (15 ML) ONTO STEW. COVER AND COOK ON HIGH FOR ABOUT 20 MINUTES, UNTIL DUMPLINGS ARE NO LONGER DOUGHY ON THE BOTTOM. SERVE IMMEDIATELY. SERVES 4 TO 6.

CHICKEN WITH 30 TO 40 CLOVES OF GARLIC

THIRTY? FORTY? OR SOMEWHERE IN BETWEEN? IT DOESN'T MAKE MUCH DIFFERENCE — IN THIS RETRO DINNER PARTY DISH, THE GARLIC MELLOWS TO A SUBLIME FLAVOR. MASHED POTATOES AND STEAMED RAPINI GO WELL WITH IT.

8	SKIN-ON BONE-IN CHICKEN THIGHS	8
	SALT AND PEPPER	
1 1/2 TSP	OLIVE OIL	7 ML
1 1/2 TSP	BUTTER	7 ML
2	ONIONS, FINELY CHOPPED	2
30 TO 40	PEELED CLOVES GARLIC	30 TO 40
1/2 CUP	DRY WHITE WINE	125 ML
1 CUP	CHICKEN BROTH	250 ML
2 TBSP	ALL-PURPOSE FLOUR	30 ML
3 TBSP	COLD WATER	45 ML
1/4 CUP	CHOPPED FRESH PARSLEY	60 ML

USE A 5- TO 6-QUART SLOW COOKER. SEASON CHICKEN WELL WITH SALT AND PEPPER. IN A SKILLET, HEAT OIL AND BUTTER OVER MEDIUM-HIGH HEAT. BROWN CHICKEN ON BOTH SIDES, IN TWO BATCHES. TRANSFER TO SLOW COOKER. DRAIN OFF ALL BUT 1 TBSP (15 ML) FAT FROM SKILLET. REDUCE HEAT TO MEDIUM. ADD ONIONS AND GARLIC; COOK, STIRRING OCCASIONALLY, FOR ABOUT 7 MINUTES, UNTIL LIGHT GOLDEN. STIR IN WINE, THEN BROTH, SCRAPING UP BROWN BITS FROM BOTTOM OF PAN; BRING TO A BOIL. POUR OVER CHICKEN. COVER AND COOK ON LOW FOR 5 TO 6 HOURS OR ON HIGH FOR 2 1/2 TO 3 HOURS, UNTIL JUICES RUN CLEAR WHEN CHICKEN IS

PIERCED. USING A SPOON, REMOVE EXCESS FAT FROM SURFACE OF SAUCE, IF NECESSARY. IN A SMALL BOWL, COMBINE FLOUR AND COLD WATER UNTIL SMOOTH. PUSH CHICKEN AND GARLIC TO ONE SIDE OF SLOW COOKER. WHISK FLOUR MIXTURE INTO COOKING LIQUID. STIR TO REDISTRIBUTE INGREDIENTS. COVER AND COOK ON HIGH FOR 15 MINUTES, UNTIL SAUCE IS THICKENED. SERVE SPRINKLED WITH PARSLEY. SERVES 4 TO 6.

TIP: WE USE SKIN-ON BONE-IN CHICKEN THIGHS FOR THE BEST FLAVOR IN THIS SIMPLE BRAISED DISH. SINCE THE SKIN GETS FLABBY DURING COOKING, WE RECOMMEND REMOVING IT BEFORE SERVING.

TIP: TO CUT DOWN ON PREP TIME, LOOK FOR READY-PEELED GARLIC CLOVES. MOST ITALIAN DELIS AND MANY SUPERMARKETS STOCK THEM IN THE PRODUCE SECTION. IF YOU CAN'T FIND THEM, YOU WILL NEED ABOUT 4 HEADS OF GARLIC.

CHICKEN SANTORINI

IT'S GREEK, BABY — YOU GOTTA LOVE IT! SERVE WITH STEAMED QUINOA AND FRESH CRUSTY BREAD TO MOP UP THE JUICES.

8	SKINLESS BONE-IN CHICKEN THIGHS	8
I TBSP	VEGETABLE OIL	15 ML
2	ONIONS, THINLY SLICED	2
I	FENNEL BULB, TRIMMED AND THINLY SLICED	I
4	CLOVES GARLIC, MINCED	4
I TSP	DRIED ITALIAN SEASONING	5 ML
	SALT AND PEPPER	
2 TBSP	ALL-PURPOSE FLOUR	30 ML
I1/2 CUPS	CHICKEN BROTH	375 ML
6	LARGE STUFFED GREEN OLIVES, SLICED (OPTIONAL)	6
2	SMALL ZUCCHINI, CHOPPED	2
I	RED BELL PEPPER, CHOPPED	I
1/4 CUP	CHOPPED FRESH PARSLEY	60 ML
	GRATED ZEST OF 1/2 LEMON	

PLACE CHICKEN IN A 5- TO 6-QUART SLOW COOKER. IN A SKILLET, HEAT OIL OVER MEDIUM HEAT. ADD ONIONS, FENNEL, GARLIC, ITALIAN SEASONING, 1/2 TSP (2 ML) SALT AND 1/4 TSP (I ML) PEPPER; COOK, STIRRING OCCASIONALLY, FOR 5 MINUTES. STIR IN FLOUR. WHISK IN BROTH AND BRING TO A BOIL. POUR OVER CHICKEN. COVER AND COOK ON LOW FOR 5 TO 6 HOURS OR ON HIGH FOR 21/2 TO 3 HOURS, UNTIL JUICES RUN CLEAR WHEN CHICKEN IS PIERCED. STIR IN OLIVES (IF USING), ZUCCHINI AND RED PEPPER. COVER AND COOK ON HIGH FOR 20 TO

30 MINUTES, UNTIL ZUCCHINI AND RED PEPPER ARE TENDER. ADJUST SEASONING WITH SALT AND PEPPER, IF DESIRED. SERVE SPRINKLED WITH PARSLEY AND LEMON ZEST. SERVES 4 TO 6.

TIP: FENNEL BULB IS LABELED "ANISE" IN SOME SUPERMARKETS. IF IT HAS FEATHERY STALKS ATTACHED, TRIM THEM OFF ABOUT 1 INCH (2.5 CM) ABOVE THE BULB. CUT THE BULB IN HALF VERTICALLY AND REMOVE THE WOODY CORE FROM EACH HALF. CUT EACH HALF CROSSWISE INTO VERY THIN STRIPS.

WATER IS COMPOSED OF TWO GINS: OXYGIN AND HYDROGIN. OXYGIN IS PURE GIN. HYDROGIN IS GIN AND WATER.
– SAM, 11 YEARS OLD

FRAGRANT CHICKEN CURRY

AN AUTHENTIC AND AROMATIC CREAMY CURRY APPEALS TO THOSE WHO PREFER MILDLY SPICED FOOD. SERVE OVER STEAMED BASMATI RICE, WITH MANGO CHUTNEY.

8	SKINLESS BONE-IN CHICKEN THIGHS	8
1 TBSP	VEGETABLE OIL	15 ML
2	BAY LEAVES	2
1	2-INCH (5 CM) CINNAMON STICK	1
2 TSP	CUMIN SEEDS	10 ML
2	ONIONS, THINLY SLICED	2
6	CLOVES GARLIC, MINCED	6
2 TBSP	MILD OR MEDIUM INDIAN CURRY PASTE	30 ML
1 TBSP	TOMATO PASTE	15 ML
1 TBSP	ALL-PURPOSE FLOUR	15 ML
1 CUP	CHICKEN BROTH	250 ML
1/2 CUP	PLAIN YOGURT OR SOUR CREAM	125 ML
1	RED BELL PEPPER, CHOPPED	1
	SALT (OPTIONAL)	
	CHOPPED TOASTED ALMONDS, CHOPPED FRESH MINT AND LIME WEDGES	

PLACE CHICKEN IN A 4- TO 6-QUART SLOW COOKER. IN A SKILLET, HEAT OIL OVER MEDIUM-HIGH HEAT. ADD BAY LEAVES, CINNAMON STICK AND CUMIN SEEDS; COOK, WITHOUT STIRRING, UNTIL CINNAMON STICK BEGINS TO UNFURL, ABOUT 30 SECONDS. REDUCE HEAT TO MEDIUM. ADD ONIONS, GARLIC, CURRY PASTE AND TOMATO PASTE; COOK, STIRRING OCCASIONALLY, FOR 5 MINUTES. STIR IN FLOUR. WHISK IN BROTH AND BRING TO A BOIL. POUR OVER

CHICKEN, TURNING CHICKEN TO COAT. COVER AND COOK ON LOW FOR 5 TO 6 HOURS OR ON HIGH FOR $2\frac{1}{2}$ TO 3 HOURS, UNTIL JUICES RUN CLEAR WHEN CHICKEN IS PIERCED. DISCARD CINNAMON STICKS AND BAY LEAVES. IN A BOWL, COMBINE YOGURT AND $\frac{1}{2}$ CUP (125 ML) OF THE COOKING LIQUID. STIR INTO SLOW COOKER. STIR IN RED PEPPER. COVER AND COOK ON HIGH FOR ABOUT 20 MINUTES, UNTIL RED PEPPER IS TENDER AND SAUCE IS BUBBLING. ADJUST SEASONING WITH SALT, IF DESIRED. SERVE GARNISHED WITH ALMONDS, MINT AND LIME WEDGES FOR SQUEEZING. SERVES 4 TO 6.

TIP: GROUND SPICES TEND TO LOSE THEIR FLAVOR IN THE LONG, MOIST HEAT OF THE SLOW COOKER. BUT WHOLE SPICES, SUCH AS CINNAMON STICKS, BAY LEAVES AND CUMIN SEEDS, FARE VERY WELL. THEY GRADUALLY RELEASE THEIR OILS INTO THE LIQUID, RESULTING IN A VERY TASTY SAUCE.

VARIATION: IF YOU LIKE MORE HEAT IN YOUR CURRY, ADD $\frac{1}{4}$ TO $\frac{1}{2}$ TSP (1 TO 2 ML) CAYENNE PEPPER WITH THE YOGURT MIXTURE. OR USE A HOT CURRY PASTE INSTEAD OF MILD OR MEDIUM.

EASY CHICKEN CURRY

THIS GOES TOGETHER FAST! SERVE WITH STEAMED BASMATI RICE AND WARM NAAN.

1 TBSP	VEGETABLE OIL	15 ML
2	ONIONS, THINLY SLICED	2
4	CLOVES GARLIC, MINCED	4
1 TBSP	FINELY CHOPPED GINGERROOT	15 ML
1/4 CUP	MILD OR MEDIUM INDIAN CURRY PASTE	60 ML
8	BONELESS SKINLESS CHICKEN THIGHS	8
1	CAN (14 OZ/398 ML) WHOLE TOMATOES, WITH JUICE	1
2 TBSP	MANGO CHUTNEY OR APRICOT JAM	30 ML
1	RED BELL PEPPER, CHOPPED	1
1 1/2 CUPS	FROZEN WHOLE GREEN BEANS, THAWED	375 ML
2 TBSP	CHOPPED FRESH CILANTRO	30 ML
	SALT (OPTIONAL)	

USE A 4- TO 6-QUART SLOW COOKER. IN A LARGE SKILLET, HEAT OIL OVER MEDIUM HEAT. ADD ONIONS, GARLIC, GINGER AND CURRY PASTE; COOK, STIRRING OCCASIONALLY, FOR 5 MINUTES. STIR IN CHICKEN. STIR IN TOMATOES AND CHUTNEY, BREAKING TOMATOES UP WITH A SPOON. TRANSFER TO SLOW COOKER. COVER AND COOK ON LOW FOR 5 TO 6 HOURS OR ON HIGH FOR 2 1/2 TO 3 HOURS, UNTIL JUICES RUN CLEAR WHEN CHICKEN IS PIERCED. STIR IN RED PEPPER, BEANS AND CILANTRO. COVER AND COOK ON HIGH FOR ABOUT 30 MINUTES, UNTIL RED PEPPER AND BEANS ARE TENDER. ADJUST SEASONING WITH SALT, IF DESIRED. *SERVES 4 TO 6.*

TIP: WE ALWAYS REACH FOR INDIAN CURRY PASTES, RATHER THAN CURRY POWDER, WHEN WE WANT TO MAKE A CURRY. THE SPICES IN THE PASTES — WHICH COME IN MILD, MEDIUM AND HOT — ARE PRESERVED IN OIL, SO THEY ARE MORE AUTHENTIC AND LESS HARSH-TASTING THAN POWDERS. WE PARTICULARLY LIKE THE PATAK'S BRAND, WHICH IS WIDELY AVAILABLE.

TIP: DARK CHICKEN MEAT, SUCH AS THIGHS AND DRUMSTICKS, WORKS BEST IN THE SLOW COOKER, AS IT STAYS MOIST AND HAS LOTS OF FLAVOR. IF YOU PREFER TO MAKE THIS CURRY (OR ANY OTHER CHICKEN RECIPE IN THIS BOOK) WITH 4 BONELESS SKINLESS CHICKEN BREASTS, COOK IT NO LONGER THAN 5 HOURS ON LOW; OTHERWISE, THE MEAT WILL BECOME DRY.

CREAMY CHICKEN AND MUSHROOMS WITH PASTA

RICH AND DELICIOUS. SERVE WITH A GREEN SALAD AND GARLIC BREAD.

8	BONELESS SKINLESS CHICKEN THIGHS, CUT INTO BITE-SIZE PIECES	8
1 TBSP	VEGETABLE OIL	15 ML
1	LARGE ONION, FINELY CHOPPED	1
1	STALK CELERY, THINLY SLICED	1
2	CLOVES GARLIC, MINCED	2
3 CUPS	SLICED MUSHROOMS	750 ML
1/2 TSP	DRIED OREGANO	2 ML
	SALT AND PEPPER	
1 TBSP	TOMATO PASTE	15 ML
2 TBSP	ALL-PURPOSE FLOUR	30 ML
2 CUPS	CHICKEN BROTH	500 ML
1/4 CUP	CHOPPED FRESH PARSLEY	60 ML
1/2 CUP	HEAVY OR WHIPPING (35%) CREAM, WARMED	125 ML
12 OZ	PENNE OR FUSILLI PASTA (ABOUT 4 CUPS/1 L)	375 G
	GRATED PARMESAN CHEESE	

PLACE CHICKEN IN A 3 1/2- TO 4-QUART SLOW COOKER. IN A SKILLET, HEAT OIL OVER MEDIUM HEAT. ADD ONION, CELERY, GARLIC, MUSHROOMS, OREGANO, 1/2 TSP (2 ML) SALT, 1/4 TSP (1 ML) PEPPER AND TOMATO PASTE; COOK, STIRRING OCCASIONALLY, FOR 5 MINUTES. STIR IN FLOUR. WHISK IN BROTH AND BRING TO A BOIL. POUR OVER CHICKEN AND STIR WELL. COVER AND COOK ON LOW FOR 5 TO 6 HOURS OR ON HIGH FOR 2 1/2 TO 3 HOURS,

UNTIL CHICKEN IS TENDER AND SAUCE IS BUBBLING.
STIR IN PARSLEY AND CREAM. MEANWHILE, IN A LARGE
POT OF BOILING WATER, COOK PASTA ACCORDING TO
PACKAGE INSTRUCTIONS. DRAIN PASTA AND ADD TO SLOW
COOKER. STIR TO COMBINE WITH CHICKEN MIXTURE.
ADJUST SEASONING WITH SALT AND PEPPER, IF DESIRED.
LET STAND, UNCOVERED, ON LOW FOR 5 MINUTES TO
LET SAUCE THICKEN SLIGHTLY. SERVE SPRINKLED WITH
PARMESAN. SERVES 4 TO 6.

TIP: FOR A DEEPER MUSHROOM FLAVOR, USE CREMINI
MUSHROOMS (SOMETIMES LABELED "BROWN
MUSHROOMS").

PANTRY RAID CHICKEN CHILI

A FEW HANDY INGREDIENTS MAKE THIS SWEET AND SAUCY CHILI SO EASY. SERVE WITH EASY CORNBREAD (PAGE 33) OR TEX-MEX CORNBREAD (PAGE 34).

8	BONELESS SKINLESS CHICKEN THIGHS, CUT INTO BITE-SIZE PIECES	8
I TBSP	VEGETABLE OIL	15 ML
I	LARGE ONION, FINELY CHOPPED	I
3	CLOVES GARLIC, CHOPPED	3
2 TSP	GROUND CUMIN	10 ML
I	CAN (14 OZ/398 ML) CHIPOTLE BARBECUE–STYLE BEANS (SEE TIP, OPPOSITE)	I
I CUP	CANNED WHOLE TOMATOES, WITH JUICE	250 ML
$\frac{1}{2}$ CUP	TOMATO-BASED CHILI SAUCE	125 ML
$\frac{1}{2}$ CUP	CANNED JELLIED CRANBERRY SAUCE	125 ML
2 TSP	CHILI POWDER	10 ML
I TBSP	FRESHLY SQUEEZED LEMON JUICE	15 ML
I	RED OR GREEN BELL PEPPER, CHOPPED	I
	SALT (OPTIONAL)	
	SHREDDED TEX-MEX CHEESE BLEND OR CHEDDAR CHEESE	

PLACE CHICKEN IN A $3\frac{1}{2}$- TO 4-QUART SLOW COOKER. IN A SKILLET, HEAT OIL OVER MEDIUM HEAT. ADD ONION, GARLIC AND CUMIN; COOK, STIRRING OCCASIONALLY, FOR 3 MINUTES. STIR IN BEANS. POUR OVER CHICKEN. ADD TOMATOES, CHILI SAUCE AND CRANBERRY SAUCE, BREAKING TOMATOES UP WITH A SPOON; STIR WELL. COVER AND COOK ON LOW FOR 5 TO 6 HOURS OR ON HIGH FOR $2\frac{1}{2}$ TO 3 HOURS, UNTIL CHICKEN IS TENDER.

IN A SMALL BOWL, COMBINE CHILI POWDER AND LEMON JUICE UNTIL SMOOTH. STIR INTO SLOW COOKER. STIR IN RED PEPPER. COVER AND COOK ON HIGH FOR ABOUT 20 MINUTES, UNTIL RED PEPPER IS TENDER. ADJUST SEASONING WITH SALT, IF DESIRED. SERVE SPRINKLED WITH CHEESE. SERVES 4 TO 6.

TIP: A CAN OF BEANS IN TOMATO SAUCE HAS LONG BEEN A SHORTCUT TO A GOOD CHILI OR STEW. WE'RE DELIGHTED THAT CANNED BEANS WITH VARIOUS FLAVORINGS ARE NOW AVAILABLE. FOR THIS RECIPE, WE PARTICULARLY LIKE THE HEINZ BRAND CHIPOTLE BBQ-STYLE BEANS. IF YOU CAN'T FIND THEM, USE REGULAR BEANS IN TOMATO SAUCE AND SUBSTITUTE ABOUT 1 TSP (5 ML) CHIPOTLE CHILE POWDER (DEPENDING ON YOUR TOLERANCE FOR HEAT!) FOR THE REGULAR CHILI POWDER.

KICKIN' CHICKEN CHILI

A SLOW COOKER VERSION OF OUR SOUTHWESTERN
CHICKEN CHILI — YOU'LL LOVE IT.

8	BONELESS SKINLESS CHICKEN THIGHS, CUT INTO BITE-SIZE PIECES	8
1	CAN (14 TO 19 OZ/398 TO 540 ML) BLACK BEANS, DRAINED AND RINSED (SEE TIP, PAGE 265)	1
1 TBSP	VEGETABLE OIL	15 ML
3	STALKS CELERY, THINLY SLICED	3
3	CARROTS, THINLY SLICED	3
2	LARGE ONIONS, CHOPPED	2
6	CLOVES GARLIC, MINCED	6
1 TBSP	GROUND CORIANDER	15 ML
2 TSP	GROUND CUMIN	10 ML
$1\frac{1}{2}$ TSP	DRIED OREGANO	7 ML
1 TSP	GRANULATED SUGAR	5 ML
	SALT AND PEPPER	
2 TBSP	TOMATO PASTE	30 ML
1	CAN (28 OZ/796 ML) DICED TOMATOES, WITH JUICE	1
2 TSP	CHILI POWDER	10 ML
2 TBSP	FRESHLY SQUEEZED LIME JUICE	30 ML
1	GREEN BELL PEPPER, CHOPPED	1
1 CUP	CORN KERNELS (NO NEED TO THAW IF FROZEN)	250 ML

PLACE CHICKEN AND BEANS IN A 5- TO 6-QUART SLOW
COOKER. IN A LARGE SKILLET, HEAT OIL OVER MEDIUM
HEAT. ADD CELERY, CARROTS, ONIONS, GARLIC, CORIANDER,
CUMIN, OREGANO, SUGAR, 1 TSP (5 ML) SALT, $\frac{1}{4}$ TSP
(1 ML) PEPPER AND TOMATO PASTE; COOK, STIRRING

OCCASIONALLY, FOR 7 MINUTES. STIR IN TOMATOES AND
BRING TO A BOIL. POUR OVER CHICKEN MIXTURE AND STIR
WELL. COVER AND COOK ON LOW FOR 5 TO 6 HOURS OR
ON HIGH FOR $2\frac{1}{2}$ TO 3 HOURS, UNTIL CHICKEN IS TENDER
AND SAUCE IS BUBBLING. IN A SMALL BOWL, COMBINE CHILI
POWDER AND LIME JUICE. STIR INTO SLOW COOKER. STIR
IN GREEN PEPPER AND CORN. COVER AND COOK ON HIGH
FOR ABOUT 20 MINUTES, UNTIL GREEN PEPPER IS TENDER.
ADJUST SEASONING WITH SALT AND PEPPER, IF DESIRED.
SERVES 4 TO 6.

TIP: THIS IS A MODERATELY HOT CHILI THAT APPEALS
TO A RANGE OF TASTES. IF YOU LIKE MORE HEAT,
INCREASE THE CHILI POWDER OR ADD CAYENNE PEPPER
OR HOT PEPPER SAUCE TO TASTE. FOR A SMOKY FLAVOR,
SUBSTITUTE ABOUT 1 TSP (5 ML) CHIPOTLE CHILE POWDER
(DEPENDING ON YOUR TOLERANCE FOR HEAT!) FOR THE
REGULAR CHILI POWDER.

CHICKEN MEATBALL STROGANOFF

SERVE THESE SAUCY MEATBALLS OVER EGG NOODLES
OR ON A KAISER BUN FOR A YUMMY WEEKNIGHT DINNER.

1/4 CUP	QUICK-COOKING ROLLED OATS OR DRY BREAD CRUMBS	60 ML
1 TSP	CRUMBLED DRIED SAGE	5 ML
	SALT AND PEPPER	
1	EGG, LIGHTLY BEATEN	1
1 LB	LEAN GROUND CHICKEN	500 G
2 TBSP	VEGETABLE OIL, DIVIDED	30 ML
1	ONION, FINELY CHOPPED	1
3	CLOVES GARLIC, MINCED	3
3 CUPS	SLICED MUSHROOMS	750 ML
2 TBSP	TOMATO PASTE	30 ML
2 TBSP	DRY SHERRY (OPTIONAL)	30 ML
2 TBSP	ALL-PURPOSE FLOUR	30 ML
1 1/2 CUPS	CHICKEN BROTH	375 ML
1/2 CUP	SOUR CREAM	125 ML
1/4 CUP	CHOPPED FRESH CHIVES	60 ML

USE A 3 1/2- TO 4-QUART SLOW COOKER. IN A BOWL,
COMBINE OATS, SAGE, 1/2 TSP (2 ML) SALT, 1/8 TSP
(0.5 ML) PEPPER AND EGG; LET STAND FOR 5 MINUTES.
ADD CHICKEN AND MIX WELL. SCOOP TABLESPOONFULS
(15 ML) OF MEAT MIXTURE AND ROLL INTO MEATBALLS.
IN A SKILLET, HEAT HALF THE OIL OVER MEDIUM-HIGH
HEAT. BROWN MEATBALLS, IN BATCHES IF NECESSARY.
TRANSFER TO SLOW COOKER. REDUCE HEAT TO MEDIUM
AND ADD REMAINING OIL TO SKILLET. ADD ONION,
GARLIC, MUSHROOMS, 1/2 TSP (2 ML) SALT, 1/8 TSP
(0.5 ML) PEPPER AND TOMATO PASTE; COOK, STIRRING

OCCASIONALLY, FOR 5 MINUTES. ADD SHERRY (IF USING) AND COOK, STIRRING, FOR 30 SECONDS. STIR IN FLOUR. WHISK IN BROTH AND BRING TO A BOIL. POUR OVER MEATBALLS. COVER AND COOK ON LOW FOR 5 TO 6 HOURS OR ON HIGH FOR $2\frac{1}{2}$ TO 3 HOURS, UNTIL MEATBALLS ARE NO LONGER PINK INSIDE. IN A BOWL, COMBINE SOUR CREAM AND $\frac{1}{2}$ CUP (125 ML) COOKING LIQUID. STIR INTO SLOW COOKER. COVER AND COOK ON HIGH FOR 15 MINUTES, UNTIL BUBBLING. SERVE SPRINKLED WITH CHIVES. MAKES ABOUT 20 MEATBALLS; SERVES 4 TO 6.

VARIATIONS

TURKEY MEATBALL STROGANOFF: SUBSTITUTE LEAN GROUND TURKEY FOR THE CHICKEN.

BEEF MEATBALL STROGANOFF: SUBSTITUTE LEAN GROUND BEEF FOR THE CHICKEN, THYME FOR THE SAGE, AND BEEF BROTH FOR THE CHICKEN BROTH.

CREAMY CHICKEN SANTA FE

ANYONE CAN MAKE THIS — TELL THE KIDS!
SERVE WITH RICE.

8	BONELESS SKINLESS CHICKEN THIGHS, CUT INTO BITE-SIZE PIECES	8
I	CAN (14 TO 19 OZ/398 TO 540 ML) BLACK BEANS, DRAINED AND RINSED (SEE TIP, PAGE 265)	I
I CUP	CORN KERNELS (NO NEED TO THAW IF FROZEN)	250 ML
I CUP	SALSA	250 ML
2 TBSP	TOMATO PASTE	30 ML
	SALT	
I TSP	CHILI POWDER (OR TO TASTE)	5 ML
2 TSP	CIDER VINEGAR	10 ML
2 OZ	CREAM CHEESE, CUBED AND SOFTENED	60 G
4	GREEN ONIONS, CHOPPED	4

IN A 3½- TO 4-QUART SLOW COOKER, COMBINE CHICKEN, BEANS, CORN, SALSA, TOMATO PASTE AND ½ TSP (2 ML) SALT. STIR WELL. COVER AND COOK ON LOW FOR 5 TO 6 HOURS OR ON HIGH FOR 2½ TO 3 HOURS, UNTIL CHICKEN IS TENDER AND SAUCE IS BUBBLING. IN A SMALL BOWL, COMBINE CHILI POWDER AND VINEGAR UNTIL SMOOTH. ADD TO SLOW COOKER, ALONG WITH CREAM CHEESE, AND STIR WELL. COVER AND COOK ON HIGH FOR 15 MINUTES, UNTIL CHEESE IS MELTED AND FLAVORS ARE BLENDED. ADJUST SEASONING WITH SALT, IF DESIRED. SERVE SPRINKLED WITH GREEN ONIONS. SERVES 4 TO 6.

TIP: THIS SAUCY DISH HOLDS WELL FOR 2 OR 3 HOURS IF YOU HAVE A MACHINE THAT AUTOMATICALLY SWITCHES TO A KEEP WARM SETTING AT THE END OF THE COOKING TIME.

MEATLESS MAINS

SIMPLY SUPER TOMATO SAUCE

MUCH BETTER THAN STORE-BOUGHT! TOSS WITH PASTA OR USE TO DRESS UP PIZZA, CHICKEN, FISH, MEATBALLS OR CUTLETS.

1 TBSP	OLIVE OIL	15 ML
1 TBSP	BUTTER	15 ML
1	LARGE ONION, FINELY CHOPPED	1
4	CLOVES GARLIC, MINCED	4
2 TSP	DRIED BASIL OR ITALIAN SEASONING	10 ML
	SALT AND PEPPER	
2	CANS (EACH 28 OZ/796 ML) WHOLE TOMATOES, WITH JUICE	2
1 TSP	GRANULATED SUGAR	5 ML
1/2 CUP	VEGETABLE BROTH	125 ML
1/4 TSP	HOT PEPPER FLAKES	1 ML
1 TBSP	BALSAMIC VINEGAR	15 ML

USE A 4- TO 6-QUART SLOW COOKER. IN A SKILLET, HEAT OIL AND BUTTER OVER MEDIUM HEAT. ADD ONION, GARLIC, BASIL, 1 TSP (5 ML) SALT AND 1/4 TSP (1 ML) PEPPER; COOK, STIRRING OCCASIONALLY, FOR 3 MINUTES. TRANSFER TO SLOW COOKER. ADD TOMATOES, SUGAR AND BROTH, BREAKING TOMATOES UP WITH A SPOON. PLACE A CLEAN TEA TOWEL, FOLDED IN HALF (SO YOU HAVE TWO LAYERS), OVER TOP OF SLOW COOKER INSERT. COVER AND COOK ON LOW FOR ABOUT 6 HOURS OR ON HIGH FOR ABOUT 3 HOURS, UNTIL SAUCE IS BUBBLING AND THICK ENOUGH TO MOUND ON A SPOON. (FOR A SMOOTHER SAUCE, PURÉE TO DESIRED CONSISTENCY WITH AN IMMERSION BLENDER OR IN A BLENDER OR FOOD PROCESSOR.) STIR IN HOT PEPPER FLAKES AND VINEGAR. COVER AND COOK ON

HIGH FOR 10 MINUTES TO BLEND THE FLAVORS. ADJUST SEASONING WITH SALT AND PEPPER, IF DESIRED. MAKES ABOUT 7 CUPS (1.75 L).

TIP: FOR THIS RECIPE, WE PREFER TO USE CANNED WHOLE PLUM (ROMA) TOMATOES IN JUICE, WITH NO ADDED SALT OR SEASONINGS. THESE ARE THE CLOSEST TO FRESH TOMATOES IN TASTE AND TEXTURE. FOR STEWS AND CHILIS, WE GENERALLY USE CANNED DICED TOMATOES BECAUSE THEY HOLD THEIR SHAPE QUITE WELL. CRUSHED TOMATOES LEND BODY AND FLAVOR TO A DISH. STEWED TOMATOES, WITH VARIOUS FLAVORINGS, PROVIDE SHORTCUTS BUT MAY BE QUITE SALTY.

TOMATO FENNEL PASTA SAUCE

A LIGHT SUPPER. SERVE OVER PENNE OR FUSILLI, AND SPRINKLE WITH LOTS OF PARMESAN CHEESE.

1 TBSP	OLIVE OIL	15 ML
1	LARGE ONION, FINELY CHOPPED	1
1	FENNEL BULB, TRIMMED AND THINLY SLICED	1
4	CLOVES GARLIC, MINCED	4
1 TSP	DRIED ITALIAN SEASONING	5 ML
	SALT AND PEPPER	
1	CAN (28 OZ/796 ML) WHOLE TOMATOES, WITH JUICE	1
1 TSP	GRANULATED SUGAR	5 ML
1/4 CUP	CHOPPED FRESH PARSLEY	60 ML
1/2 TSP	GRATED LEMON ZEST (OPTIONAL)	2 ML
1/4 TSP	HOT PEPPER FLAKES	1 ML
2 TSP	CIDER VINEGAR OR LEMON JUICE	10 ML

USE A 4- TO 6-QUART SLOW COOKER. IN A SKILLET, HEAT OIL OVER MEDIUM HEAT. ADD ONION AND FENNEL; COOK, STIRRING OCCASIONALLY, FOR 5 MINUTES. ADD GARLIC, ITALIAN SEASONING, 1 TSP (5 ML) SALT AND 1/4 TSP (1 ML) PEPPER; COOK, STIRRING, FOR 15 SECONDS. TRANSFER TO SLOW COOKER. ADD TOMATOES AND SUGAR, BREAKING TOMATOES UP WITH A SPOON. COVER AND COOK ON LOW FOR ABOUT 6 HOURS OR ON HIGH FOR ABOUT 3 HOURS, UNTIL SAUCE IS BUBBLING AND THICK ENOUGH TO MOUND ON A SPOON. STIR IN PARSLEY, LEMON ZEST (IF USING), HOT PEPPER FLAKES AND VINEGAR. ADJUST SEASONING WITH SALT AND PEPPER, IF DESIRED. SERVES 3 OR 4.

TIP: FENNEL BULB IS LABELED "ANISE" IN SOME SUPERMARKETS. IF IT HAS FEATHERY STALKS ATTACHED, TRIM THEM OFF ABOUT 1 INCH (2.5 CM) ABOVE THE BULB. CUT THE BULB IN HALF VERTICALLY AND REMOVE THE WOODY CORE FROM EACH HALF. CUT EACH HALF CROSSWISE INTO VERY THIN STRIPS.

VARIATION

TOMATO, FENNEL AND CHICKPEA PASTA SAUCE: ADD 1 CAN (14 TO 19 OZ/398 TO 540 ML) CHICKPEAS, DRAINED AND RINSED (SEE TIP, PAGE 261) WITH THE TOMATOES.

IF THE SHOE FITS, BUY IT!

PUTTANESCA PASTA SAUCE

THE WORKING GIRL'S PASTA SAUCE!

1 TBSP	OLIVE OIL	15 ML
1	LARGE ONION, FINELY CHOPPED	1
4	CLOVES GARLIC, MINCED	4
1/2 TSP	DRIED OREGANO	2 ML
	SALT AND PEPPER	
1	CAN (28 OZ/796 ML) WHOLE TOMATOES, WITH JUICE	1
1 TSP	GRANULATED SUGAR	5 ML
1/2 CUP	CHOPPED PITTED BLACK OLIVES	125 ML
1/2 CUP	SLICED STUFFED GREEN OLIVES	125 ML
1/4 CUP	CHOPPED FRESH PARSLEY	60 ML
2 TBSP	DRAINED CAPERS	30 ML
1/4 TSP	HOT PEPPER FLAKES	1 ML

USE A 4- TO 6-QUART SLOW COOKER. IN A SKILLET, HEAT OIL OVER MEDIUM HEAT. ADD ONION, GARLIC, OREGANO, 1/2 TSP (2 ML) SALT AND 1/4 TSP (1 ML) PEPPER; COOK, STIRRING OCCASIONALLY, FOR 3 MINUTES. TRANSFER TO SLOW COOKER. ADD TOMATOES AND SUGAR, BREAKING TOMATOES UP WITH A SPOON. COVER AND COOK ON LOW FOR ABOUT 6 HOURS OR ON HIGH FOR ABOUT 3 HOURS, UNTIL SAUCE IS BUBBLING AND THICK ENOUGH TO MOUND ON A SPOON. ADD BLACK OLIVES, GREEN OLIVES, PARSLEY, CAPERS AND HOT PEPPER FLAKES, STIRRING A FEW TIMES, UNTIL HEATED THROUGH. ADJUST SEASONING WITH SALT AND PEPPER, IF DESIRED. SERVES 3 OR 4.

SWEET POTATO CANNELLONI

3 CUPS	TOMATO SAUCE	750 ML
1 CUP	EVAPORATED MILK	250 ML
1/2 TSP	SALT	2 ML
1/4 TSP	GROUND NUTMEG	1 ML
1/8 TSP	PEPPER	0.5 ML
1	EGG, LIGHTLY BEATEN	1
1 1/4 CUPS	RICOTTA CHEESE	300 ML
1/4 CUP	GRATED PARMESAN CHEESE	60 ML
1 1/4 CUPS	GRATED PEELED SWEET POTATO	300 ML
1 CUP	PACKED BABY SPINACH, CHOPPED	250 ML
12	OVEN-READY CANNELLONI SHELLS	12
1 CUP	SHREDDED MOZZARELLA CHEESE	250 ML

GREASE THE INSERT OF A 3 1/2- TO 4-QUART SLOW
COOKER. IN A BOWL, WHISK TOGETHER TOMATO SAUCE
AND MILK. SPREAD 1 CUP (250 ML) SAUCE MIXTURE IN
BOTTOM OF SLOW COOKER. IN ANOTHER BOWL, WHISK
TOGETHER SALT, NUTMEG, PEPPER, EGG, RICOTTA AND
PARMESAN. STIR IN SWEET POTATO AND SPINACH.
USING YOUR FINGERS, FILL CANNELLONI SHELLS WITH
RICOTTA MIXTURE. PLACE FILLED SHELLS SIDE BY SIDE
IN SLOW COOKER, MAKING TWO LAYERS IF NECESSARY.
POUR REMAINING SAUCE OVER SHELLS. COVER AND COOK
ON LOW FOR ABOUT 6 HOURS OR ON HIGH FOR ABOUT
3 HOURS, UNTIL BUBBLING. SPRINKLE WITH MOZZARELLA.
COVER AND COOK ON HIGH FOR ABOUT 15 MINUTES, UNTIL
MOZZARELLA IS MELTED. SERVES 4.

TIP: USE OVEN-READY CANNELLONI FOR THIS RECIPE. IT
STANDS UP BETTER TO THE LONG, MOIST COOKING THAN
FRESH OR REGULAR DRIED PASTA.

NEW GOURMET MACARONI AND CHEESE

HURRAH! THIS HAS THE SAME CREAMY, CHEESY APPEAL AS OUR ORIGINAL GOURMET MACARONI AND CHEESE, BUT IT'S WAY QUICKER TO ASSEMBLE.

1/4 CUP	BUTTER	60 ML
1 CUP	FRESH BREAD CRUMBS	250 ML
2 CUPS	MACARONI	500 ML
1 TSP	DRY MUSTARD	5 ML
PINCH	CAYENNE PEPPER	PINCH
2	EGGS, LIGHTLY BEATEN	2
1 1/2 CUPS	COTTAGE CHEESE	375 ML
1 CUP	SOUR CREAM	250 ML
8 OZ	BLOCK PROCESSED CHEESE (SUCH AS VELVEETA), CUBED	250 G
2 CUPS	SHREDDED EXTRA-SHARP (EXTRA-OLD) OR SHARP (OLD) CHEDDAR CHEESE	500 ML

GREASE THE INSERT OF A 3 1/2- TO 4-QUART SLOW COOKER. IN A SKILLET, MELT BUTTER OVER MEDIUM HEAT. ADD BREAD CRUMBS AND COOK, STIRRING, UNTIL GOLDEN AND CRISPY. TRANSFER TO A BOWL AND LET COOL; COVER AND SET ASIDE. IN A POT OF BOILING WATER, COOK MACARONI ACCORDING TO PACKAGE INSTRUCTIONS; DRAIN. IN A LARGE BOWL, WHISK TOGETHER MUSTARD, CAYENNE, EGGS, COTTAGE CHEESE AND SOUR CREAM. STIR IN PROCESSED CHEESE AND CHEDDAR. STIR IN COOKED MACARONI. TRANSFER TO PREPARED SLOW COOKER. COVER AND COOK ON HIGH FOR 2 TO 2 1/2 HOURS, UNTIL BUBBLING. STIR GENTLY. SPRINKLE WITH RESERVED TOASTED BREAD CRUMBS. SERVE IMMEDIATELY. *SERVES 4 TO 6.*

TIP: FRESH BREAD CRUMBS CAN BE MADE EASILY IN A FOOD PROCESSOR WITH WHATEVER SLIGHTLY STALE BREAD YOU HAVE LYING AROUND, SUCH AS SANDWICH LOAF, ENGLISH MUFFINS, DINNER ROLLS OR PITA BREAD. NO MACHINE? SIMPLY RUB THE BREAD ON A BOX GRATER. FROZEN BREAD IS EASIER TO GRATE THAN ROOM TEMPERATURE BREAD. FREEZE EXTRA BREAD CRUMBS IN SEALABLE PLASTIC BAGS.

TIP: BLOCK PROCESSED CHEESE, SUCH AS VELVEETA, IS A BLAST FROM THE PAST, BUT IT'S GOT WHAT IT TAKES WHEN IT COMES TO MELTING QUALITIES. IT'S PERFECT IN RECIPES WHERE YOU WANT A REALLY SMOOTH AND CREAMY TEXTURE. YOU CAN SUBSTITUTE 1 CUP (250 ML) SHREDDED EXTRA-SHARP (EXTRA-OLD) CHEDDAR CHEESE IN THIS RECIPE, IF YOU PREFER.

BARLEY CAPONATA

CAPONATA IS A SICILIAN VEGETABLE DISH. PAIRED WITH BARLEY, IT BECOMES A SATISFYING VEGETARIAN MAIN COURSE. SERVE WITH TOMATO SALAD DRESSED WITH OLIVE OIL, BALSAMIC VINEGAR AND SHREDDED FRESH BASIL.

1	EGGPLANT, PEELED AND CUT INTO $1/2$-INCH (1 CM) CUBES	1
	SALT	
3 TBSP	OLIVE OIL	45 ML
2	SMALL ZUCCHINI, QUARTERED LENGTHWISE AND CUT INTO $1/2$-INCH (1 CM) CHUNKS	2
1	RED BELL PEPPER, CHOPPED	1
1	LARGE ONION, THINLY SLICED	1
4	CLOVES GARLIC, MINCED	4
1 TSP	DRIED ITALIAN SEASONING	5 ML
	PEPPER	
2 TBSP	TOMATO PASTE	30 ML
$1/2$ CUP	BARLEY, RINSED	125 ML
2 CUPS	VEGETABLE BROTH	500 ML
1 CUP	TOMATO SAUCE	250 ML
$1/4$ CUP	CHOPPED PITTED BLACK OLIVES	60 ML
1 TBSP	BALSAMIC VINEGAR	15 ML
$1/4$ CUP	CHOPPED FRESH PARSLEY	60 ML

USE A $3^1/2$- TO 4-QUART SLOW COOKER. PLACE EGGPLANT IN A COLANDER AND SPRINKLE GENEROUSLY WITH SALT. LET STAND FOR ABOUT 30 MINUTES, UNTIL MOISTURE COMES TO THE SURFACE. RINSE EGGPLANT WELL IN COLD WATER AND SQUEEZE OUT EXCESS WATER. PAT DRY WITH PAPER TOWELS. SET ASIDE. IN A SKILLET, HEAT 1 TBSP

(15 ML) OIL OVER MEDIUM HEAT. ADD ZUCCHINI AND RED PEPPER; COOK, STIRRING OCCASIONALLY, UNTIL LIGHTLY BROWNED, ABOUT 5 MINUTES. TRANSFER TO A BOWL AND LET COOL; COVER AND REFRIGERATE. ADD REMAINING OIL TO SKILLET; ADD DRAINED EGGPLANT AND ONION; COOK, STIRRING OCCASIONALLY, UNTIL STARTING TO BROWN, ABOUT 5 MINUTES. ADD GARLIC, ITALIAN SEASONING, $\frac{1}{2}$ TSP (2 ML) SALT, $\frac{1}{4}$ TSP (1 ML) PEPPER AND TOMATO PASTE; COOK, STIRRING, FOR 30 SECONDS. STIR IN BARLEY, BROTH AND TOMATO SAUCE; BRING TO A BOIL. POUR INTO SLOW COOKER. COVER AND COOK ON LOW FOR 5 TO 6 HOURS OR ON HIGH FOR $2\frac{1}{2}$ TO 3 HOURS, UNTIL BARLEY IS TENDER AND SAUCE IS THICKENED. STIR IN OLIVES, VINEGAR AND RESERVED ZUCCHINI AND RED PEPPER. COVER AND COOK ON HIGH FOR ABOUT 15 MINUTES, UNTIL VEGETABLES ARE HOT. SERVE SPRINKLED WITH PARSLEY. SERVES 4.

VEGETABLE POLENTA CASSEROLE

POLENTA IS A VERSATILE ITALIAN GRAIN DISH MADE BY COOKING CORNMEAL IN BROTH OR WATER. HERE, IT'S TRANSFORMED INTO A HEARTY VEGETARIAN ENTRÉE. START THE MEAL WITH A SALAD.

I CUP	CORNMEAL	250 ML
1/2 TSP	SALT	2 ML
1/8 TSP	PEPPER	0.5 ML
3 CUPS	BOILING WATER	750 ML
4 OZ	CREAM CHEESE, CUBED AND SOFTENED	125 G
I CUP	SHREDDED MOZZARELLA CHEESE, DIVIDED	250 ML
1/2 CUP	GRATED PARMESAN CHEESE, DIVIDED	125 ML
I TBSP	VEGETABLE OIL	15 ML
2	ONIONS, THINLY SLICED	2
I	RED BELL PEPPER, THINLY SLICED	I
4	CLOVES GARLIC, MINCED	4
3 CUPS	SLICED MUSHROOMS	750 ML
2 CUPS	TOMATO-BASED PASTA SAUCE	500 ML

GREASE THE INSERT OF A 3 1/2- TO 4-QUART SLOW COOKER. GREASE A 13- BY 9-INCH (33 BY 23 CM) BAKING DISH. PLACE CORNMEAL, SALT AND PEPPER IN PREPARED SLOW COOKER. GRADUALLY ADD BOILING WATER, WHISKING CONSTANTLY UNTIL BLENDED. COVER AND COOK ON LOW FOR 1 1/2 TO 3 HOURS, UNTIL LIQUID IS ABSORBED AND CORNMEAL IS TENDER. TRANSFER SLOW COOKER INSERT TO A HEAT-RESISTANT SURFACE. STIR IN CREAM CHEESE, 3/4 CUP (175 ML) MOZZARELLA AND 1/4 CUP (60 ML) PARMESAN. SPREAD TWO-THIRDS OF THE POLENTA IN PREPARED BAKING DISH; SET ASIDE. MEANWHILE, PREHEAT OVEN

CONTINUED ON PAGE 257...

Sweet Potato Cannelloni (page 251)

Vegetable Polenta Casserole (page 256)

Red Lentil and Vegetable Curry (page 258)

Spicy Orange Squash (page 278)

TO 400°F (200°C). IN A SKILLET, HEAT OIL OVER MEDIUM HEAT. ADD ONIONS, RED PEPPER, GARLIC AND MUSHROOMS; COOK, STIRRING OCCASIONALLY, FOR 5 MINUTES. STIR IN PASTA SAUCE. SPREAD OVER POLENTA IN BAKING DISH. DROP REMAINING POLENTA BY SPOONFULS OVER TOP. SPRINKLE WITH REMAINING MOZZARELLA AND PARMESAN. BAKE, UNCOVERED, FOR ABOUT 25 MINUTES, UNTIL HEATED THROUGH AND BROWNED. SERVES 6.

MAKE AHEAD: PREPARE THE POLENTA BASE AND SPREAD IN THE BAKING DISH. COVER AND REFRIGERATE OVERNIGHT. PLACE REMAINING POLENTA IN ANOTHER CONTAINER, COVER AND REFRIGERATE. PREPARE THE VEGETABLE MIXTURE AND TRANSFER TO A SEPARATE CONTAINER. LET COOL, COVER AND REFRIGERATE OVERNIGHT. THE NEXT DAY, ASSEMBLE CASSEROLE AND PROCEED WITH THE RECIPE.

RED LENTIL AND VEGETABLE CURRY

THIS CURRY IS DELIGHTFUL. SERVE AS A VEGETARIAN MAIN COURSE OVER STEAMED RICE, OR AS PART OF AN INDIAN-THEMED DINNER WITH PORK VINDALOO (PAGE 184) OR BEEF MADRAS (PAGE 137).

1 TBSP	VEGETABLE OIL	15 ML
1	LARGE ONION, FINELY CHOPPED	1
4	CLOVES GARLIC, MINCED	4
3 TBSP	MILD OR MEDIUM INDIAN CURRY PASTE	45 ML
1 1/2 CUPS	GRATED PEELED SWEET POTATO	375 ML
1 CUP	DRIED RED LENTILS, RINSED	250 ML
1 1/2 CUPS	TOMATO SAUCE	375 ML
2 CUPS	VEGETABLE BROTH	500 ML
3 CUPS	PACKED BABY SPINACH	750 ML
1 1/4 CUPS	DRAINED ROASTED RED PEPPERS, CHOPPED	300 ML
	SALT (OPTIONAL)	
2 TBSP	CHOPPED FRESH CILANTRO	30 ML
	CHOPPED TOMATO	

USE A 3 1/2- TO 4-QUART SLOW COOKER. IN A SKILLET, HEAT OIL OVER MEDIUM HEAT. ADD ONION, GARLIC AND CURRY PASTE; COOK, STIRRING OCCASIONALLY, FOR 3 MINUTES. STIR IN SWEET POTATO AND LENTILS. STIR IN TOMATO SAUCE AND BRING TO A BOIL. TRANSFER TO SLOW COOKER. STIR IN BROTH. COVER AND COOK ON LOW FOR 6 TO 8 HOURS OR ON HIGH FOR 3 TO 4 HOURS, UNTIL LENTILS ARE VERY SOFT. STIR IN SPINACH AND RED PEPPERS. COVER AND COOK ON HIGH FOR ABOUT 20 MINUTES, UNTIL SPINACH IS WILTED AND RED PEPPERS

ARE HOT. ADJUST SEASONING WITH SALT, IF DESIRED. SERVE GARNISHED WITH CILANTRO AND TOMATO. SERVES 4 TO 6.

TIP: HEAT SEEKERS CAN USE HOT INDIAN CURRY PASTE OR ADD CAYENNE PEPPER TO TASTE WITH THE SPINACH.

TIP: CURRY PASTES CAN BE QUITE SALTY. TASTE THE CURRY AT THE END OF THE COOKING TIME AND ADD SALT IF NECESSARY.

VARIATION: USE 1 CUP (250 ML) FROZEN PEAS INSTEAD OF THE SPINACH.

WHO ARE "THEY" ANYWAY?

SQUASH AND CHICKPEA COCONUT CURRY

A MILDLY SPICED, COLORFUL VEGETARIAN DISH TO SERVE AS A MAIN COURSE WITH STEAMED BASMATI RICE, NAAN AND A DOLLOP OF MANGO CHUTNEY.

1 TBSP	VEGETABLE OIL	15 ML
2	ONIONS, FINELY CHOPPED	2
4	CLOVES GARLIC, MINCED	4
1 TBSP	MINCED GINGERROOT	15 ML
2 TBSP	MILD OR MEDIUM INDIAN CURRY PASTE	30 ML
1/2 CUP	VEGETABLE BROTH	125 ML
1	CAN (14 OZ/400 ML) LIGHT COCONUT MILK, DIVIDED	1
4 CUPS	CUBED PEELED BUTTERNUT SQUASH (1-INCH/2.5 CM CUBES)	1 L
1	CAN (14 TO 19 OZ/398 TO 540 ML) CHICKPEAS, DRAINED AND RINSED (SEE TIP, OPPOSITE)	1
1	RED BELL PEPPER, CHOPPED	1
1 CUP	FROZEN PEAS (NO NEED TO THAW)	250 ML
2 TBSP	CHOPPED FRESH CILANTRO	30 ML
1 TBSP	FRESHLY SQUEEZED LIME JUICE	15 ML
	SALT (OPTIONAL)	
	TOASTED SLIVERED ALMONDS	

USE A 4- TO 6-QUART SLOW COOKER. IN A SKILLET, HEAT OIL OVER MEDIUM HEAT. ADD ONIONS, GARLIC, GINGER AND CURRY PASTE; COOK, STIRRING OCCASIONALLY, FOR 3 MINUTES. STIR IN BROTH AND 1 1/2 CUPS (375 ML) COCONUT MILK; BRING TO A BOIL. TRANSFER TO SLOW COOKER. STIR IN SQUASH AND CHICKPEAS. COVER AND COOK ON LOW FOR 5 TO 6 HOURS OR ON HIGH FOR 2 1/2 TO

3 HOURS, UNTIL SQUASH IS TENDER. STIR IN RED PEPPER, PEAS AND REMAINING COCONUT MILK. COVER AND COOK ON HIGH FOR ABOUT 20 MINUTES, UNTIL RED PEPPER IS TENDER. STIR IN CILANTRO AND LIME JUICE. ADJUST SEASONING WITH SALT, IF DESIRED. SERVE GARNISHED WITH TOASTED ALMONDS. SERVES 6.

TIP: CURRY PASTES CAN BE QUITE SALTY. TASTE THE CURRY AT THE END OF THE COOKING TIME AND ADD SALT IF NECESSARY.

TIP: IF YOU PREFER TO USE COOKED DRIED CHICKPEAS INSTEAD OF CANNED, SEE BASIC BEANS (PAGE 282). YOU'LL NEED 2 CUPS (500 ML) COOKED CHICKPEAS FOR THIS RECIPE.

FAY'S FAVORITE CHICKPEA CURRY

AS A TEENAGE VEGETARIAN, FAY THRIVED ON THIS.
A DECADE LATER, SHE ORDERS HER STEAKS MEDIUM-
RARE BUT STILL LOVES CHICKPEAS.

I TBSP	VEGETABLE OIL	15 ML
2	ONIONS, FINELY CHOPPED	2
I TBSP	CHOPPED GINGERROOT	15 ML
2 TBSP	MILD OR MEDIUM INDIAN CURRY PASTE	30 ML
I	CAN (14 OZ/398 ML) TOMATO SAUCE	I
I	CAN (14 TO 19 OZ/398 TO 540 ML) CHICKPEAS, DRAINED AND RINSED (SEE TIP, PAGE 261)	I
2 TBSP	CHOPPED FRESH CILANTRO	30 ML
I TBSP	FRESHLY SQUEEZED LIME JUICE	15 ML
I TSP	LIQUID HONEY	5 ML
	SALT (OPTIONAL)	

USE A $3\frac{1}{2}$- TO 4-QUART SLOW COOKER. IN A SKILLET,
HEAT OIL OVER MEDIUM HEAT. ADD ONIONS, GINGER AND
CURRY PASTE; COOK, STIRRING OCCASIONALLY, FOR 3
MINUTES. STIR IN TOMATO SAUCE AND BRING TO A BOIL.
TRANSFER TO SLOW COOKER. STIR IN CHICKPEAS. COVER
AND COOK ON LOW FOR 5 TO 6 HOURS OR ON HIGH FOR
$2\frac{1}{2}$ TO 3 HOURS, UNTIL BUBBLING. STIR IN CILANTRO, LIME
JUICE AND HONEY. ADJUST SEASONING WITH SALT, IF
DESIRED. SERVES 3 TO 4.

TIP: CURRY PASTES CAN BE QUITE SALTY. TASTE THE
CURRY AT THE END OF THE COOKING TIME AND ADD SALT
IF NECESSARY.

MEDITERRANEAN CHICKPEA STEW

A MEATLESS DINNER ONCE OR TWICE A WEEK IS A GOOD THING. SERVE WITH A GREEN SALAD AND WARMED PITAS.

1 TBSP	OLIVE OIL	15 ML
1	LARGE ONION, FINELY CHOPPED	1
4	CLOVES GARLIC, MINCED	4
1½ TSP	DRIED ITALIAN SEASONING	7 ML
	SALT AND PEPPER	
1	CAN (28 OZ/796 ML) DICED TOMATOES, WITH JUICE	1
1	CAN (14 TO 19 OZ/398 TO 540 ML) CHICKPEAS, DRAINED AND RINSED (SEE TIP, PAGE 261)	1
2	SMALL ZUCCHINI, CUT INTO ½-INCH (1 CM) CHUNKS	2
1	YELLOW OR RED BELL PEPPER, CHOPPED	1
1⅓ CUPS	CHOPPED PITTED BLACK OLIVES	325 ML
2 TBSP	CHOPPED FRESH MINT	30 ML
	GRATED ZEST OF ½ LEMON	

USE A 3½- TO 4-QUART SLOW COOKER. IN A SKILLET, HEAT OIL OVER MEDIUM HEAT. ADD ONION, GARLIC, ITALIAN SEASONING, 1 TSP (5 ML) SALT AND ¼ TSP (1 ML) PEPPER; COOK, STIRRING OCCASIONALLY, FOR 3 MINUTES. TRANSFER TO SLOW COOKER. STIR IN TOMATOES AND CHICKPEAS. COVER AND COOK ON LOW FOR 4 TO 6 HOURS OR ON HIGH FOR 2 TO 3 HOURS, UNTIL BUBBLING. STIR IN ZUCCHINI, BELL PEPPER AND OLIVES. COVER AND COOK ON HIGH FOR 20 TO 30 MINUTES, UNTIL VEGETABLES ARE TENDER. ADJUST SEASONING WITH SALT, IF DESIRED. SERVE SPRINKLED WITH MINT AND LEMON ZEST. SERVES 4.

SWEET POTATO AND BLACK BEAN CHILI

IT LOOKS AS GOOD AS IT TASTES! EASY CORNBREAD (PAGE 33) OR TEX-MEX CORNBREAD (PAGE 34) ROUND OUT THE MEAL.

I TBSP	VEGETABLE OIL	15 ML
2	ONIONS, FINELY CHOPPED	2
4	CLOVES GARLIC, MINCED	4
2 TSP	GROUND CUMIN	10 ML
I TSP	DRIED OREGANO	5 ML
	SALT AND PEPPER	
2 TBSP	TOMATO PASTE	30 ML
I	CAN (28 OZ/796 ML) DICED TOMATOES, WITH JUICE	I
I	CAN (14 TO 19 OZ/398 TO 540 ML) BLACK BEANS, DRAINED AND RINSED (SEE TIP, OPPOSITE)	I
I	LARGE SWEET POTATO, PEELED AND CUT INTO I-INCH (2.5 CM) CUBES	I
I TSP	CHIPOTLE CHILE POWDER	5 ML
2 TBSP	FRESHLY SQUEEZED LIME JUICE	30 ML
I CUP	CORN KERNELS (NO NEED TO THAW IF FROZEN)	250 ML
2 TBSP	CHOPPED FRESH CILANTRO	30 ML
	CHOPPED TOMATO, CHOPPED AVOCADO AND SOUR CREAM	

USE A 4- TO 6-QUART SLOW COOKER. IN A SKILLET, HEAT OIL OVER MEDIUM HEAT. ADD ONIONS, GARLIC, CUMIN, OREGANO, I TSP (5 ML) SALT, $\frac{1}{4}$ TSP (I ML) PEPPER AND TOMATO PASTE; COOK, STIRRING OCCASIONALLY, FOR 5 MINUTES. TRANSFER TO SLOW COOKER. STIR IN

TOMATOES, BEANS AND SWEET POTATO. COVER AND COOK ON LOW FOR 7 TO 8 HOURS OR ON HIGH FOR $3\frac{1}{2}$ TO 4 HOURS, UNTIL SWEET POTATO IS TENDER AND MIXTURE IS BUBBLING. IN A BOWL, COMBINE CHIPOTLE CHILE POWDER AND LIME JUICE UNTIL SMOOTH. STIR INTO SLOW COOKER. STIR IN CORN AND CILANTRO. COVER AND COOK ON HIGH FOR 30 MINUTES, UNTIL STEAMING. ADJUST SEASONING WITH SALT AND PEPPER, IF DESIRED. SERVE GARNISHED WITH TOMATOES, AVOCADO AND DOLLOPS OF SOUR CREAM. SERVES 6.

TIP: IF YOU PREFER TO USE COOKED DRIED BEANS INSTEAD OF CANNED, SEE BASIC BEANS (PAGE 282). YOU'LL NEED 2 CUPS (500 ML) COOKED BEANS FOR THIS RECIPE.

TIP: WHEN SQUEEZING JUICE FROM A LEMON, LIME OR ORANGE, AIM TO HAVE THE FRUIT AT ROOM TEMPERATURE — IT WILL GIVE UP JUICE MORE EASILY THAN IF SQUEEZED STRAIGHT FROM THE REFRIGERATOR. IF YOU FORGET TO REMOVE IT FROM THE FRIDGE AHEAD OF TIME, PRICK THE FRUIT WITH A FORK AND MICROWAVE IT ON HIGH FOR ABOUT 20 SECONDS TO WARM IT SLIGHTLY.

BLACK BEAN VEGETARIAN TACOS

HEALTHY AND HEARTY! THEY WON'T MISS THE MEAT.

1 TBSP	VEGETABLE OIL	15 ML
1	LARGE ONION, FINELY CHOPPED	1
3	CLOVES GARLIC, MINCED	3
1 TSP	GROUND CUMIN	5 ML
1	CAN (14 OZ/398 ML) CHILI-STYLE STEWED TOMATOES	1
1 TBSP	GRANULATED SUGAR	15 ML
1	CAN (14 TO 19 OZ/398 TO 540 ML) BLACK BEANS, DRAINED AND RINSED (SEE TIP, PAGE 265)	1
1 TSP	CHILI POWDER, OR TO TASTE	5 ML
1 TBSP	CIDER VINEGAR	15 ML
1	RED BELL PEPPER, CHOPPED	1
1	ZUCCHINI, QUARTERED LENGTHWISE AND CUT INTO $1/2$-INCH (1 CM) CHUNKS	1
1 CUP	CORN KERNELS (NO NEED TO THAW IF FROZEN)	250 ML
12	TACO SHELLS, WARMED	12
	REAL GUACAMOLE (OPPOSITE)	
	SHREDDED CHEESE, DICED AVOCADO, DICED TOMATO, SLICED RADISHES, SOUR CREAM	

USE A $3^1/_2$- TO 4-QUART SLOW COOKER. IN A SKILLET, HEAT OIL OVER MEDIUM HEAT. ADD ONION, GARLIC AND CUMIN; COOK, STIRRING OCCASIONALLY, FOR 3 MINUTES. STIR IN TOMATOES AND SUGAR. TRANSFER TO SLOW COOKER. STIR IN BEANS. COVER AND COOK ON LOW FOR 6 HOURS OR ON HIGH FOR 3 HOURS, UNTIL BUBBLING. IN A SMALL BOWL, COMBINE CHILI POWDER AND VINEGAR UNTIL SMOOTH. STIR INTO SLOW COOKER. STIR IN RED PEPPER, ZUCCHINI AND CORN. COVER

AND COOK ON HIGH FOR 30 MINUTES, UNTIL VEGETABLES ARE TENDER-CRISP. SET OUT THE SLOW COOKER INSERT, WARMED TACO SHELLS, GUACAMOLE AND OTHER TOPPINGS AND LET EVERYONE HELP THEMSELVES. SERVES 4 TO 6.

VARIATION: IF YOU ENJOY A SMOKY FLAVOR, REPLACE THE CHILI POWDER WITH AN EQUAL AMOUNT OF CHIPOTLE CHILE POWDER.

REAL GUACAMOLE

A BREEZE TO MAKE AND MUCH TASTIER THAN STORE-BOUGHT VERSIONS. SERVE WITH BLACK BEAN VEGETARIAN TACOS (PAGE 266) OR BLACK BEAN VEGETARIAN BURRITOS (PAGE 270), OR AS AN APPETIZER.

1	RIPE AVOCADO	1
1	RIPE PLUM (ROMA) TOMATO, SEEDED AND FINELY CHOPPED	1
1	SMALL RED OR GREEN CHILE PEPPER, SEEDED AND FINELY CHOPPED	1
1	CLOVE GARLIC, MINCED	1
1/4 CUP	CHOPPED FRESH CILANTRO	60 ML
	SALT	
1 TBSP	FRESHLY SQUEEZED LIME JUICE (APPROX.)	15 ML

CUT AVOCADO IN HALF AND REMOVE THE PIT. USING A SPOON, SCOOP THE FLESH INTO A BOWL. USING A FORK, LIGHTLY MASH AVOCADO TO A CHUNKY PASTE. STIR IN TOMATO, CHILE PEPPER, GARLIC, CILANTRO, 1/2 TSP (2 ML) SALT AND LIME JUICE. ADJUST SEASONING WITH ADDITIONAL SALT AND LIME JUICE, IF DESIRED. SERVE IMMEDIATELY. MAKES ABOUT 1 CUP (250 ML).

MEXICAN BEAN AND CORN PIE

A CRISPY CORNMEAL TOPPING HELPS THE VEGETABLES GO DOWN! SERVE WITH SALSA AND SOUR CREAM.

2	STALKS CELERY, THINLY SLICED	2
1	LARGE CARROT, QUARTERED LENGTHWISE AND THINLY SLICED	1
1	LARGE ONION, FINELY CHOPPED	1
1	CAN (14 OZ/398 ML) CHILI-STYLE STEWED TOMATOES	1
1	CAN (14 TO 19 OZ/398 TO 540 ML) BLACK BEANS, DRAINED AND RINSED (SEE TIP, PAGE 265)	1
1 CUP	CORN KERNELS (NO NEED TO THAW IF FROZEN)	250 ML
2 TBSP	CHOPPED FRESH CILANTRO	30 ML
1 TSP	CHILI POWDER, OR TO TASTE	5 ML
	SALT (OPTIONAL)	

TOPPING

1 CUP	ALL-PURPOSE FLOUR	250 ML
1/2 CUP	CORNMEAL	125 ML
3/4 TSP	BAKING POWDER	3 ML
1/2 TSP	SALT	2 ML
1/4 TSP	BAKING SODA	1 ML
1	EGG, LIGHTLY BEATEN	1
3/4 CUP	BUTTERMILK	175 ML
3 TBSP	MELTED BUTTER, SLIGHTLY COOLED	45 ML
1/2 CUP	SHREDDED TEX-MEX CHEESE BLEND OR CHEDDAR CHEESE	125 ML

IN A 3½- TO 4-QUART SLOW COOKER, COMBINE CELERY, CARROT, ONION, TOMATOES, BEANS AND CORN. COVER AND COOK ON LOW FOR ABOUT 6 HOURS OR ON HIGH

FOR ABOUT 3 HOURS, UNTIL BUBBLING. STIR IN CILANTRO AND CHILI POWDER. ADJUST SEASONING WITH SALT AND ADDITIONAL CHILI POWDER, IF DESIRED.

TOPPING: IN A BOWL, COMBINE FLOUR, CORNMEAL, BAKING POWDER, SALT AND BAKING SODA. MAKE A WELL IN THE CENTER OF THE FLOUR MIXTURE. ADD EGG, BUTTERMILK AND BUTTER TO WELL. STIR JUST UNTIL EVENLY COMBINED. SPRINKLE CHEESE OVER BEAN MIXTURE, THEN DROP SPOONFULS OF BATTER ON TOP. USING A FORK, SPREAD BATTER EVENLY OVER BEAN MIXTURE. COVER AND COOK ON HIGH FOR ABOUT 40 MINUTES, UNTIL A TESTER INSERTED IN THE CENTER OF THE TOPPING COMES OUT CLEAN. SERVE IMMEDIATELY. SERVES 4 TO 6.

TIP: CONVENIENT BAGS OF SHREDDED TEX-MEX CHEESE BLEND CAN BE FOUND IN THE REFRIGERATED SECTION OF THE SUPERMARKET. THE BLEND USUALLY INCLUDES CHEDDAR, MOZZARELLA AND JALAPEÑO-FLAVORED MONTEREY JACK CHEESE. IF YOU PREFER, SHRED YOUR OWN CHEESE USING ONE OR A COMBINATION OF THE TYPES SUGGESTED.

BLACK BEAN VEGETARIAN BURRITOS

MAKE A BATCH, THEN WRAP AND FREEZE INDIVIDUALLY. PERFECT FOR LUNCH BOXES AND LAST-MINUTE DINNERS. SERVE WITH REAL GUACAMOLE (PAGE 267).

1	BATCH BLACK BEAN VEGETARIAN TACO FILLING (PAGE 266)	1
10	9-INCH (23 CM) FLOUR TORTILLAS	10
2 CUPS	SHREDDED TEX-MEX CHEESE BLEND OR CHEDDAR CHEESE (APPROX.)	500 ML
	SALSA AND SOUR CREAM (OPTIONAL)	

LET TACO FILLING COOL FOR 15 MINUTES. MEANWHILE, PREHEAT OVEN TO 400°F (200°C) AND GREASE A BAKING SHEET. PLACE A TORTILLA ON A WORK SURFACE. SPOON $1/3$ CUP (75 ML) FILLING JUST BELOW THE CENTER OF THE TORTILLA. SPRINKLE WITH 3 TBSP (45 ML) CHEESE. FOLD UP BOTTOM EDGE OF TORTILLA, THEN FOLD IN SIDES AND ROLL UP. PLACE SEAM SIDE DOWN ON PREPARED BAKING SHEET. REPEAT WITH REMAINING TORTILLAS, FILLING AND CHEESE. BAKE BURRITOS FOR ABOUT 20 MINUTES, UNTIL BROWNED. CUT IN HALF DIAGONALLY AND SERVE WITH SALSA AND SOUR CREAM, IF DESIRED. MAKES 10 BURRITOS.

TIP: IF YOU'RE PREPARING THE BURRITOS FOR THE FREEZER, YOU CAN SKIP THE BAKING INSTRUCTIONS. LET THE FILLING COOL COMPLETELY BEFORE ASSEMBLING THE BURRITOS. WRAP INDIVIDUAL BURRITOS IN PLASTIC WRAP AND FREEZE FOR UP TO 1 MONTH. REHEAT FROM FROZEN IN THE MICROWAVE.

SIDE DISHES

SPICED MANGOS

ADDS PIZZAZZ TO PORK CHOPS, GRILLED PORK TENDERLOIN OR PAN-FRIED SALMON.

1 TBSP	FINELY CHOPPED GINGERROOT	15 ML
1 TBSP	PACKED BROWN SUGAR	15 ML
1/2 TSP	CHINESE FIVE-SPICE POWDER	2 ML
1/8 TSP	SALT	0.5 ML
1/8 TSP	CAYENNE PEPPER	0.5 ML
1 TBSP	MELTED BUTTER	15 ML
2	FIRM RIPE MANGOS, PEELED AND CUT INTO THICK WEDGES	2
2 TBSP	FRESHLY SQUEEZED LIME JUICE (APPROX.)	30 ML

IN A 2- TO $3\frac{1}{2}$-QUART SLOW COOKER, COMBINE GINGER, BROWN SUGAR, FIVE-SPICE POWDER, SALT, CAYENNE AND BUTTER. STIR IN MANGOS. COVER AND COOK ON HIGH FOR 2 TO 3 HOURS, STIRRING HALFWAY THROUGH, UNTIL MANGOS ARE TENDER AND GLAZED. SPRINKLE WITH LIME JUICE. STIR. ADD MORE LIME JUICE, IF DESIRED (IT WILL DEPEND ON THE SWEETNESS OF THE MANGOS). SERVE IMMEDIATELY. SERVES 3 TO 4.

TIP: WHEN SELECTING A MANGO, SQUEEZE IT GENTLY. IF IT'S RIPE, IT WILL BE SLIGHTLY SOFT. TO PEEL A MANGO, STAND IT STEM END DOWN ON A CUTTING BOARD. WITH A SHARP KNIFE, CUT AWAY THE PEEL, WORKING FROM TOP TO BOTTOM. THEN CUT A THICK SLICE OFF EACH SIDE OF THE PIT. SLICE OFF ANY REMAINING FLESH AND CHOP ALL PIECES AS DESIRED.

BALSAMIC-GLAZED BEETS

*SWEET RUBY NUGGETS. AMAZING WITH GRILLED
SALMON. OR USE TO MAKE BEET, SPINACH AND
GOAT CHEESE SALAD (PAGE 274).*

2 LBS	LARGE BEETS, PEELED AND CUT INTO $1/2$-INCH (1 CM) CUBES	1 KG
2	CLOVES GARLIC, MINCED	2
2 TBSP	PACKED BROWN SUGAR	30 ML
	SALT	
2 TBSP	BALSAMIC VINEGAR	30 ML
1 TBSP	OLIVE OIL	15 ML
1 TBSP	CORNSTARCH	15 ML
1 TBSP	COLD WATER	15 ML
1	GREEN ONION, CHOPPED	1

IN A $31/2$- TO 4-QUART SLOW COOKER, COMBINE BEETS,
GARLIC, BROWN SUGAR, $1/4$ TSP (1 ML) SALT, VINEGAR AND
OIL. COVER AND COOK ON LOW FOR 5 TO 6 HOURS, UNTIL
BEETS ARE TENDER. MOVE BEETS TO ONE SIDE OF THE
SLOW COOKER. IN A BOWL, COMBINE CORNSTARCH AND
COLD WATER UNTIL SMOOTH. STIR INTO SAUCE IN SLOW
COOKER. STIR BEETS BACK INTO SAUCE. COVER AND
COOK ON HIGH FOR ABOUT 10 MINUTES, UNTIL SAUCE IS
THICKENED AND BEETS ARE GLAZED. ADJUST SEASONING
WITH SALT, IF DESIRED. SERVE SPRINKLED WITH GREEN
ONION. SERVES 6 TO 8.

TIP: YOU CAN ALSO MAKE THIS RECIPE USING SMALL
SUMMER BEETS FRESH FROM THE GARDEN, IN WHICH
CASE LEAVE THEM WHOLE AFTER PEELING. CUT MEDIUM-
SIZED BEETS INTO QUARTERS.

BEET, SPINACH AND GOAT CHEESE SALAD

AN EXCELLENT DINNER PARTY APPETIZER. FOLLOW IT WITH ROCKIN' ROULADEN (PAGE 126). CUE THE APPLAUSE.

CRANBERRY VINAIGRETTE

3 TBSP	GRANULATED SUGAR	45 ML
1 CUP	CRANBERRY COCKTAIL	250 ML
5 TBSP	FRESHLY SQUEEZED LEMON JUICE, DIVIDED	75 ML
	SALT AND PEPPER	
1/4 CUP	OLIVE OIL	60 ML

SALAD

4 CUPS	PACKED BABY SPINACH	1 L
1 1/2 CUPS	BALSAMIC-GLAZED BEETS (PAGE 273), CHILLED	375 ML
2 TBSP	CHOPPED FRESH DILL	30 ML
1/2 CUP	CRUMBLED GOAT OR FETA CHEESE	125 ML
1/4 CUP	TOASTED GREEN PUMPKIN SEEDS (PEPITAS)	60 ML
1/4 CUP	DRIED CRANBERRIES	60 ML

VINAIGRETTE: IN A SMALL SAUCEPAN, WHISK TOGETHER SUGAR, CRANBERRY COCKTAIL AND 3 TBSP (45 ML) OF THE LEMON JUICE; BRING TO A BOIL. REDUCE HEAT AND SIMMER, STIRRING OCCASIONALLY, FOR ABOUT 25 MINUTES, UNTIL JUICE IS REDUCED BY TWO-THIRDS AND IS SYRUPY. LET COOL COMPLETELY. *(THIS CAN BE DONE AHEAD. REFRIGERATE SYRUP IN AN AIRTIGHT CONTAINER FOR UP TO 2 WEEKS.)* IN A SMALL BOWL, WHISK TOGETHER 2 TBSP (30 ML) OF THE CRANBERRY

SYRUP AND THE REMAINING LEMON JUICE. GRADUALLY WHISK IN OIL. SEASON TO TASTE WITH SALT AND PEPPER.

SALAD: IN A SHALLOW SERVING BOWL, GENTLY TOSS SPINACH WITH HALF THE VINAIGRETTE. SPOON BEETS INTO THE CENTER OF THE SPINACH. SPRINKLE DILL OVER BEETS. SPRINKLE GOAT CHEESE, PUMPKIN SEEDS AND CRANBERRIES OVER BEETS AND SPINACH. TRANSFER REMAINING VINAIGRETTE TO A SMALL SERVING JUG. LET GUESTS HELP THEMSELVES TO SALAD AND DRIZZLE EXTRA DRESSING OVER TOP, IF DESIRED. SERVES 4.

TIP: LEFTOVER CRANBERRY SYRUP CAN BE DRIZZLED OVER GRILLED CHICKEN, PORK OR SALMON. IT'S SUPERB AS A TOPPING FOR VANILLA ICE CREAM.

PARSNIP BUTTERMILK CHIVE PURÉE

*A PLATE BUDDY FOR BEST-EVER BRAISED SHORT RIBS
(PAGE 162), BARBECUE-BRAISED RIBS, ROAST BEEF
OR GRILLED STEAK.*

4 CUPS	THINLY SLICED PARSNIPS (ABOUT 2 LBS/1 KG)	1 L
1½ CUPS	CUBED PEELED POTATOES (½-INCH/1 CM CUBES)	375 ML
	SALT	
1 CUP	WATER	250 ML
2 TSP	PACKED BROWN SUGAR	10 ML
¼ TSP	PEPPER	1 ML
4 OZ	CREAM CHEESE, CUBED AND SOFTENED	125 G
1 CUP	BUTTERMILK, WARMED	250 ML
¼ CUP	CHOPPED FRESH CHIVES	60 ML

IN A 3½- TO 4-QUART SLOW COOKER, COMBINE PARSNIPS,
POTATOES AND 1 TSP (5 ML) SALT. STIR IN WATER. PLACE
A PIECE OF PARCHMENT PAPER ON TOP OF THE PARSNIP
MIXTURE AND UP THE SIDES OF THE SLOW COOKER.
COVER AND COOK ON LOW FOR 6 HOURS OR ON HIGH
FOR 3 HOURS, UNTIL VEGETABLES ARE TENDER. REMOVE
PARCHMENT PAPER. DRAIN VEGETABLES AND RETURN
TO SLOW COOKER. ADD BROWN SUGAR, PEPPER, CREAM
CHEESE AND BUTTERMILK. USING AN IMMERSION BLENDER,
PURÉE UNTIL SMOOTH. (OR TRANSFER IN BATCHES TO
A BLENDER OR FOOD PROCESSOR AND PURÉE UNTIL
SMOOTH.) STIR IN CHIVES. SERVE IMMEDIATELY. SERVES 6
TO 8.

TIP: LOOK FOR FIRM PARSNIPS THAT ARE HEAVY FOR THEIR SIZE. AVOID PARSNIPS WITH WRINKLED SKIN OR LONG, SKINNY TAIL ENDS. PEEL WITH A VEGETABLE PEELER BEFORE SLICING. SOME RECIPES SUGGEST REMOVING THE WOODY CORE, BUT WE DON'T BOTHER FOR THIS RECIPE, AS THE CORE SOFTENS DURING COOKING.

MASHED MAPLE GINGER SQUASH

EXCELLENT AS A SIDE DISH FOR ROAST PORK, CHICKEN OR TURKEY, OR FOR BAKED HAM.

4 CUPS	CHOPPED BUTTERNUT SQUASH	1 L
1 TBSP	FINELY CHOPPED GINGERROOT	15 ML
	SALT AND PEPPER	
1/4 CUP	UNSWEETENED APPLE JUICE	60 ML
2 TBSP	PURE MAPLE SYRUP	30 ML
1 TBSP	BUTTER	

IN A 3 1/2- TO 4-QUART SLOW COOKER, COMBINE SQUASH, GINGER, 1/2 TSP (2 ML) SALT, 1/4 TSP (1 ML) PEPPER AND APPLE JUICE. COVER AND COOK ON LOW FOR ABOUT 4 HOURS, UNTIL SQUASH IS VERY TENDER. USING A POTATO MASHER, MASH SQUASH TO DESIRED CONSISTENCY. STIR IN MAPLE SYRUP AND BUTTER. ADJUST SEASONING WITH SALT AND PEPPER, IF DESIRED. SERVES 4.

SPICY ORANGE SQUASH

A SIMPLE SIDE DISH FOR GRILLED PORK CHOPS, CHICKEN OR SALMON.

1	SMALL ACORN SQUASH, HALVED, SEEDS AND MEMBRANE REMOVED	1
1/2 CUP	WATER	125 ML
2 TBSP	PACKED BROWN SUGAR	30 ML
1/4 TSP	SALT	1 ML
1/4 TSP	HOT PEPPER FLAKES	1 ML
2 TBSP	MELTED BUTTER	30 ML
	GRATED ZEST OF 1/2 ORANGE	
	FRESHLY SQUEEZED JUICE OF 1 ORANGE	

PLACE SQUASH CUT SIDE UP IN A 5- TO 6-QUART SLOW COOKER. POUR WATER AROUND SQUASH. IN A BOWL, COMBINE BROWN SUGAR, SALT, HOT PEPPER FLAKES, BUTTER, ORANGE ZEST AND ORANGE JUICE. POUR INTO SQUASH HALVES. COVER AND COOK ON LOW FOR 4 TO 5 HOURS, UNTIL SQUASH IS TENDER. CUT EACH HALF INTO 2 WEDGES. SERVE WITH JUICES SPOONED OVER SQUASH.

SERVES 4.

GINGER-GLAZED CARROTS

A GREAT RECIPE FOR HOLIDAY MEALS — ONE LESS DISH TO FUSS OVER.

2 LBS	CARROTS, SLICED	1 KG
1	ONION, THINLY SLICED	1
2 TSP	GRANULATED SUGAR	10 ML
1/4 TSP	GROUND CORIANDER	1 ML
	SALT AND PEPPER	
1/3 CUP	WATER	75 ML
1/3 CUP	GINGER MARMALADE	75 ML
2 TBSP	BUTTER	30 ML
1 TBSP	CHOPPED FRESH PARSLEY	15 ML

IN A 3 1/2- TO 4-QUART SLOW COOKER, COMBINE CARROTS, ONION, SUGAR, CORIANDER, 1/2 TSP (2 ML) SALT AND 1/4 TSP (1 ML) PEPPER. STIR IN WATER. COVER AND COOK ON LOW FOR ABOUT 4 HOURS OR ON HIGH FOR ABOUT 2 HOURS, UNTIL CARROTS ARE TENDER. ADD MARMALADE AND BUTTER, STIRRING UNTIL BUTTER MELTS AND CARROTS ARE COATED AND GLOSSY. ADJUST SEASONING WITH SALT AND PEPPER, IF DESIRED. SERVE SPRINKLED WITH PARSLEY. SERVES 4 TO 6.

TIP: GINGER MARMALADE PUTS A SWEETLY EXOTIC SPIN ON YOUR COOKING. (IT'S JOLLY GOOD ON BUTTERED TOAST, TOO!) IT'S WIDELY AVAILABLE IN SUPERMARKETS.

VARIATION: ORANGE-GLAZED CARROTS: REPLACE THE GINGER MARMALADE WITH ORANGE MARMALADE.

ROASTED GARLIC

MAKE A BATCH — IT KEEPS WELL — AND USE IT TO ENLIVEN MASHED POTATOES, PIZZAS, PASTA DISHES, SOUPS AND STEWS. OR MAKE ROASTED GARLIC CAESAR DRESSING (PAGE 281).

6	HEADS GARLIC	6
1/2 CUP	WATER	125 ML
1 TBSP	OLIVE OIL	15 ML

USE A MAXIMUM 4-QUART SLOW COOKER. CUT A THIN SLICE OFF THE TOP OF THE GARLIC HEADS, EXPOSING THE CLOVES. POUR WATER INTO SLOW COOKER. PLACE GARLIC, CUT SIDE UP, IN SLOW COOKER. SPOON 1/2 TSP (2 ML) OIL OVER EACH HEAD. COVER AND COOK ON LOW FOR 4 TO 5 HOURS, UNTIL GARLIC IS VERY TENDER. LET COOL SLIGHTLY. SQUEEZE THE INDIVIDUAL CLOVES OUT OF THEIR PAPERY SKIN.

MAKE AHEAD: LET COOL AND REFRIGERATE IN AN AIRTIGHT CONTAINER FOR UP TO 1 WEEK. OR MASH THE ROASTED GARLIC CLOVES WITH A FORK AND PLACE TABLESPOONFULS (15 ML) INTO ICE CUBE TRAYS; FREEZE UNTIL HARD. TRANSFER TO FREEZER BAGS AND FREEZE FOR UP TO 2 MONTHS.

ROASTED GARLIC CAESAR DRESSING

A RICH, CREAMY AND LOWER-FAT VERSION OF A
FAVORITE SALAD DRESSING. THE SECRET? ROASTED
GARLIC REPLACES RAW EGGS OR MAYONNAISE.

1	HEAD ROASTED GARLIC (PAGE 280)	1
	SALT AND PEPPER	
2 TBSP	CIDER VINEGAR	30 ML
1 TBSP	COLD WATER (APPROX.)	15 ML
1 TBSP	FRESHLY SQUEEZED LEMON JUICE	15 ML
1 TSP	DIJON MUSTARD	5 ML
$1/2$ TSP	WORCESTERSHIRE SAUCE	2 ML
$1/4$ CUP	OLIVE OIL	60 ML
2 TBSP	GRATED PARMESAN CHEESE	30 ML

SQUEEZE THE INDIVIDUAL CLOVES OUT OF THEIR PAPERY
SKIN AND PLACE IN A FOOD PROCESSOR. ADD $1/2$ TSP
(2 ML) SALT, $1/4$ TSP (1 ML) PEPPER, VINEGAR, COLD WATER,
LEMON JUICE, MUSTARD AND WORCESTERSHIRE SAUCE.
PULSE A FEW TIMES, UNTIL MIXTURE IS SMOOTH. ADD
OIL AND PULSE UNTIL CREAMY. STIR IN CHEESE. ADJUST
SEASONING WITH SALT AND PEPPER, IF DESIRED. WHISK IN
1 TO 2 TSP (5 TO 10 ML) MORE COLD WATER IF YOU DESIRE
A LOOSER CONSISTENCY. MAKES ABOUT $2/3$ CUP (150 ML).

TIP: TO MAKE THE DRESSING IN A BOWL, MASH THE
ROASTED GARLIC CLOVES WITH A FORK, THEN WHISK IN
THE REMAINING INGREDIENTS.

NO MORE EXCUSES! IT'S TIME TO START COOKING WITH DRIED LEGUMES, SUCH AS KIDNEY BEANS, CHICKPEAS AND LENTILS. THEY'RE GOOD FOR YOU, THEY'RE CHEAP, AND THEY'RE A BREEZE TO PREPARE IN THE SLOW COOKER. MOST DRIED LEGUMES — APART FROM LENTILS — NEED TO BE SOAKED AND THEN COOKED. HERE'S WHAT TO DO.

1. SOAK

LONG SOAK: RINSE BEANS. IN A BOWL, COMBINE BEANS WITH THREE TIMES THEIR VOLUME OF WATER (E.G., 1 CUP/250 ML BEANS AND 3 CUPS/750 ML WATER). SOAK FOR AT LEAST 6 HOURS OR OVERNIGHT. DRAIN AND RINSE. BEANS ARE NOW READY FOR COOKING.

SHORT SOAK: RINSE BEANS. IN A SAUCEPAN, COMBINE BEANS WITH THREE TIMES THEIR VOLUME OF WATER (E.G., 1 CUP/250 ML BEANS AND 3 CUPS/750 ML WATER). BRING TO A BOIL. REDUCE HEAT TO LOW, COVER AND SIMMER FOR 3 MINUTES. TURN OFF HEAT AND LET SOAK FOR 1 HOUR. DRAIN AND RINSE. BEANS ARE NOW READY FOR COOKING.

2. COOK

IN SLOW COOKER, COMBINE SOAKED BEANS WITH THREE TIMES THEIR NEW VOLUME OF WATER. (BEANS MAY DOUBLE OR MORE IN VOLUME DURING SOAKING, WITH 2 CUPS/500 ML DRIED BEANS YIELDING 4 TO 5 CUPS/1 TO 1.25 L SOAKED BEANS.) ADD SEASONINGS, IF YOU LIKE, SUCH AS 2 BAY LEAVES, AN ONION STUCK WITH 3 WHOLE CLOVES OR AN HERB BAG MADE FROM FRESH HERBS SUCH AS PARSLEY AND THYME TIED IN A SMALL PIECE OF

CHEESECLOTH. (DO NOT ADD SALT TO BEANS UNTIL THEY ARE FULLY COOKED, AS IT CAN MAKE THEM TOUGH). COVER AND COOK ON LOW FOR 10 TO 12 HOURS OR ON HIGH FOR 5 TO 6 HOURS, UNTIL BEANS ARE TENDER BUT NOT MUSHY. DRAIN AND RINSE, DISCARDING SEASONINGS. THE BEANS ARE NOW READY TO USE IN YOUR FAVORITE RECIPE.

MAKE AHEAD: COOKED LEGUMES CAN BE STORED IN AN AIRTIGHT CONTAINER IN THE REFRIGERATOR FOR UP TO 5 DAYS OR IN THE FREEZER FOR UP TO 6 MONTHS.

SUBSTITUTION: CANNED BEANS ARE A QUICK AND EASY SUBSTITUTION FOR COOKED DRIED BEANS. ALTHOUGH CAN SIZES VARY, THE DIFFERENCE IN AMOUNT WON'T AFFECT THE RESULTS OF MOST RECIPES. TO REPLACE 2 CUPS (500 ML) COOKED BEANS, USE A 14- TO 19-OZ (398 TO 540 ML) CAN. RINSE CANNED BEANS WELL BEFORE ADDING THEM TO A RECIPE.

OLD-FASHIONED BAKED BEANS

*FOR BARBECUES, FAMILY GET-TOGETHERS
OR A COMFORTING MIDWEEK SUPPER.*

6	SLICES BACON, CHOPPED	6
1	ONION, FINELY CHOPPED	1
2	CLOVES GARLIC, MINCED	2
1	CAN (14 OZ/398 ML) WHOLE TOMATOES, WITH JUICE	1
2	CANS (EACH 14 TO 19 OZ/398 TO 540 ML) SMALL WHITE BEANS, DRAINED AND RINSED (SEE TIP, PAGE 265)	2
2 TBSP	PACKED BROWN SUGAR	30 ML
1 TBSP	INSTANT COFFEE GRANULES	15 ML
2 TSP	DRY MUSTARD	10 ML
1/4 TSP	PEPPER	1 ML
1/2 CUP	KETCHUP	125 ML
1/4 CUP	LIGHT (FANCY) MOLASSES	60 ML
	HOT WATER (IF NEEDED)	
1 TBSP	CIDER VINEGAR, OR TO TASTE	15 ML

USE A 3 1/2- TO 4-QUART SLOW COOKER. IN A SKILLET,
COOK BACON OVER MEDIUM-HIGH HEAT UNTIL CRISPY.
USING A SLOTTED SPOON, TRANSFER BACON TO A PLATE
LINED WITH PAPER TOWELS. COVER AND REFRIGERATE.
REDUCE HEAT TO MEDIUM. ADD ONION AND GARLIC
TO SKILLET AND COOK, STIRRING OCCASIONALLY, FOR
3 MINUTES. SCRAPE INTO SLOW COOKER. ADD TOMATOES
AND COARSELY MASH WITH A POTATO MASHER. STIR
IN BEANS, BROWN SUGAR, COFFEE, MUSTARD, PEPPER,
KETCHUP AND MOLASSES. COVER AND COOK ON LOW FOR
6 TO 8 HOURS OR ON HIGH FOR 3 TO 4 HOURS, UNTIL

MIXTURE IS BUBBLING AND THICK ENOUGH TO HEAP ON A SPOON. ADJUST CONSISTENCY WITH HOT WATER, IF DESIRED. STIR IN VINEGAR. ADD RESERVED BACON AND STIR A FEW TIMES, UNTIL HEATED THROUGH. SERVE IMMEDIATELY. SERVES 6.

TIP: MOLASSES IS A THICK, SWEET, DARK BROWN LIQUID THAT IS A BY-PRODUCT OF SUGAR REFINING. IT IS OFTEN USED IN BAKED GOODS. THERE ARE A NUMBER OF GRADES OF MOLASSES. LIGHT, OR FANCY, MOLASSES HAS THE BEST FLAVOR. IF YOU SUBSTITUTE DARK (COOKING) OR BLACKSTRAP MOLASSES, YOU WILL GET A MORE INTENSE AND SOMEWHAT BITTER FLAVOR.

VARIATION
SMOKY VEGETARIAN BAKED BEANS: OMIT THE BACON. ADD 1 TSP (5 ML) SWEET SMOKED PAPRIKA WITH THE VINEGAR. COVER AND COOK ON HIGH FOR 15 MINUTES TO BLEND THE FLAVORS.

CREAMY CHEESE AND ONION POTATOES

OUTSTANDING WITH BAKED HAM — AND PRETTY MUCH ANYTHING ELSE.

2 LBS	YELLOW-FLESHED POTATOES (SUCH AS YUKON GOLD), PEELED AND CUT INTO 1-INCH (2.5 CM) CUBES	1 KG
1 TSP	SALT	5 ML
1 CUP	WATER	250 ML
1 TSP	PAPRIKA	5 ML
$\frac{1}{8}$ TSP	CAYENNE PEPPER	0.5 ML
1 CUP	HALF-AND-HALF (10%) CREAM, WARMED	250 ML
3	GREEN ONIONS, CHOPPED	3
$\frac{1}{2}$ CUP	GRATED PARMESAN CHEESE	125 ML
$\frac{3}{4}$ CUP	SHREDDED SHARP (OLD) CHEDDAR CHEESE	175 ML

IN A $3\frac{1}{2}$- TO 4-QUART SLOW COOKER, COMBINE POTATOES, SALT AND WATER. COVER AND COOK ON LOW FOR 5 TO 6 HOURS OR ON HIGH FOR $2\frac{1}{2}$ TO 3 HOURS, UNTIL POTATOES ARE TENDER. DRAIN POTATOES AND RETURN TO SLOW COOKER. IN A BOWL, COMBINE PAPRIKA, CAYENNE AND CREAM. POUR OVER POTATOES. GENTLY STIR IN GREEN ONIONS AND PARMESAN. SPRINKLE CHEDDAR OVER TOP. COVER AND COOK ON HIGH FOR 15 MINUTES, UNTIL CHEESE IS MELTED AND FLAVORS HAVE BLENDED. TURN OFF SLOW COOKER AND LET STAND FOR 10 MINUTES BEFORE SERVING. SERVES 4.

TIP: YOU CAN BUY GRATED PARMESAN CHEESE AT THE SUPERMARKET, BUT WE RECOMMEND GRATING YOUR OWN. WEDGES OF FRESH PARMESAN MAY SEEM EXPENSIVE, BUT THEY TASTE SO MUCH BETTER THAN THE PACKAGED STUFF. TO GRATE, USE A RASP-STYLE GRATER, SUCH AS A MICROPLANE, OR THE SMALLEST HOLES OF A BOX GRATER. WRAPPED IN PLASTIC WRAP, FRESH PARMESAN WILL KEEP FOR WEEKS IN THE REFRIGERATOR. BEST OF ALL, THE "HEEL," OR RIND, AT THE END OF THE WEDGE CAN BE THROWN INTO A SOUP OR STEW FOR ADDED FLAVORING.

AMBIVALENT? WELL ... YES AND NO.

BEST-EVER GARLIC MASHED POTATOES

THESE POTATOES ARE CREAMIER THAN THOSE COOKED IN A POT OF BOILING WATER, AND THE SLOW COOKER FREES UP SPACE ON THE STOVETOP.

3 LBS	YELLOW-FLESHED POTATOES (SUCH AS YUKON GOLD), PEELED AND CUT INTO 1-INCH (2.5 CM) CUBES	1.5 KG
6	WHOLE CLOVES GARLIC, PEELED	6
	SALT	
1½ CUPS	WATER	375 ML
	PEPPER	
¾ CUP	HALF-AND-HALF (10%) CREAM (APPROX.), WARMED	175 ML
⅓ CUP	BUTTER	75 ML
2 TBSP	CHOPPED FRESH CHIVES	30 ML

IN A 4- TO 6-QUART SLOW COOKER, COMBINE POTATOES, GARLIC, 1 TSP (2 ML) SALT AND WATER, PUSHING GARLIC DOWN TO ENSURE THAT IT IS SUBMERGED IN WATER. COVER AND COOK ON LOW FOR 5 TO 6 HOURS OR ON HIGH FOR 2½ TO 3 HOURS, UNTIL POTATOES AND GARLIC ARE TENDER. DRAIN POTATOES AND GARLIC AND RETURN TO SLOW COOKER. ADD ¼ TSP (1 ML) PEPPER, CREAM AND BUTTER; MASH TO DESIRED SMOOTHNESS. STIR IN CHIVES. ADD MORE CREAM TO REACH DESIRED CONSISTENCY. ADJUST SEASONING WITH SALT AND PEPPER, IF DESIRED. SERVES 6.

VARIATIONS: FOR LIGHTER MASHED POTATOES, REPLACE THE CREAM WITH MILK. YOU CAN ALSO OMIT THE GARLIC, IF YOU PREFER.

HORSERADISH MASHED POTATOES: OMIT THE GARLIC. JUST BEFORE SERVING, STIR IN 1 TBSP (15 ML) PREPARED CREAMED HORSERADISH (OR TO TASTE). MAGNIFICENT WITH ANY BEEF DISH.

NO-FUSS WILD RICE MEDLEY

AHH! THE NUTTY TEXTURE AND SUPERB AROMA OF WHOLESOME WILD AND BROWN RICE SIMMERED IN A SLOW COOKER. IT ALWAYS WORKS, AND IT'S ALWAYS A HIT!

1/2 CUP	WILD RICE, RINSED	125 ML
1/2 CUP	LONG-GRAIN BROWN RICE, RINSED	125 ML
1/2 TSP	SALT	2 ML
2 CUPS	WATER	500 ML
1 TBSP	BUTTER	15 ML

IN A 3 1/2- TO 4-QUART SLOW COOKER, COMBINE WILD RICE, BROWN RICE, SALT, WATER AND BUTTER. COVER AND COOK ON HIGH FOR ABOUT 1 1/2 HOURS, UNTIL RICE IS TENDER AND LIQUID IS ABSORBED. FLUFF WITH A FORK. SERVE IMMEDIATELY. SERVES 4.

TIP: PACKAGES OF WILD RICE BLEND, WHICH MAY INCLUDE WILD, BROWN, RED AND BLACK SWEET RICE, ARE WIDELY AVAILABLE IN SUPERMARKETS. USE THE METHOD ABOVE TO COOK THESE BLENDS IN THE SLOW COOKER.

WILD RICE AND ARTICHOKE HEARTS

A SPECIAL OCCASION DISH.

I CUP	WILD RICE, RINSED	250 ML
$\frac{1}{2}$ TSP	SALT	2 ML
2 CUPS	WATER	500 ML
3 TBSP	BUTTER, DIVIDED	45 ML
I	SMALL ONION, FINELY CHOPPED	I
2	CLOVES GARLIC, MINCED	2
2	JARS (EACH 6 OZ/170 ML) MARINATED ARTICHOKE HEARTS, DRAINED AND CHOPPED	2
2 TBSP	CHOPPED FRESH PARSLEY	30 ML

IN A $3\frac{1}{2}$- TO 4-QUART SLOW COOKER, COMBINE WILD RICE, SALT, WATER AND I TBSP (15 ML) BUTTER. COVER AND COOK ON HIGH FOR ABOUT $1\frac{1}{2}$ HOURS, UNTIL WILD RICE IS TENDER AND LIQUID IS ABSORBED. FLUFF WITH A FORK. MEANWHILE, IN A SKILLET, MELT REMAINING BUTTER OVER MEDIUM HEAT. ADD ONION AND GARLIC; COOK, STIRRING OCCASIONALLY, FOR 3 MINUTES. ADD ARTICHOKES AND COOK, STIRRING, UNTIL HEATED THROUGH, ABOUT 2 MINUTES. STIR INTO WILD RICE, ALONG WITH PARSLEY. SERVE IMMEDIATELY. SERVES 4 TO 6.

TIP: USE A MIXTURE OF WILD RICE AND LONG-GRAIN BROWN RICE, IF YOU PREFER. OR SUBSTITUTE ONE OF THE WILD RICE BLENDS THAT ARE NOW WIDELY AVAILABLE IN SUPERMARKETS.

INDIAN-SPICED BROWN RICE

SIMPLY PERFECT WITH BUTTER CHICKEN (PAGE 211), EASY CHICKEN CURRY (PAGE 234) OR BEEF MADRAS (PAGE 137).

1 TBSP	VEGETABLE OIL	30 ML
1 TBSP	CUMIN SEEDS	15 ML
1	LARGE ONION, FINELY CHOPPED	1
3	CLOVES GARLIC, MINCED	3
1 TSP	SALT	5 ML
1/2 TSP	GROUND CARDAMOM	2 ML
1 1/2 CUPS	LONG-GRAIN BROWN RICE, RINSED	375 ML
3	WHOLE CLOVES	3
1	2-INCH (5 CM) CINNAMON STICK	1
2 1/4 to 2 1/2 CUPS	BOILING WATER	550 to 625 ML
1/4 CUP	UNSALTED ROASTED CASHEWS	60 ML

USE A 3 1/2 TO 4-QUART SLOW COOKER. IN A SKILLET, HEAT OIL OVER MEDIUM-HIGH HEAT. ADD CUMIN SEEDS AND COOK, STIRRING, FOR ABOUT 1 MINUTE, UNTIL FRAGRANT. REDUCE HEAT TO MEDIUM. ADD ONION, GARLIC, SALT AND CARDAMOM; COOK, STIRRING OCCASIONALLY, FOR 3 MINUTES. ADD RICE AND STIR TO COAT. SCRAPE INTO SLOW COOKER. ADD CLOVES AND CINNAMON STICK. POUR IN 2 1/4 CUPS (550 ML) BOILING WATER AND STIR WELL. COVER AND COOK ON HIGH FOR 1 1/2 HOURS, UNTIL LIQUID IS ABSORBED AND RICE IS TENDER. IF RICE IS NOT YET TENDER BUT LIQUID IS ABSORBED AFTER 1 1/2 HOURS, ADD 1/4 CUP (60 ML) BOILING WATER, COVER AND COOK FOR 15 TO 30 MINUTES. USING A FORK, GENTLY STIR IN CASHEWS. SERVE IMMEDIATELY. *SERVES 6.*

BARLEY PARMESAN RISOTTO

BARLEY IS AN EXCELLENT CHOICE FOR THE SLOW COOKER — IT GETS TENDER WHILE HOLDING ITS SHAPE. SERVE THIS WITH GRILLED MEAT OR PAN-FRIED FISH. USE LEFTOVERS TO MAKE AMAZING BARLEY RISOTTO FRITTERS (PAGE 294).

3 TBSP	BUTTER, DIVIDED	45 ML
1	ONION, FINELY CHOPPED	1
3	CLOVES GARLIC, MINCED	3
1/2 TSP	SALT	2 ML
1/4 TSP	PEPPER	1 ML
3 TBSP	TOMATO PASTE	45 ML
1 CUP	BARLEY, RINSED	250 ML
4 CUPS	CHICKEN OR VEGETABLE BROTH	1 L
3/4 CUP	GRATED PARMESAN CHEESE	175 ML
1/4 CUP	CHOPPED FRESH PARSLEY	60 ML

USE A 3 1/2- TO 4-QUART SLOW COOKER. IN A SKILLET, MELT 2 TBSP (30 ML) BUTTER OVER MEDIUM HEAT. ADD ONION, GARLIC, SALT, PEPPER AND TOMATO PASTE; COOK, STIRRING OCCASIONALLY, FOR 3 MINUTES. STIR IN BARLEY. STIR IN BROTH AND BRING TO A BOIL. TRANSFER TO SLOW COOKER. COVER AND COOK ON LOW FOR 5 TO 6 HOURS OR ON HIGH FOR 2 1/2 TO 3 HOURS, UNTIL BARLEY IS TENDER AND MIXTURE IS CREAMY. STIR IN CHEESE, PARSLEY AND REMAINING BUTTER. SERVES 4 TO 6.

TIP: WHOLE, POT OR PEARL BARLEY ALL WORK WELL IN THIS RECIPE. WHOLE BARLEY IS THE MOST NUTRITIOUS FORM, BUT RESULTS IN A LESS CREAMY RISOTTO.

TIP: WE USE TOMATO PASTE IN MANY OF OUR SLOW COOKER RECIPES BECAUSE IT GREATLY BOOSTS FLAVOR AND RICHNESS. THE LONG, MOIST COOKING DULLS OTHER AROMATIC INGREDIENTS, SUCH AS ONIONS, GARLIC AND HERBS. MICROWAVING OR BROWNING A DOLLOP OR TWO OF TOMATO PASTE WITH THESE INGREDIENTS MAKES ALL THE DIFFERENCE.

VARIATION

BARLEY TOMATO RISOTTO: OMIT THE PARSLEY. WHEN RISOTTO IS COOKED, STIR IN 2 DICED SEEDED TOMATOES, $\frac{1}{4}$ CUP (60 ML) CHOPPED FRESH CHIVES AND AN ADDITIONAL $\frac{1}{3}$ CUP (75 ML) BROTH. COVER AND COOK ON HIGH FOR 15 MINUTES, UNTIL TOMATOES ARE HEATED THROUGH AND FLAVORS ARE BLENDED. STIR IN CHEESE AND REMAINING BUTTER.

BARLEY RISOTTO FRITTERS

A GREAT WAY TO USE UP LEFTOVER BARLEY PARMESAN RISOTTO. SERVE WITH FRIED EGGS FOR A LIGHT SUPPER, OR WITH PAN-FRIED FISH.

3	SLICES BACON, CHOPPED	3
3	GREEN ONIONS, CHOPPED	3
3 CUPS	CHILLED BARLEY PARMESAN RISOTTO (PAGE 292)	750 ML
1/4 TSP	CAYENNE PEPPER	1 ML
1	EGG, LIGHTLY BEATEN	1
1 TBSP	VEGETABLE OIL (APPROX.)	15 ML

IN A SKILLET, COOK BACON OVER MEDIUM-HIGH HEAT UNTIL CRISPY. USING A SLOTTED SPOON, TRANSFER BACON TO A PLATE LINED WITH PAPER TOWELS. DRAIN FAT FROM SKILLET AND WIPE CLEAN WITH A PAPER TOWEL. IN A BOWL, COMBINE COOKED BACON, GREEN ONIONS, RISOTTO, CAYENNE AND EGG. SHAPE INTO 6 PATTIES. (USE A 1/2 CUP/125 ML MEASURING CUP TO DIVIDE THE MIXTURE EQUALLY.) ADD OIL TO SKILLET AND HEAT OVER MEDIUM HEAT. ADD 3 FRITTERS AND COOK FOR 3 TO 4 MINUTES PER SIDE, UNTIL BROWN AND CRISPY. TRANSFER TO A PLATE LINED WITH PAPER TOWELS AND KEEP WARM. REPEAT WITH REMAINING FRITTERS, ADDING MORE OIL TO SKILLET AS NECESSARY. MAKES 6 FRITTERS.

BUTTERNUT SQUASH BARLEY RISOTTO

FABULOUS FALL FLAVORS TO SERVE WITH GRILLED PORK CHOPS, PORK TENDERLOIN OR PAN-FRIED WHITE FISH, SUCH AS HALIBUT OR TILAPIA.

3 TBSP	BUTTER, DIVIDED	45 ML
1	ONION, FINELY CHOPPED	1
1/2 TSP	CRUMBLED DRIED SAGE	2 ML
1/2 TSP	SALT	2 ML
1/4 TSP	PEPPER	1 ML
2 CUPS	CUBED BUTTERNUT SQUASH (1/2-INCH/1 CM CUBES)	500 ML
1 CUP	BARLEY, RINSED	250 ML
1/4 CUP	DRY WHITE WINE	60 ML
4 CUPS	CHICKEN OR VEGETABLE BROTH	1 L
3/4 CUP	GRATED PARMESAN CHEESE	175 ML
1/3 CUP	CHOPPED TOASTED HAZELNUTS	75 ML
1 TBSP	CHOPPED FRESH SAGE (OPTIONAL)	15 ML

USE A 3½- TO 4-QUART SLOW COOKER. IN A SKILLET, MELT 2 TBSP (30 ML) BUTTER OVER MEDIUM HEAT. ADD ONION, DRIED SAGE, SALT AND PEPPER; COOK, STIRRING, FOR 3 MINUTES. STIR IN SQUASH AND BARLEY. STIR IN WINE AND COOK, STIRRING, FOR A FEW SECONDS, UNTIL WINE IS ALMOST EVAPORATED. TRANSFER TO SLOW COOKER. STIR IN BROTH. COVER AND COOK ON LOW FOR 5 TO 6 HOURS OR ON HIGH FOR 2½ TO 3 HOURS, UNTIL BARLEY AND SQUASH ARE TENDER AND MIXTURE IS CREAMY. STIR IN CHEESE, HAZELNUTS, FRESH SAGE (IF USING) AND REMAINING BUTTER. SERVES 4 TO 6.

MUSHROOM HERB BREAD STUFFING

THE WORRY-FREE WAY TO COOK STUFFING WHEN THE TURKEY IS OCCUPYING THE OVEN!

10 CUPS	CUBED FRENCH OR OTHER WHITE BREAD	2.5 L
1/4 CUP	BUTTER OR OLIVE OIL	60 ML
2	ONIONS, CHOPPED	2
2	STALKS CELERY, THINLY SLICED	2
2	LEEKS (WHITE TO MEDIUM GREEN PARTS ONLY), THINLY SLICED	2
4	CLOVES GARLIC, MINCED	4
6 CUPS	SLICED MUSHROOMS	1.5 L
1/2 CUP	CHOPPED FRESH PARSLEY	125 ML
1/4 CUP	CHOPPED FRESH SAGE (OR 1 TBSP/15 ML DRIED)	60 ML
2 TBSP	CHOPPED FRESH THYME (OR 1 TSP/5 ML DRIED)	30 ML
1 TSP	SALT	5 ML
1/4 TSP	PEPPER	1 ML
2	EGGS, LIGHTLY BEATEN	2
1 1/2 CUPS	CHICKEN OR VEGETABLE BROTH	375 ML

GREASE A 5- TO 6-QUART SLOW COOKER. PLACE BREAD CUBES IN A LARGE BOWL. IN A LARGE SKILLET, MELT BUTTER OVER MEDIUM HEAT. ADD ONIONS, CELERY, LEEKS AND GARLIC; COOK, STIRRING OCCASIONALLY, FOR 5 MINUTES. ADD MUSHROOMS AND COOK, STIRRING OCCASIONALLY, FOR 10 MINUTES. SCRAPE OVER BREAD CUBES. STIR IN PARSLEY, SAGE, THYME, SALT, PEPPER, EGGS AND BROTH. TRANSFER TO SLOW COOKER, SPREADING EVENLY. COVER AND COOK ON LOW FOR ABOUT 4 HOURS OR ON HIGH FOR ABOUT 2 HOURS, UNTIL HEATED THROUGH. SERVES 10.

TIP: FOR BEST RESULTS, USE STALE BREAD. AN EASY WAY TO STALE BREAD IS TO SPREAD THE SLICES IN A SINGLE LAYER ON A COUPLE OF BAKING SHEETS AND LEAVE THEM UNCOVERED ON THE COUNTER OVERNIGHT.

TIP: RINSE LEEKS WELL, AS THEY OFTEN HAVE SOIL TRAPPED BETWEEN THEIR LAYERS. TO CLEAN THEM THOROUGHLY, SWIRL CHOPPED OR SLICED LEEKS IN A LARGE BOWL OF WATER. LET THE DIRT FALL TO THE BOTTOM AND REMOVE LEEKS WITH A SLOTTED SPOON. REPEAT IF NECESSARY. YOU CAN USE BOTH THE WHITE AND THE PALE TO MEDIUM GREEN PARTS OF THE LEEK. ONLY THE VERY DARK GREEN TOP 1 TO 2 INCHES (2.5 TO 5 CM) SHOULD BE DISCARDED.

MUSHROOM PARMESAN POLENTA

A SIMPLIFIED VERSION OF THE TRADITIONAL ITALIAN SIDE DISH, AND NO SCORCHED PAN! SERVE WARM WITH STEWS, POT ROASTS OR BRAISED SHORT RIBS.

1 CUP	CORNMEAL	250 ML
1/4 CUP	CHOPPED DRIED MUSHROOMS, RINSED IN LUKEWARM WATER	60 ML
1/2 TSP	SALT	2 ML
1/8 TSP	PEPPER	0.5 ML
1 TBSP	BUTTER	15 ML
3 CUPS	BOILING WATER	750 ML
1/2 CUP	GRATED PARMESAN CHEESE	125 ML
2 TBSP	CHOPPED FRESH PARSLEY	30 ML

GREASE A 3 1/2- TO 4-QUART SLOW COOKER. PLACE CORNMEAL, MUSHROOMS, SALT, PEPPER AND BUTTER IN SLOW COOKER. GRADUALLY ADD BOILING WATER, WHISKING CONSTANTLY UNTIL BLENDED. COVER AND COOK ON LOW FOR 1 1/2 TO 3 HOURS, UNTIL GRAINS ARE TENDER AND MIXTURE HAS THICKENED. STIR IN CHEESE AND PARSLEY. SERVE IMMEDIATELY. SERVES 6.

DESSERTS

BANOFFEE PIE

AN IRRESISTIBLE BRITISH DESSERT. THE TOFFEE SAUCE IS EASY TO MAKE IN THE SLOW COOKER.

1	CAN (14 OZ OR 300 ML) SWEETENED CONDENSED MILK	1
	VERY HOT WATER	
2 CUPS	CRUSHED DIGESTIVE COOKIES	500 ML
1/2 CUP	MELTED BUTTER	125 ML
2	BANANAS, SLICED	2
1 CUP	HEAVY OR WHIPPING (35%) CREAM	250 ML
	GRATED CHOCOLATE	

USE A 4- TO 6-QUART SLOW COOKER. POUR MILK INTO A 2-CUP (500 ML) GLASS MEASURING CUP, COVER WITH FOIL AND PLACE IN SLOW COOKER. ADD VERY HOT WATER TO THE SLOW COOKER UNTIL IT REACHES THE LEVEL OF THE MILK. COVER AND COOK ON LOW FOR ABOUT 9 HOURS, UNTIL MILK IS VERY THICK AND CARAMEL-COLORED. WHISK THOROUGHLY, THEN LET COOL TO ROOM TEMPERATURE. MEANWHILE, IN A BOWL, COMBINE COOKIES AND BUTTER. PAT INTO THE BASE AND UP THE SIDES OF AN 8-INCH (20 CM) PIE PLATE. REFRIGERATE FOR 1 HOUR. ARRANGE BANANAS OVER CHILLED BASE. POUR TOFFEE SAUCE OVER BANANAS. REFRIGERATE FOR AT LEAST 1 HOUR, UNTIL CHILLED, OR OVERNIGHT. IN A BOWL, WHIP CREAM UNTIL SOFT PEAKS FORM. SPREAD OVER PIE. SPRINKLE WITH GRATED CHOCOLATE. SERVES 6.

MAKE AHEAD: TRANSFER THE COOLED TOFFEE SAUCE TO AN AIRTIGHT CONTAINER AND REFRIGERATE FOR UP TO

5 DAYS OR FREEZE FOR UP TO I MONTH. THAW OVERNIGHT IN THE REFRIGERATOR.

TIP: FOR BEST RESULTS WHEN WHIPPING CREAM, BE SURE THAT THE CREAM IS VERY COLD. ALSO, CHILL THE BOWL AND BEATERS IN THE FREEZER FOR A SHORT WHILE BEFOREHAND. USE A DEEP BOWL TO PREVENT SPATTERS. RECIPES USUALLY SPECIFY WHIPPING THE CREAM TO SOFT PEAKS (WHICH BEND OVER SLIGHTLY) OR FIRM PEAKS (WHICH ARE MORE POINTY AND UPRIGHT). BE CAREFUL NOT TO OVER-WHIP CREAM. IF IT STARTS TO LOOK GRAINY, YOU HAVE GONE TOO FAR. YOU MAY BE ABLE TO RESCUE OVER-WHIPPED CREAM BY ADDING A LITTLE MORE UNWHIPPED CREAM TO THE BOWL AND WHIPPING ON LOW SPEED.

VARIATION
CARAMEL CRUNCH PIE: OMIT THE BANANAS AND GRATED CHOCOLATE. SPRINKLE TOP OF PIE WITH I MILK CHOCOLATE TOFFEE CANDY BAR (SUCH AS SKOR), COARSELY CHOPPED.

TOO MUCH π CAN GIVE YOU
A LARGE CIRCUMFERENCE.

BLUEBERRY UPSIDE-DOWN GINGER CAKE

A YEAR-ROUND WINNER. SERVE WARM WITH WHIPPED CREAM OR A DOLLOP OF PLAIN GREEK YOGURT.

TOPPING

1/2 CUP	PACKED BROWN SUGAR	125 ML
1/4 CUP	MELTED BUTTER	60 ML
4 CUPS	BLUEBERRIES (THAWED IF FROZEN)	1 L
1 TBSP	FRESHLY SQUEEZED LIME JUICE	15 ML

CAKE

1 1/2 CUPS	ALL-PURPOSE FLOUR	375 ML
2 TSP	GROUND GINGER	10 ML
1 TSP	GROUND CINNAMON	5 ML
1 TSP	BAKING POWDER	5 ML
1/2 TSP	BAKING SODA	2 ML
1/8 TSP	GROUND CLOVES	0.5 ML
1 CUP	PACKED BROWN SUGAR	250 ML
1/2 CUP	BUTTER, SOFTENED	125 ML
1/2 CUP	LIGHT (FANCY) MOLASSES	125 ML
1/2 CUP	BUTTERMILK	125 ML
2	EGGS, AT ROOM TEMPERATURE	2

TOPPING: GREASE THE INSERT OF A 3 1/2- TO 4-QUART SLOW COOKER. SPREAD BROWN SUGAR AND BUTTER OVER BOTTOM OF SLOW COOKER. SPREAD BLUEBERRIES ON TOP. SPRINKLE WITH LIME JUICE.

CAKE: IN A BOWL, WHISK TOGETHER FLOUR, GINGER, CINNAMON, BAKING POWDER, BAKING SODA AND CLOVES. IN A LARGE BOWL, CREAM BROWN SUGAR AND BUTTER

UNTIL LIGHT AND FLUFFY. BEAT IN MOLASSES AND BUTTERMILK UNTIL BLENDED. BEAT IN EGGS, ONE AT A TIME. (DON'T WORRY IF IT LOOKS CURDLED.) BEAT IN FLOUR MIXTURE UNTIL SMOOTH. SPREAD BATTER OVER BLUEBERRIES. PLACE A CLEAN TEA TOWEL, FOLDED IN HALF (SO YOU HAVE TWO LAYERS), OVER TOP OF INSERT. COVER AND COOK ON HIGH FOR 2 TO 3 HOURS, UNTIL A TESTER INSERTED IN THE CENTER OF THE CAKE COMES OUT CLEAN. WHEN READY TO SERVE, SLICE AND INVERT ONTO A PLATE. SERVES 6.

TIP: MOLASSES IS A THICK, SWEET, DARK BROWN LIQUID THAT IS A BY-PRODUCT OF SUGAR REFINING. IT IS OFTEN USED IN BAKED GOODS. THERE ARE A NUMBER OF GRADES OF MOLASSES. LIGHT, OR FANCY, MOLASSES HAS THE BEST FLAVOR. IF YOU SUBSTITUTE DARK (COOKING) OR BLACKSTRAP MOLASSES, YOU WILL GET A MORE INTENSE AND SOMEWHAT BITTER FLAVOR.

CARIBBEAN FRUIT UPSIDE-DOWN CAKE

TASTES OF THE TROPICS. SERVE WARM, WITH A SCOOP OF VANILLA ICE CREAM.

TOPPING

1/4 CUP	MELTED BUTTER	60 ML
1/2 CUP	PACKED DARK BROWN SUGAR	125 ML
1/2 TSP	GROUND CINNAMON	2 ML
2 TBSP	DARK RUM (OPTIONAL)	30 ML
2	FIRM RIPE BANANAS, CUT INTO 1/2-INCH (1 CM) SLICES	2
2 CUPS	FROZEN MANGO CUBES, THAWED	500 ML

CAKE

1 1/2 CUPS	ALL-PURPOSE FLOUR	375 ML
2 TSP	BAKING POWDER	10 ML
1 TSP	GROUND CINNAMON	5 ML
1/4 TSP	SALT (OPTIONAL)	1 ML
1/8 TSP	GROUND CLOVES	0.5 ML
3/4 CUP	GRANULATED SUGAR	175 ML
1/2 CUP	BUTTER, SOFTENED	125 ML
2	EGGS, AT ROOM TEMPERATURE	2
1 TSP	VANILLA EXTRACT	5 ML
1 CUP	WHOLE MILK	250 ML

TOPPING: GREASE THE INSERT OF A 3 1/2- TO 4-QUART SLOW COOKER. POUR BUTTER INTO SLOW COOKER. ADD BROWN SUGAR, CINNAMON AND RUM (IF USING); STIR WELL, SPREADING EVENLY OVER BOTTOM OF SLOW COOKER. ARRANGE BANANAS AND MANGOS ON TOP.

CAKE: IN A BOWL, WHISK TOGETHER FLOUR, BAKING POWDER, CINNAMON, SALT (IF USING) AND CLOVES. IN A LARGE BOWL, CREAM SUGAR AND BUTTER UNTIL LIGHT AND FLUFFY. BEAT IN EGGS, ONE A TIME, AND VANILLA. BEAT IN FLOUR MIXTURE ALTERNATELY WITH MILK, MAKING TWO ADDITIONS OF EACH. SPREAD BATTER OVER FRUIT. PLACE A CLEAN TEA TOWEL, FOLDED IN HALF (SO YOU HAVE TWO LAYERS), OVER TOP OF INSERT. COVER AND COOK ON HIGH FOR 2 TO 3 HOURS, UNTIL A TESTER INSERTED IN THE CENTER OF THE CAKE COMES OUT CLEAN. WHEN READY TO SERVE, SLICE AND INVERT ONTO A PLATE.

SERVES 6.

TIP: FROZEN PEELED MANGO CUBES ARE SOLD IN MOST SUPERMARKETS. KEEP A BAG IN THE FREEZER AND YOU'LL FIND WAYS TO USE MANGO IN SOUPS, STIR-FRIES, DESSERTS AND SMOOTHIES. YOU CAN SUBSTITUTE 2 CHOPPED RIPE MANGOS IN THIS RECIPE, IF YOU PREFER.

VARIATION
KID-FRIENDLY BANANA UPSIDE-DOWN CAKE: OMIT THE MANGOS AND USE 4 BANANAS. REPLACE THE RUM WITH 2 TBSP (30 ML) ORANGE JUICE.

APPLE CRANBERRY CAKE

THE PERFECT FALL DESSERT. YOU CAN NAP WHILE IT COOKS. SERVE WITH VANILLA ICE CREAM OR WHIPPED CREAM.

1 1/4 CUPS	ALL-PURPOSE FLOUR	300 ML
3/4 CUP	GRANULATED SUGAR	175 ML
2 TSP	BAKING POWDER	10 ML
1 TSP	GROUND CINNAMON	5 ML
1/2 TSP	SALT	2 ML
1	EGG, AT ROOM TEMPERATURE	1
1/2 CUP	2% OR WHOLE MILK	125 ML
1 TSP	VANILLA EXTRACT	5 ML
	GRATED ZEST OF 1 ORANGE	
2	APPLES, PEELED AND CHOPPED	2
1 CUP	CRANBERRIES (THAWED IF FROZEN)	250 ML
1/4 CUP	ORANGE MARMALADE	60 ML
1/4 CUP	MELTED BUTTER	60 ML

GREASE THE INSERT OF A 3 1/2- TO 4-QUART SLOW COOKER. IN A LARGE BOWL, WHISK TOGETHER FLOUR, SUGAR, BAKING POWDER, CINNAMON AND SALT. IN ANOTHER BOWL, WHISK TOGETHER EGG, MILK, VANILLA AND ORANGE ZEST. POUR OVER FLOUR MIXTURE AND STIR JUST UNTIL EVENLY COMBINED. SPREAD BATTER IN PREPARED SLOW COOKER. IN A BOWL, COMBINE APPLES, CRANBERRIES AND MARMALADE. ARRANGE ON TOP OF BATTER. POUR BUTTER OVER TOP. COVER AND COOK ON HIGH FOR 2 TO 2 1/2 HOURS, UNTIL APPLES ARE TENDER AND A TESTER INSERTED IN THE CENTER OF THE CAKE COMES OUT CLEAN. TURN OFF SLOW COOKER, REMOVE LID AND LET STAND FOR 15 MINUTES BEFORE REMOVING CAKE. SERVES 4 TO 6.

APPLE BLACKBERRY CRISP

KEEP FROZEN BLACKBERRIES ON HAND TO MAKE THIS COMFORTING DESSERT ANY TIME OF THE YEAR.

BASE

4	APPLES, PEELED AND THINLY SLICED	4
2 CUPS	BLACKBERRIES (NO NEED TO THAW IF FROZEN)	500 ML
$\frac{1}{2}$ CUP	PACKED BROWN SUGAR	125 ML
2 TBSP	ALL-PURPOSE FLOUR	30 ML
2 TSP	GROUND CINNAMON	10 ML
2 TBSP	ORANGE JUICE	30 ML

TOPPING

$\frac{1}{2}$ CUP	ALL-PURPOSE FLOUR	125 ML
$\frac{1}{2}$ CUP	PACKED BROWN SUGAR	125 ML
$\frac{1}{2}$ CUP	GROUND ALMONDS	125 ML
$\frac{1}{4}$ CUP	LARGE-FLAKE (OLD-FASHIONED) ROLLED OATS	60 ML
$\frac{1}{4}$ CUP	MELTED BUTTER	60 ML

BASE: GREASE THE INSERT OF A $3\frac{1}{2}$- TO 4-QUART SLOW COOKER. IN SLOW COOKER, GENTLY STIR TOGETHER APPLES, BLACKBERRIES, BROWN SUGAR, FLOUR, CINNAMON AND ORANGE JUICE.

TOPPING: IN A BOWL, COMBINE FLOUR, BROWN SUGAR, ALMONDS AND OATS. STIR IN BUTTER. SPRINKLE EVENLY OVER APPLE MIXTURE. PLACE A CLEAN TEA TOWEL, FOLDED IN HALF (SO YOU HAVE TWO LAYERS), OVER TOP OF INSERT. COVER AND COOK ON HIGH FOR ABOUT 3 HOURS, UNTIL BUBBLING. TURN OFF SLOW COOKER, REMOVE LID AND LET STAND FOR AT LEAST 45 MINUTES TO ALLOW FRUIT TO THICKEN. SERVES 6.

APPLE CRISP WITH HAZELNUT TOPPING

YOU CAN MAKE FRUIT CRISP IN THE SLOW COOKER. SERVE WITH RUM PECAN CARAMEL SAUCE (PAGE 336) AND WHIPPED CREAM.

BASE

6	APPLES, PEELED AND THINLY SLICED	6
1/2 CUP	PACKED BROWN SUGAR	125 ML
2 TBSP	ALL-PURPOSE FLOUR	30 ML
2 TSP	GROUND CINNAMON	10 ML
2 TBSP	FRESHLY SQUEEZED LEMON JUICE	30 ML

HAZELNUT TOPPING

1/2 CUP	ALL-PURPOSE FLOUR	125 ML
1/2 CUP	PACKED BROWN SUGAR	125 ML
1/2 CUP	CHOPPED TOASTED HAZELNUTS	125 ML
1/4 CUP	LARGE-FLAKE (OLD-FASHIONED) ROLLED OATS	60 ML
1/4 CUP	MELTED BUTTER	60 ML

BASE: GREASE THE INSERT OF A 3½- TO 4-QUART SLOW COOKER. IN SLOW COOKER, GENTLY STIR TOGETHER APPLES, BROWN SUGAR, FLOUR, CINNAMON AND LEMON JUICE.

TOPPING: IN A BOWL, COMBINE FLOUR, BROWN SUGAR, HAZELNUTS AND OATS. STIR IN BUTTER. SPRINKLE EVENLY OVER APPLE MIXTURE. PLACE A CLEAN TEA TOWEL, FOLDED IN HALF (SO YOU HAVE TWO LAYERS), OVER TOP OF INSERT. COVER AND COOK ON HIGH FOR ABOUT 3 HOURS, UNTIL BUBBLING. TURN OFF SLOW

COOKER, REMOVE LID AND LET STAND FOR AT LEAST 45 MINUTES TO ALLOW FRUIT TO THICKEN. SERVES 6.

TIP: WHEN SQUEEZING JUICE FROM A LEMON, LIME OR ORANGE, AIM TO HAVE THE FRUIT AT ROOM TEMPERATURE — IT WILL GIVE UP JUICE MORE EASILY THAN IF SQUEEZED STRAIGHT FROM THE REFRIGERATOR. IF YOU FORGET TO REMOVE IT FROM THE FRIDGE AHEAD OF TIME, PRICK THE FRUIT WITH A FORK AND MICROWAVE IT ON HIGH FOR ABOUT 20 SECONDS TO WARM IT SLIGHTLY.

TIP: IF YOU BUY WHOLE HAZELNUTS, YOU WILL NOTICE THAT THEY ARE SOLD EITHER WITH SKINS ON (A DARK BROWN COLOR) OR BLANCHED (A CREAMY WHITE COLOR). WE'VE TRIED VARIOUS METHODS FOR REMOVING THE SKIN OF HAZELNUTS, AND NONE WORK VERY WELL, SO WE TRY TO BUY THE BLANCHED ONES.

MANGO STRAWBERRY CRISP

*SWEETLY EXOTIC! SERVE WITH VANILLA BEAN
ICE CREAM OR WHIPPED CREAM.*

BASE

3 CUPS	FROZEN MANGO CUBES (NO NEED TO THAW)	750 ML
2 CUPS	STRAWBERRIES (NO NEED TO THAW IF FROZEN), HALVED	500 ML
1/2 CUP	GRANULATED SUGAR	125 ML
2 TBSP	ALL-PURPOSE FLOUR	30 ML
1 TSP	GROUND CINNAMON	5 ML
	GRATED ZEST OF 1/2 LIME	
2 TBSP	FRESHLY SQUEEZED LIME JUICE	30 ML

TOPPING

1/2 CUP	ALL-PURPOSE FLOUR	125 ML
1/2 CUP	PACKED BROWN SUGAR	125 ML
1/4 CUP	TOASTED SWEETENED FLAKED OR SHREDDED COCONUT (SEE TIP, OPPOSITE)	60 ML
1/4 CUP	LARGE-FLAKE (OLD-FASHIONED) ROLLED OATS	60 ML
1/4 CUP	MELTED BUTTER	60 ML

BASE: GREASE THE INSERT OF A 3 1/2- TO 4-QUART SLOW COOKER. IN SLOW COOKER, GENTLY STIR TOGETHER MANGOS, STRAWBERRIES, SUGAR, FLOUR, CINNAMON, LIME ZEST AND LIME JUICE.

TOPPING: IN A BOWL, COMBINE FLOUR, BROWN SUGAR, COCONUT AND OATS. STIR IN BUTTER. SPRINKLE EVENLY OVER MANGO MIXTURE. PLACE A CLEAN TEA TOWEL, FOLDED IN HALF (SO YOU HAVE TWO LAYERS), OVER

TOP OF INSERT. COVER AND COOK ON HIGH FOR ABOUT 3 HOURS, UNTIL BUBBLING. TURN OFF SLOW COOKER, REMOVE LID AND LET STAND FOR AT LEAST 45 MINUTES TO ALLOW FRUIT TO THICKEN. SERVES 6.

TIP: TOASTING COCONUT HELPS TO BRING OUT ITS FLAVOR. SPREAD COCONUT IN A DRY NONSTICK SKILLET AND COOK OVER MEDIUM HEAT, SHAKING OR STIRRING FREQUENTLY, FOR 4 TO 5 MINUTES OR UNTIL FRAGRANT AND LIGHTLY BROWNED. TRANSFER COCONUT TO A COLD PLATE TO STOP THE COOKING PROCESS AND LET COOL COMPLETELY.

GREY IS THE NEW BLONDE.

FESTIVE FRUIT CRISP

NOVICE COOKS WILL LOVE THIS FUSS-FREE CHRISTMAS FINALE! SERVE WITH CHANTILLY CREAM (OPPOSITE).

BASE

2	APPLES, PEELED AND CHOPPED	2
2 CUPS	MINCEMEAT	500 ML
I CUP	FRESH OR FROZEN CRANBERRIES	250 ML
3 TBSP	RUM OR BRANDY	45 ML
	GRATED ZEST OF I ORANGE	

TOPPING

1/2 CUP	ALL-PURPOSE FLOUR	125 ML
1/2 CUP	PACKED BROWN SUGAR	125 ML
1/2 CUP	LARGE-FLAKE (OLD-FASHIONED) ROLLED OATS	125 ML
I TSP	GROUND CINNAMON	5 ML
1/8 TSP	GROUND CLOVES	0.5 ML
1/8 TSP	GROUND NUTMEG	0.5 ML
1/4 CUP	MELTED BUTTER	60 ML

BASE: GREASE THE INSERT OF A 3½- TO 4-QUART SLOW COOKER. IN SLOW COOKER, STIR TOGETHER APPLES, MINCEMEAT, CRANBERRIES, RUM AND ORANGE ZEST.

TOPPING: IN A BOWL, COMBINE FLOUR, BROWN SUGAR, OATS, CINNAMON, CLOVES AND NUTMEG. STIR IN BUTTER. SPRINKLE EVENLY OVER APPLE MIXTURE. PLACE A CLEAN TEA TOWEL, FOLDED IN HALF (SO YOU HAVE TWO LAYERS), OVER TOP OF INSERT. COVER AND COOK ON HIGH FOR ABOUT 3 HOURS, UNTIL BUBBLING. TURN OFF SLOW COOKER, REMOVE LID AND LET STAND FOR AT LEAST 45 MINUTES TO ALLOW FRUIT TO THICKEN. SERVES 6.

TIP: MINCEMEAT IS A RICH MIXTURE OF CHOPPED DRIED FRUIT, NUTS AND SPICES USED AS THE FILLING IN CHRISTMAS MINCE PIES. TRADITIONALLY, IT CONTAINED LEAN MEAT — HENCE ITS NAME. LOOK FOR JARS OF MINCEMEAT IN THE SUPERMARKET BAKING AISLE OR BAKERY DEPARTMENT.

CHANTILLY CREAM

HERE'S AN EASY WAY TO MAKE WHIPPED CREAM EVEN MORE DELICIOUS. DOLLOP ON TOP OF FRUIT CRISPS, PIES AND YOUR FAVORITE PUDDINGS.

I CUP	HEAVY OR WHIPPING (35%) CREAM	250 ML
2 TBSP	CONFECTIONERS' (ICING) SUGAR	30 ML
I TSP	VANILLA EXTRACT	5 ML

IN A LARGE BOWL, WHIP CREAM, SUGAR AND VANILLA UNTIL SOFT PEAKS FORM. MAKES ABOUT 2 CUPS (500 ML).

BUMBLEBERRY COBBLER

"BUMBLEBERRY" IS A COMBINATION OF BERRIES AND OTHER FRUIT. THIS ONE INCLUDES RHUBARB, BUT YOU CAN CREATE YOUR OWN BLEND FOR THIS COMFORTING DESSERT. SERVE WITH WHIPPED CREAM OR ICE CREAM.

BASE

4 CUPS	BLACKBERRIES, BLUEBERRIES, RASPBERRIES OR A COMBINATION	1 L
1 CUP	CHOPPED RHUBARB	250 ML
1/2 CUP	PACKED BROWN SUGAR	125 ML
1 TBSP	CORNSTARCH (SEE TIP, OPPOSITE)	15 ML
1 TSP	GROUND CINNAMON	5 ML
	GRATED ZEST OF 1 ORANGE OR LEMON	

TOPPING

1 1/2 CUPS	ALL-PURPOSE FLOUR	375 ML
1/4 CUP	GRANULATED SUGAR	60 ML
1 TSP	BAKING POWDER	5 ML
1/2 TSP	BAKING SODA	2 ML
1/4 TSP	SALT	1 ML
2/3 CUP	BUTTERMILK	150 ML
1/4 CUP	BUTTER, MELTED AND COOLED	60 ML

BASE: GREASE THE INSERT OF A 3 1/2- TO 4-QUART SLOW COOKER. IN SLOW COOKER, GENTLY COMBINE BERRIES, RHUBARB, BROWN SUGAR, CORNSTARCH, CINNAMON AND ORANGE ZEST.

TOPPING: IN A BOWL, WHISK TOGETHER FLOUR, SUGAR, BAKING POWDER, BAKING SODA AND SALT. MAKE A WELL IN THE CENTER OF THE FLOUR MIXTURE. ADD BUTTERMILK

AND BUTTER TO THE WELL. STIR JUST UNTIL EVENLY COMBINED. DROP SPOONFULS OF BATTER OVER BERRY MIXTURE. COVER AND COOK ON HIGH FOR $3\frac{1}{2}$ TO 4 HOURS, UNTIL A TESTER INSERTED IN THE CENTER OF THE TOPPING COMES OUT CLEAN. TURN OFF SLOW COOKER, REMOVE LID AND LET STAND FOR 1 HOUR TO ALLOW FRUIT TO THICKEN. SERVES 4 TO 6.

TIP: IF USING FROZEN BERRIES, INCREASE THE CORNSTARCH TO $1\frac{1}{2}$ TBSP (22 ML). THERE IS NO NEED TO THAW FROZEN BERRIES BEFORE ASSEMBLING THE COBBLER — THE SLOW COOKER WILL TAKE CARE OF THAT AND WILL COOK THE FRUIT EVENLY.

WILD BLUEBERRY CORNMEAL COBBLER

A DELICIOUS OLD-FASHIONED DESSERT THAT WORKS WELL WITH FRESH OR FROZEN BLUEBERRIES.

BASE

5 CUPS	FROZEN WILD BLUEBERRIES	1.25 L
1/2 CUP	GRANULATED SUGAR	125 ML
2 TBSP	ALL-PURPOSE FLOUR	30 ML
	GRATED ZEST OF 1/2 LEMON	
2 TBSP	FRESHLY SQUEEZED LEMON JUICE	30 ML

TOPPING

3/4 CUP	CORNMEAL	175 ML
3/4 CUP	ALL-PURPOSE FLOUR	175 ML
1/3 CUP	GRANULATED SUGAR	75 ML
1 TSP	BAKING POWDER	5 ML
1/2 TSP	BAKING SODA	2 ML
1/2 TSP	GROUND CINNAMON	2 ML
1/4 TSP	SALT	1 ML
1	EGG, LIGHTLY BEATEN	1
2/3 CUP	BUTTERMILK	150 ML
1/4 CUP	MELTED BUTTER	60 ML

BASE: GREASE THE INSERT OF A 3 1/2- TO 4-QUART SLOW COOKER. IN SLOW COOKER, GENTLY COMBINE BLUEBERRIES, SUGAR, FLOUR, LEMON ZEST AND LEMON JUICE.

TOPPING: IN A BOWL, WHISK TOGETHER CORNMEAL, FLOUR, SUGAR, BAKING POWDER, BAKING SODA, CINNAMON AND SALT. MAKE A WELL IN THE CENTER OF THE CORNMEAL MIXTURE. ADD EGG, BUTTERMILK AND BUTTER

TO THE WELL. STIR JUST UNTIL EVENLY COMBINED. DROP SPOONFULS OF BATTER OVER BERRY MIXTURE. COVER AND COOK ON HIGH FOR $3\frac{1}{2}$ TO 4 HOURS, UNTIL A TESTER INSERTED IN THE CENTER OF THE TOPPING COMES OUT CLEAN. TURN OFF SLOW COOKER, REMOVE LID AND LET STAND FOR 1 HOUR TO ALLOW FRUIT TO THICKEN. SERVES 4 TO 6.

TIP: WE FIRST MADE THIS DESSERT AFTER DISCOVERING FROZEN WILD BLUEBERRIES BEING SOLD — AT A VERY REASONABLE PRICE — IN A COUPLE OF MAJOR SUPERMARKET CHAINS. WILD BLUEBERRIES ARE SMALLER, WITH A MORE INTENSE, SWEETER FLAVOR THAN CULTIVATED BLUEBERRIES.

RHUBARB BROWN BETTY

DATING FROM AMERICAN COLONIAL DAYS, A BETTY IS A BAKED PUDDING OF LAYERED FRUIT AND BREAD CRUMBS. SERVE WITH WHIPPED CREAM OR A BERRY-FLAVORED ICE CREAM.

4 CUPS	CHOPPED RHUBARB	1 L
3/4 CUP	PACKED BROWN SUGAR OR GRANULATED SUGAR	175 ML
2 TSP	GROUND CINNAMON	10 ML
1 TSP	GRATED ORANGE ZEST	5 ML
2 CUPS	FRESH WHOLE WHEAT OR WHITE BREAD CRUMBS	500 ML
1/2 CUP	MELTED BUTTER	125 ML

GREASE THE INSERT OF A 3½- TO 4-QUART SLOW COOKER. IN A BOWL, COMBINE RHUBARB, SUGAR, CINNAMON AND ORANGE ZEST. IN ANOTHER BOWL, COMBINE BREAD CRUMBS AND BUTTER. SPREAD HALF THE RHUBARB MIXTURE IN PREPARED SLOW COOKER. SPRINKLE HALF THE BREAD CRUMB MIXTURE ON TOP. REPEAT LAYERS. PLACE A CLEAN TEA TOWEL, FOLDED IN HALF (SO YOU HAVE TWO LAYERS), OVER TOP OF INSERT. COVER AND COOK ON HIGH FOR 3 HOURS, UNTIL BUBBLING. TURN OFF SLOW COOKER, REMOVE LID AND LET STAND FOR AT LEAST 45 MINUTES TO ALLOW FRUIT TO THICKEN. SERVES 4 TO 6.

PEACH CINNAMON BROWN BETTY

A SWEET AND JUICY DESSERT TO MAKE WHEN PEACHES ARE IN SEASON.

4 CUPS	SLICED PEELED FRESH OR FROZEN PEACHES	1 L
1/3 CUP	GRANULATED SUGAR	75 ML
2 TBSP	ALL-PURPOSE FLOUR	30 ML
1 TBSP	FRESHLY SQUEEZED LEMON JUICE	15 ML
2 CUPS	FRESH WHOLE WHEAT BREAD CRUMBS	500 ML
1 TSP	GROUND CINNAMON	5 ML
1/4 TSP	GROUND NUTMEG	1 ML
1/8 TSP	GROUND CLOVES	0.5 ML
1/2 CUP	MELTED BUTTER	125 ML

GREASE THE INSERT OF A 3 1/2- TO 4-QUART SLOW COOKER. IN A BOWL, COMBINE PEACHES, SUGAR, FLOUR AND LEMON JUICE. IN ANOTHER BOWL, COMBINE BREAD CRUMBS, CINNAMON, NUTMEG AND CLOVES. STIR IN BUTTER. SPREAD HALF THE PEACH MIXTURE IN PREPARED SLOW COOKER. SPRINKLE HALF THE BREAD CRUMB MIXTURE ON TOP. REPEAT LAYERS. PLACE A CLEAN TEA TOWEL, FOLDED IN HALF (SO YOU HAVE TWO LAYERS), OVER TOP OF INSERT. COVER AND COOK ON HIGH FOR 3 HOURS, UNTIL BUBBLING. TURN OFF SLOW COOKER, REMOVE LID AND LET STAND FOR AT LEAST 45 MINUTES TO ALLOW FRUIT TO THICKEN. SERVES 4 TO 6.

TIP: YOU CAN SUBSTITUTE TWO 28-OZ (796 ML) CANS OF SLICED PEACHES. BE SURE TO DRAIN THE PEACHES WELL AND BLOT THEM DRY WITH PAPER TOWELS.

PEARS POACHED IN RED WINE

ANOTHER CLASSIC ADAPTED FOR YOUR SLOW COOKER. SERVE WITH WHIPPED CREAM.

8	FIRM RIPE PEARS, PEELED, HALVED LENGTHWISE AND CORED	8
	GRATED ZEST OF I LEMON	
2 TBSP	FRESHLY SQUEEZED LEMON JUICE	30 ML
I	2-INCH (5 CM) CINNAMON STICK	I
I CUP	GRANULATED SUGAR	250 ML
I TSP	VANILLA EXTRACT	5 ML
2 CUPS	DRY RED WINE	500 ML

IN A 5- TO 6-QUART SLOW COOKER, GENTLY TOSS PEARS AND LEMON JUICE. IN A SAUCEPAN, OVER LOW HEAT, COMBINE CINNAMON STICK, SUGAR, VANILLA, LEMON ZEST AND WINE, STIRRING UNTIL SUGAR DISSOLVES. POUR OVER PEARS. COVER AND COOK ON LOW FOR ABOUT 4 HOURS OR ON HIGH FOR ABOUT 2 HOURS, TURNING PEARS ONCE, UNTIL PEARS ARE TENDER. DISCARD CINNAMON STICK. USING A SLOTTED SPOON, TRANSFER PEARS TO A SERVING DISH. POUR COOKING LIQUID INTO A SMALL SAUCEPAN AND BRING TO A BOIL. BOIL UNTIL LIQUID IS REDUCED BY ABOUT TWO-THIRDS AND IS SYRUPY. POUR OVER PEARS. SERVE WARM OR AT ROOM TEMPERATURE, OR COVER AND REFRIGERATE FOR AT LEAST 2 HOURS, UNTIL CHILLED, OR FOR UP TO 3 DAYS. SERVE PEARS WITH SOME OF THE SYRUP SPOONED OVER TOP. SERVES 6 TO 8.

Parsnip Buttermilk Chive Purée (page 276)
and Ginger-Glazed Carrots (page 279)

Apple Cranberry Cake (page 306)

Banoffee Pie (page 300)

Old-Fashioned Lemon Pudding (page 328)

MAPLE ORANGE GLAZED PEARS

A SPLASH OF ORANGE LIQUEUR LENDS DINNER PARTY APPEAL TO THIS EASY DESSERT. OMIT THE BOOZE IF YOU PREFER — IT'LL STILL TASTE WONDERFUL.

6	FIRM RIPE PEARS, PEELED, HALVED LENGTHWISE AND CORED	6
4	WHOLE CLOVES	4
1	2-INCH (5 CM) CINNAMON STICK	1
1/2 CUP	PACKED BROWN SUGAR	125 ML
1/2 CUP	CRANBERRY COCKTAIL OR UNSWEETENED APPLE JUICE	125 ML
1/3 CUP	PURE MAPLE SYRUP	75 ML
3 TBSP	ORANGE LIQUEUR, DIVIDED	45 ML

PLACE PEARS IN A 5- TO 6-QUART SLOW COOKER. IN A SAUCEPAN, OVER LOW HEAT, COMBINE CLOVES, CINNAMON STICK, BROWN SUGAR, CRANBERRY COCKTAIL, MAPLE SYRUP AND 2 TBSP (30 ML) LIQUEUR, STIRRING UNTIL SUGAR IS DISSOLVED. POUR OVER PEARS. COVER AND COOK ON LOW FOR ABOUT 4 HOURS OR ON HIGH FOR ABOUT 2 HOURS, TURNING PEARS ONCE, UNTIL PEARS ARE TENDER. DISCARD CLOVES AND CINNAMON STICK. STIR IN REMAINING LIQUEUR. SERVE WARM OR AT ROOM TEMPERATURE, OR COVER AND REFRIGERATE FOR AT LEAST 2 HOURS, UNTIL CHILLED, OR FOR UP TO 3 DAYS. SERVE PEARS WITH SOME OF THE SYRUP SPOONED OVER TOP. SERVES 4 TO 6.

SPICED PLUM DESSERT

A SWEET AND JUICY FALL TREAT. SERVE WARM OR CHILLED, WITH A DOLLOP OF PLAIN GREEK YOGURT. TOP WITH TOASTED ALMONDS OR GRANOLA.

2 LBS	FIRM RIPE PLUMS, HALVED AND PITTED	1 KG
1/4 CUP	PACKED BROWN SUGAR	60 ML
1 TSP	CHINESE FIVE-SPICE POWDER	5 ML
	GRATED ZEST OF 1 ORANGE	
1 TBSP	PORT WINE (OPTIONAL)	15 ML

GREASE THE INSERT OF A 3½- TO 4-QUART SLOW COOKER. IN SLOW COOKER, GENTLY COMBINE PLUMS, BROWN SUGAR, FIVE-SPICE POWDER, ORANGE ZEST AND PORT (IF USING). COVER AND COOK ON LOW FOR ABOUT 4 HOURS OR ON HIGH FOR ABOUT 2 HOURS, UNTIL PLUMS ARE TENDER BUT STILL HOLD THEIR SHAPE. SERVE PLUMS WITH COOKING LIQUID SPOONED OVER TOP. SERVES 4 TO 6.

TIP: FIVE-SPICE POWDER IS A BLEND THAT GENERALLY INCLUDES GROUND CINNAMON, CLOVES, FENNEL SEEDS, STAR ANISE AND SZECHUAN PEPPER. YOU'LL FIND IT WITH OTHER BOTTLED HERBS AND SPICES IN MOST GROCERY STORES. IF YOU DON'T HAVE IT, SUBSTITUTE 1 TSP (5 ML) GROUND CINNAMON AND A PINCH OF GROUND NUTMEG IN THIS RECIPE.

VERY CHOCOLATEY RICE PUDDING

SILKY, SENSATIONAL AND SIMPLE. SERVE WARM FROM THE SLOW COOKER. ALTERNATIVELY, CHILL THE PUDDING AND DRESS IT UP WITH WHIPPED CREAM IN PRETTY PARFAIT GLASSES.

1/3 CUP	SHORT-GRAIN WHITE RICE (SUCH AS ARBORIO)	75 ML
3 CUPS	SWEETENED CHOCOLATE-FLAVORED ALMOND MILK	750 ML
1/4 CUP	HAZELNUT CHOCOLATE SPREAD (SUCH AS NUTELLA)	60 ML

IN A 2- TO 3½-QUART SLOW COOKER, COMBINE RICE, ALMOND MILK AND HAZELNUT CHOCOLATE SPREAD. STIR WELL. PLACE A CLEAN TEA TOWEL, FOLDED IN HALF (SO YOU HAVE TWO LAYERS), OVER TOP OF INSERT. COVER AND COOK ON HIGH FOR 2½ TO 3 HOURS, UNTIL RICE IS VERY TENDER AND PUDDING IS CREAMY. STIR WELL. SERVES 4.

TIP: UNLIKE REGULAR MILK, WHICH CAN CURDLE IN THE SLOW COOKER, ALMOND MILK STANDS UP WELL TO THE HIGH TEMPERATURES AND LONG COOKING TIMES. ALMOND MILK MAY BE LABELED "ALMOND NON-DAIRY BEVERAGE." IT IS AVAILABLE SWEETENED AND UNSWEETENED, IN SEVERAL FLAVORS, AND CAN USUALLY BE FOUND IN THE REFRIGERATED FOODS SECTION OF THE SUPERMARKET.

CHOCOLATE POTS DE CRÈME

TRÈS ÉLÉGANTS! USE GOOD-QUALITY CHOCOLATE FOR THESE INDIVIDUAL SILKEN CHOCOLATE PUDDINGS.

1 CUP	WHOLE MILK	250 ML
2/3 CUP	HEAVY OR WHIPPING (35%) CREAM	150 ML
4 OZ	BITTERSWEET (DARK) OR SEMISWEET CHOCOLATE, CHOPPED	125 G
3 TBSP	GRANULATED SUGAR	45 ML
4	EGG YOLKS	4
3/4 TSP	VANILLA EXTRACT	3 ML
	WHIPPED CREAM	

USE A 6- TO 7-QUART SLOW COOKER. GREASE FOUR 6-OZ (175 ML) RAMEKINS. IN A SAUCEPAN, OVER LOW HEAT, WHISK MILK, CREAM AND CHOCOLATE UNTIL CHOCOLATE MELTS AND MIXTURE IS WARM; DO NOT LET BOIL. REMOVE FROM HEAT. IN A BOWL, WHISK TOGETHER SUGAR AND EGG YOLKS. SLOWLY WHISK IN WARM CHOCOLATE MIXTURE, WHISKING CONSTANTLY UNTIL SUGAR IS DISSOLVED. STIR IN VANILLA. STRAIN INTO A LARGE GLASS MEASURING CUP AND SKIM BUBBLES OFF SURFACE. POUR INTO RAMEKINS, DIVIDING EVENLY. COVER EACH RAMEKIN TIGHTLY WITH FOIL. PLACE RAMEKINS IN SLOW COOKER. POUR ENOUGH HOT WATER INTO SLOW COOKER TO COME HALFWAY UP THE SIDES OF THE RAMEKINS. COVER AND COOK ON HIGH FOR 1 TO 2 HOURS, UNTIL CUSTARDS ARE SET BUT STILL JIGGLE SLIGHTLY WHEN SHAKEN. TRANSFER TO A WIRE RACK, UNCOVER AND LET COOL COMPLETELY. COVER AND REFRIGERATE FOR AT LEAST 3 HOURS, UNTIL CHILLED, OR OVERNIGHT. SERVE GARNISHED WITH WHIPPED CREAM. SERVES 4.

TIP: SINCE SOME SLOW COOKERS RUN HOTTER AND FASTER THAN OTHERS, AND SINCE BAKED CUSTARDS ARE SENSITIVE, WE RECOMMEND CHECKING THE POTS DE CRÈME AFTER 1 HOUR OF COOKING. IF THEY OVERCOOK, THEY END UP LOOKING LIKE SCRAMBLED EGGS!

TIP: DON'T DISCARD THE LEFTOVER EGG WHITES YOU'LL HAVE WHEN YOU MAKE THIS RECIPE. EGG WHITES FREEZE WELL AND CAN BE USED IN OMELETS, COOKIES AND MERINGUES. PLACE EACH EGG WHITE IN AN ICE CUBE TRAY. ONCE FROZEN, TRANSFER THE CUBES TO AN AIRTIGHT CONTAINER AND STORE IN THE FREEZER FOR UP TO 1 MONTH. LET THAW OVERNIGHT IN THE REFRIGERATOR BEFORE USE. LEFTOVER EGG WHITES WILL ALSO KEEP IN THE FRIDGE FOR UP TO 3 DAYS.

WE DON'T STAND FOR GOSSIP,
SO SIT DOWN AND GET COMFY.

ORANGE CRÈME CARAMEL

TRUST US – THIS GOURMET DESSERT IS EASIER THAN YOU THINK!

CARAMEL

3 TBSP	GRANULATED SUGAR	45 ML

CUSTARD

1½ CUPS	HALF-AND-HALF (10%) CREAM OR WHOLE MILK	375 ML
⅓ CUP	GRANULATED SUGAR	75 ML
3	EGGS	3
1 TSP	GRATED ORANGE ZEST	5 ML
1 TBSP	ORANGE LIQUEUR	15 ML

CARAMEL: GREASE FOUR 6-OZ (175 ML) RAMEKIN DISHES. SPREAD SUGAR EVENLY IN A SMALL, HEAVY-BOTTOMED SAUCEPAN. PLACE PAN OVER MEDIUM HEAT AND COOK, WITHOUT STIRRING, FOR 4 TO 5 MINUTES, UNTIL SUGAR DISSOLVES AND SYRUP TURNS A DEEP AMBER COLOR. (WATCH CLOSELY, AS THE SYRUP CAN EASILY BURN). QUICKLY DIVIDE CARAMEL AMONG PREPARED RAMEKINS, TILTING THE RAMEKINS SO THE CARAMEL COVERS THE BOTTOM. IT WILL HARDEN.

CUSTARD: USE A 6- TO 7-QUART SLOW COOKER. IN THE SAME SAUCEPAN (NO NEED TO WASH IT), WARM CREAM OVER MEDIUM HEAT UNTIL SMALL BUBBLES APPEAR AROUND THE EDGE. IN A BOWL, WHISK TOGETHER SUGAR, EGGS AND ORANGE ZEST. GRADUALLY WHISK WARM CREAM INTO EGG MIXTURE, WHISKING UNTIL SUGAR DISSOLVES. STIR IN ORANGE LIQUEUR. DIVIDE MILK MIXTURE AMONG RAMEKINS. COVER EACH RAMEKIN TIGHTLY WITH FOIL.

PLACE RAMEKINS IN SLOW COOKER. POUR ENOUGH HOT WATER INTO THE SLOW COOKER TO COME HALFWAY UP THE SIDES OF THE RAMEKINS. COVER AND COOK ON HIGH FOR 1 TO 2 HOURS, UNTIL CUSTARDS ARE SET BUT STILL JIGGLE SLIGHTLY WHEN SHAKEN. TRANSFER TO A WIRE RACK, UNCOVER AND LET COOL COMPLETELY. COVER AND REFRIGERATE FOR AT LEAST 3 HOURS, UNTIL CHILLED, OR OVERNIGHT. TO UNMOLD, RUN A KNIFE AROUND THE EDGE OF EACH RAMEKIN AND INVERT ONTO A PLATE. SERVE IMMEDIATELY. SERVES 4.

TIP: SINCE SOME SLOW COOKERS RUN HOTTER AND FASTER THAN OTHERS, AND SINCE BAKED CUSTARDS ARE SENSITIVE, WE RECOMMEND CHECKING THE CRÈME CARAMELS AFTER 1 HOUR OF COOKING. IF THEY OVERCOOK, THEY END UP LOOKING LIKE SCRAMBLED EGGS!

VARIATION
VANILLA CRÈME CARAMEL: REPLACE THE ORANGE ZEST AND ORANGE LIQUEUR WITH 2 TSP (10 ML) VANILLA EXTRACT.

OLD-FASHIONED LEMON PUDDING

AN OLDIE THAT'S STILL A GOODIE. THE TOP TURNS TO LIGHT SPONGE CAKE, AND THE BOTTOM TURNS TO A CREAMY LEMON SAUCE.

1 CUP	GRANULATED SUGAR	250 ML
2 TBSP	ALL-PURPOSE FLOUR	30 ML
2	EGGS, SEPARATED	2
1 CUP	MILK	250 ML
1 TBSP	GRATED LEMON ZEST	15 ML
1/4 CUP	FRESHLY SQUEEZED LEMON JUICE	60 ML
3 TBSP	MELTED BUTTER	45 ML

GREASE THE INSERT OF A 3 1/2- TO 4-QUART SLOW COOKER. IN A BOWL, WHISK TOGETHER SUGAR AND FLOUR. WHISK IN EGG YOLKS, MILK, LEMON ZEST, LEMON JUICE AND BUTTER. IN A SEPARATE BOWL, BEAT EGG WHITES UNTIL STIFF PEAKS FORM. GENTLY FOLD EGG WHITES INTO LEMON MIXTURE. TRANSFER TO SLOW COOKER. COVER AND COOK ON HIGH FOR 2 TO 2 1/2 HOURS, UNTIL PUFFY AND SET. TURN OFF SLOW COOKER, REMOVE LID AND LET COOL FOR 30 MINUTES. SERVE WARM OR COOL COMPLETELY. SERVES 4 TO 6.

IF LIFE GIVES YOU MELONS,
YOU MIGHT BE DYSLEXIC.

UPSIDE-DOWN CHOCOLATE FUDGE PUDDING

GENERATIONS OF OUR FAMILIES HAVE VOTED THIS THEIR FAVORITE WINTER DESSERT.

PUDDING

1 CUP	ALL-PURPOSE FLOUR	250 ML
3/4 CUP	GRANULATED SUGAR	175 ML
3 TBSP	UNSWEETENED COCOA POWDER	45 ML
2 TSP	BAKING POWDER	10 ML
1/2 CUP	MILK	125 ML
2 TBSP	MELTED BUTTER	30 ML
1/4 CUP	FINELY CHOPPED TOASTED PECANS (OPTIONAL)	60 ML

FUDGE SAUCE

3/4 CUP	PACKED BROWN SUGAR	175 ML
1/2 CUP	UNSWEETENED COCOA POWDER	125 ML
2 CUPS	BOILING WATER	500 ML

PUDDING: GREASE THE INSERT OF A 3½- TO 4-QUART SLOW COOKER. IN A BOWL, WHISK TOGETHER FLOUR, SUGAR, COCOA AND BAKING POWDER. MAKE A WELL IN THE CENTER OF THE FLOUR MIXTURE. ADD MILK AND BUTTER TO THE WELL. STIR UNTIL A STIFF BATTER FORMS. STIR IN PECANS, IF USING. SPOON INTO PREPARED SLOW COOKER AND LEVEL THE TOP.

FUDGE SAUCE: IN ANOTHER BOWL, WHISK TOGETHER BROWN SUGAR, COCOA AND BOILING WATER. POUR SLOWLY OVER BATTER. COVER AND COOK ON HIGH FOR 2 TO 2½ HOURS, UNTIL A TOOTHPICK INSERTED IN THE CENTER OF THE PUDDING COMES OUT CLEAN. SERVES 6.

A LITTLE CHRISTMAS PUDDING

FOR EMPTY NESTERS AND SINGLETONS.
SERVE WITH WHIPPED CREAM.

2/3 CUP	CRUSHED GINGERSNAP COOKIES, DIVIDED	150 ML
1/2 CUP	CRUSHED CRISP LADYFINGER COOKIES	125 ML
1/2 TSP	GROUND CINNAMON	2 ML
1/4 TSP	GROUND CLOVES	1 ML
1/8 TSP	GROUND GINGER	0.5 ML
PINCH	GROUND NUTMEG	PINCH
1/4 CUP	CONFECTIONERS' (ICING) SUGAR	60 ML
1/2 TSP	GRATED LEMON ZEST	2 ML
1/4 CUP	BUTTER, SOFTENED	60 ML
3	EGGS, SEPARATED	3
3 TBSP	GRANULATED SUGAR	45 ML
1/4 CUP	DRIED CURRANTS	60 ML
2 TBSP	CHOPPED CANDIED LEMON OR ORANGE PEEL	30 ML
	BOILING WATER	

USE A MINIMUM 6-QUART SLOW COOKER. GREASE A 4-CUP
(1 L) PUDDING BOWL OR ROUND BAKING DISH. SPRINKLE
2 TBSP (30 ML) GINGERSNAP CRUMBS INTO THE BOWL AND
TILT TO COAT. IN A SMALL BOWL, COMBINE REMAINING
GINGERSNAP CRUMBS, LADYFINGER CRUMBS, CINNAMON,
CLOVES, GINGER AND NUTMEG. IN ANOTHER BOWL, CREAM
CONFECTIONERS' SUGAR, LEMON ZEST AND BUTTER
UNTIL LIGHT AND FLUFFY. BEAT IN EGG YOLKS, ONE AT
A TIME. STIR IN HALF THE CRUMB MIXTURE. IN A CLEAN
BOWL, WHIP EGG WHITES UNTIL FROTHY. GRADUALLY ADD
GRANULATED SUGAR, WHIPPING UNTIL SOFT PEAKS FORM.

FOLD IN THE REMAINING CRUMB MIXTURE. FOLD THE EGG WHITE MIXTURE INTO THE EGG YOLK MIXTURE. FOLD IN CURRANTS AND CANDIED LEMON. SCRAPE BATTER INTO PREPARED BOWL. COVER DISH TIGHTLY WITH FOIL AND SECURE WITH KITCHEN STRING. PLACE IN SLOW COOKER AND POUR IN ENOUGH BOILING WATER TO COME HALFWAY UP THE SIDES OF THE BOWL. COVER AND COOK ON HIGH FOR $2\frac{1}{2}$ TO 3 HOURS, UNTIL A TOOTHPICK INSERTED IN THE CENTER OF THE PUDDING COMES OUT CLEAN. TRANSFER BOWL TO A WIRE RACK, REMOVE FOIL AND LET COOL FOR 15 MINUTES. USING A RUBBER SPATULA, LOOSEN SIDES OF PUDDING. INVERT ONTO A SERVING PLATE. SERVE IMMEDIATELY. SERVES 2 TO 3.

TIP: LADYFINGER COOKIES ARE DRIED STRIPS OF SPONGE CAKE BEST KNOWN FOR THEIR USE IN THE ITALIAN DESSERT TIRAMISU. THEY'RE AVAILABLE IN SOFT AND CRISPY VARIETIES AND ARE USUALLY FOUND IN THE COOKIE AISLE, BAKERY OR FROZEN FOODS SECTION OF THE SUPERMARKET.

BRITISH STICKY SPONGE PUDDING

THE BRITS CALL IT TREACLE SPONGE PUDDING. WE CALL IT YUMMY! SERVE WITH WHIPPED CREAM.

1/2 CUP	GOLDEN SYRUP (SEE TIP, OPPOSITE), DIVIDED	125 ML
1 1/2 CUPS	ALL-PURPOSE FLOUR	375 ML
2 TSP	BAKING POWDER	10 ML
1/4 TSP	SALT	1 ML
1 CUP	PACKED BROWN SUGAR	250 ML
1/2 CUP	BUTTER, SOFTENED	125 ML
3	EGGS	3
	GRATED ZEST OF 1 LEMON	
	BOILING WATER	

USE A MINIMUM 6-QUART SLOW COOKER. GREASE A 6-CUP (1.5 L) PUDDING BOWL OR OVENPROOF MIXING BOWL. POUR HALF THE GOLDEN SYRUP INTO PREPARED BOWL. IN A BOWL, COMBINE FLOUR, BAKING POWDER AND SALT. IN ANOTHER BOWL, CREAM BROWN SUGAR AND BUTTER UNTIL LIGHT AND FLUFFY. BEAT IN EGGS, ONE AT A TIME, AND LEMON ZEST UNTIL BLENDED. STIR IN FLOUR MIXTURE. SPOON BATTER OVER TOP OF GOLDEN SYRUP. COVER DISH TIGHTLY WITH FOIL AND SECURE WITH KITCHEN STRING. PLACE IN SLOW COOKER AND POUR IN ENOUGH BOILING WATER TO COME 1 INCH (2.5 CM) UP THE SIDES OF THE BOWL. COVER AND COOK ON HIGH FOR 2 1/2 TO 3 HOURS, UNTIL A TOOTHPICK INSERTED IN THE CENTER COMES OUT CLEAN. TRANSFER BOWL TO A WIRE RACK, REMOVE FOIL AND LET COOL FOR 5 MINUTES. USING A RUBBER SPATULA, LOOSEN SIDES OF PUDDING. INVERT ONTO A

SERVING PLATE AND DRIZZLE REMAINING GOLDEN SYRUP OVER TOP. SERVE IMMEDIATELY. SERVES 6.

TIP: GOLDEN SYRUP IS A SUGAR BY-PRODUCT USED IN BAKING. IT RESEMBLES AN AMBER-COLORED CORN SYRUP. SAMPLE ITS TOFFEE-LIKE SWEETNESS, AND YOU'LL UNDERSTAND WHY THE BRITS ARE SO ADDICTED. BOTH IMPORTED AND CANADIAN GOLDEN SYRUP ARE WIDELY AVAILABLE: LOOK FOR THEM IN THE BAKING OR PRESERVES SECTION, OR WHERE BRITISH PRODUCTS ARE SHELVED.

LIFE CYCLE OF MEN: THEY'RE BORN,
THEY'RE WRONG, THEY DIE.

PEAR GINGER BREAD PUDDING

PEARS AND GINGER ARE PERFECT PARTNERS.
SERVE WARM WITH WHIPPED CREAM.

4 TBSP	PACKED BROWN SUGAR, DIVIDED	60 ML
1/2 TSP	GROUND CINNAMON	2 ML
1/4 TSP	GROUND GINGER	1 ML
3	EGGS	3
1 CUP	WHOLE OR 2% MILK	250 ML
1/3 CUP	HEAVY OR WHIPPING (35%) CREAM	75 ML
1/4 CUP	BUTTER, SOFTENED	60 ML
6	SLICES WHITE BREAD (SEE TIP, PAGE 335)	6
1/2 CUP	GINGER MARMALADE	125 ML
2	RIPE PEARS, PEELED AND CHOPPED	2

GREASE THE INSERT OF A 3½- TO 4-QUART SLOW COOKER. IN A BOWL, WHISK TOGETHER 2 TBSP (30 ML) BROWN SUGAR, CINNAMON, GINGER, EGGS, MILK AND CREAM; SET ASIDE. BUTTER ONE SIDE OF EACH BREAD SLICE. SPREAD MARMALADE THICKLY OVER BUTTER. CUT EACH SLICE INTO QUARTERS. ARRANGE HALF THE BREAD IN PREPARED SLOW COOKER, OVERLAPPING PIECES. POUR HALF THE EGG MIXTURE OVER TOP. SPRINKLE WITH PEARS. ARRANGE THE REMAINING BREAD ON TOP. POUR REMAINING EGG MIXTURE OVER BREAD, PUSHING DOWN GENTLY TO ENSURE ALL BREAD IS SUBMERGED. SPRINKLE WITH REMAINING BROWN SUGAR. COVER AND REFRIGERATE FOR AT LEAST 30 MINUTES, UNTIL CHILLED, OR OVERNIGHT. PLACE INSERT IN SLOW COOKER, COVER AND COOK ON HIGH FOR 2½ TO 3 HOURS, UNTIL A TOOTHPICK INSERTED IN THE CENTER COMES OUT CLEAN. SERVES 4 TO 6.

CHOCOLATE BANANA BREAD PUDDING

HEAVENLY! SERVE WARM WITH RUM PECAN CARAMEL SAUCE (PAGE 336).

4 CUPS	CUBED WHITE BREAD	1 L
2 OZ	SEMISWEET OR BITTERSWEET (DARK) CHOCOLATE, CHOPPED	60 G
1	BANANA, CHOPPED	1
1/2 CUP	GRANULATED SUGAR	125 ML
1 TSP	GROUND CINNAMON	5 ML
2	EGGS	2
2 CUPS	HALF-AND-HALF (10%) CREAM	500 ML
1 TSP	VANILLA EXTRACT	5 ML
2 TBSP	TOFFEE BITS	30 ML

GREASE THE INSERT OF A 3½- TO 4-QUART SLOW COOKER. PLACE BREAD CUBES IN SLOW COOKER. STIR IN CHOCOLATE AND BANANA. IN A BOWL, WHISK TOGETHER SUGAR, CINNAMON, EGGS, CREAM AND VANILLA. POUR OVER BREAD MIXTURE, PUSHING DOWN GENTLY TO ENSURE ALL BREAD IS SUBMERGED. SPRINKLE WITH TOFFEE BITS. COVER AND REFRIGERATE FOR AT LEAST 30 MINUTES, UNTIL CHILLED, OR OVERNIGHT. PLACE INSERT IN SLOW COOKER, COVER AND COOK ON HIGH FOR 2½ TO 3 HOURS, UNTIL A TOOTHPICK INSERTED IN THE CENTER COMES OUT CLEAN. SERVES 4 TO 6.

TIP: FOR BEST RESULTS, USE STALE BREAD. AN EASY WAY TO STALE BREAD IS TO SPREAD THE SLICES IN A SINGLE LAYER ON A COUPLE OF BAKING SHEETS AND LEAVE THEM UNCOVERED ON THE COUNTER OVERNIGHT.

RUM PECAN CARAMEL SAUCE

AN ESSENTIAL TOPPING FOR SOME OF THE DESSERTS IN THIS CHAPTER, PARTICULARLY CHOCOLATE BANANA BREAD PUDDING (PAGE 335) AND APPLE CRISP WITH HAZELNUT TOPPING (PAGE 308).

1/2 CUP	COLD WATER	125 ML
1 CUP	GRANULATED SUGAR	250 ML
1 CUP	HEAVY OR WHIPPING (35%) CREAM	250 ML
2 TBSP	DARK RUM	30 ML
1/2 TSP	VANILLA EXTRACT	2 ML
1 CUP	CHOPPED TOASTED PECANS	250 ML

POUR COLD WATER INTO A HEAVY-BOTTOMED SAUCEPAN. ADD SUGAR, BEING CAREFUL NOT TO LET IT STICK TO THE SIDES OF THE PAN. BRING TO A BOIL OVER HIGH HEAT, WITHOUT STIRRING. BOIL FOR 6 TO 7 MINUTES, UNTIL SUGAR IS DISSOLVED AND SYRUP IS A PALE GOLDEN COLOR. REMEMBER — DON'T STIR! REDUCE HEAT TO MEDIUM AND COOK FOR 1 TO 2 MINUTES, UNTIL SYRUP IS A DEEP AMBER COLOR. (WATCH CLOSELY, AS THE SYRUP CAN TURN FROM TOFFEE-COLORED TO HORRIBLY BURNED IN SECONDS.) REMOVE FROM HEAT. CAREFULLY ADD 1/4 CUP (60 ML) CREAM. THE SYRUP WILL BUBBLE DRAMATICALLY. WHEN THE BUBBLING HAS SUBSIDED, WHISK IN THE REMAINING CREAM, RUM AND VANILLA. (IF THE SAUCE LOOKS A BIT LUMPY, HEAT IT OVER LOW HEAT, STIRRING CONSTANTLY, UNTIL SMOOTH). IF USING RIGHT AWAY, STIR IN PECANS. OTHERWISE, LET COOL, TRANSFER TO AN AIRTIGHT CONTAINER AND REFRIGERATE FOR UP TO 2 WEEKS. REHEAT OVER LOW HEAT AND STIR IN PECANS JUST BEFORE SERVING. MAKES ABOUT 1 1/2 CUPS (375 ML).

TIP: DON'T BE TEMPTED TO SUBSTITUTE ARTIFICIAL RUM FLAVORING FOR THE REAL THING — IT WON'T TASTE GOOD!

TIP: THE SYRUP WILL INITIALLY TURN GOLDEN AT THE EDGES OF THE PAN. AS IT CONTINUES TO COOK, THE GOLDEN COLOR WILL "CREEP" TOWARD THE MIDDLE. ONCE THE SYRUP IN THE CENTER TURNS GOLDEN, REDUCE THE HEAT TO MEDIUM.

VARIATION

SIMPLE CARAMEL SAUCE: OMIT THE RUM AND PECANS.

IT'S NOT SHOPPING
IF YOU BUY 10 ITEMS OR LESS.

Library and Archives Canada Cataloguing in Publication

Best of Bridge slow cooker cookbook : 200 brand-new recipes / Best of Bridge Cookbooks.

Includes index.
ISBN 978-0-7788-0413-0

1. Electric cooking, Slow. 2. Cookbooks. I. Best of Bridge Publishing Ltd
II. Title: Slow cooker cookbook.

TX827.B438 2012   641.5'884   C2012-902533-X

INDEX